Primitive Mental States

Traditional psychoanalysis relies on the presence of certain meaning-making capacities in the patient for its effectiveness. *Primitive Mental States* examines how particular capacities, including those for symbolizing, fantasizing, dreaming, experiencing and finding meanings in those experiences, can be taken for granted. Many of us lack these capacities in certain dimensions of our minds, making traditional psychoanalysis ineffective.

In this book, international contributors are brought together to consider a radical evolution in contemporary psychoanalytic theory developed from a combination of ultrasound studies, infant analysis, and observation of mothers and babies. These findings demonstrate how much mental life exists even before birth and considers unevolved, unborn and barely born aspects of the self such as the birth of emotion and the birth of alpha functioning.

Topics covered include:

- prenatal imprints on the mind and body
- difficult to treat patients
- non-verbal, non-symbolic, disembodied states of being
- early relational and attachment trauma.

Illustrated throughout with original data and extensive clinical discussions from some of the biggest names in the field, *Primitive Mental States* will be a useful resource for students and seasoned analysts alike.

Jane Van Buren is a psychoanalyst in full time private practice in Los Angeles, California and a training and supervising analyst at the Psychoanalytic Centre of California. She has written widely on the themes of women and children, culture and psychoanalysis.

Shelley Alhanati is a psychoanalyst in northern California, and is a supervising analyst and faculty member of the Psychoanalytic Institute of Northern California. She has lectured and written widely on various topics in psychoanalytic theory as well as on fetal, infant, and child developmental research.

Primitive Mental States

A Psychoanalytic Exploration of the Origins of Meaning

Edited by Jane Van Buren and Shelley Alhanati

Routledge
Taylor & Francis Group
LONDON AND NEW YORK

First published 2010
by Routledge
27 Church Road, Hove, East Sussex BN3 2FA

Simultaneously published in the USA and Canada
by Routledge
270 Madison Avenue, New York, NY 10016

Routledge is an imprint of the Taylor & Francis Group, an Informa business

Typeset in Times by Garfield Morgan, Swansea, West Glamorgan
Printed and bound in Great Britain by TJ International Ltd, Padstow, Cornwall
Paperback cover design by Andy Ward

British Library Cataloguing in Publication Data
A catalogue record for this book is available from the British Library

Library of Congress Cataloging-in-Publication Data
Primitive mental states / edited by Jane Van Buren and Shelley Alhanati.
p. cm.
Includes bibliographical references and index.
ISBN 978-0-415-46893-0 (hbk.) – ISBN 978-0-415-46894-7 (pbk.) 1. Psychoanalysis. 2. Mother and child–Psychological aspects. I. Van Buren, Jane. II. Alhanati, Shelley.
BF173.P6715 2009
150.19'5–dc22

2009022148

ISBN: 978-0-415-46893-0 (hbk)
ISBN: 978-0-415-46894-7 (pbk)

This book is dedicated to James Grotstein, whose boundless generosity and creativity have profoundly influenced several generations of analysts

Contents

Contributors

Arnaldo Chuster (achuster@centroin.com.br) is a Training Analyst at the Psychoanalytic Association of Rio de Janeiro, Brazil.

Antonino Ferro (ninoferro3@aol.com) is a Training Analyst at the Italian Psychoanalytical Society.

Celia Fix Korbivcher (celiafix@uol.com.br) is a Training Analyst at the Brazilian Psychoanalytical Society.

Francisco Gonzalez (f.j.g@comcast.net) is a Psychoanalyst at the Psychoanalytic Institute of Northern California.

James S. Grotstein (jgrotstein@earthlink.com) is a Training Analyst at the Psychoanalytic Center of California and the New Center for Psychoanalysis.

Johan Norman (deceased) was a former President of the Swedish Psychoanalytic Society.

Annie Reiner (anniereine@aol.com) is a faculty member of the Psychoanalytic Center of California.

Marianne Robinson (mrobins@nwlink.com) is a Training Analyst at the Northwestern Psychoanalytic Society.

Björn Salomonsson (bjorn.salomonsson@ki.se) is a Training Analyst at the Swedish Psychoanalytic Society.

Jane Van Buren (janevburen@aol.com) is a Training Analyst at the Psychoanalytic Center of California.

Joanna Wilheim (joannawilheim@uol.com.br) is a Training Analyst at the Brazilian Psychoanalytic Society, São Paolo.

Paul Williams (pw@pwilliams.eu) is a Training Analyst at the British Psycho-Analytical Society.

Foreword

Birth of meaning: Wild thoughts, protomental states and disembodied experience

Editors: Jane Van Buren, Shelley Alhanati

In this volume, we are concerned with making contact with unborn, barely born, un-embodied, un-mentalized aspects of the self; what we might conceive of as the lost subject, the birth of being, the origins of meaning.

We are looking at aspects of our patients that have not been able to be touched, or have even sometimes been made worse, by the more traditional analytic approaches that have relied on the presence of certain meaning-making capacities in the patient for their effectiveness.

The capacity for symbolizing, fantasizing, verbalizing, having affects and thoughts, feelings and dreams; the capacity for experiencing different aspects of oneself in conflict with other aspects; the capacity for projective identification, for making links; the capacity for living inside of one's body, for experiencing one's experiences, for finding meaning in those experiences; the capacity to relate to another person: these are not capacities that can be taken for granted. Not everyone has these capacities, and for that matter, there are dimensions of all of our minds that do not have these capacities.

There has been a radical evolution in contemporary psychoanalytic theory; in its practice, in the range of patients accessible to treatment, in the range of states of mind and body that can be dealt with in psychoanalysis, and in the whole underlying assumption of what constitutes a psychoanalytic enterprise. One of the strengths of the psychoanalytic approach is that it is, first and foremost, a very practical job. Most of the revolutionary changes have come through the simple expedient of certain patients who were not growing or developing in their analyses. At each step in our development as analysts, something that had been taken for granted when working with certain states was found to be something that could not be taken for granted at all.

Each of the contributors to this volume struggles with these difficulties in his/her own way. Some of the integrating clinical discussions that emerge throughout the papers in this book are related to: working with protomental states (i.e. states of mind that are not yet differentiated from states of body); prenatal/neonatal imprints on the mind and body; early attachment trauma; and the evolution of signs, symbols, and language as a precursor to laying the foundations for development of mentalization, embodiment, reflection and meaning.

We hope they will help to create a context for the analyst to hold and build on the more elemental forms of contact that we sometimes encounter in our work as we begin to help people weave a rich tapestry of complex and meaningful experience in their lives.

Introduction

Primitive mental states and the origins of meaning

The designation of primitive mental states is an outcome of interesting and powerful elaborations of notions of the unconscious in psychoanalytic theory. Freud originally elaborated and explored the notion of two consciousnesses, but he felt largely that the unconscious needed to be tamed as well as understood. His theory of neurosis and dreams is based on the idea that the forces of the unconscious, the instincts, needed to find expression. Dream work and neurotic structures were felt to be either helpful or disturbing compromise formations. As the 20th century unfolded, Melanie Klein, in particular, but others as well, developed an interest in the mental functioning of infants and children. With Klein's notions of unconscious infantile phantasy, psychoanalysis was able to understand more about the very early time in a person's life during which meaning began to develop. Melanie Klein outlined a developmental schema, including what was called the Oedipus Complex, and brought forward the idea that mental life began at birth, not before, and that early phantasies were developed around the vicissitudes of object relations rather than through the release of instinctual forces. However, as is well known, she carried forward the idea that at birth the child was faced with annihilation anxiety, which she felt was a product of the death instinct. Gradually, she believed that the anxieties and fears of the early infant, now thought to be capable of mapping out his or her experience, were projected into the "mothering one" as a way of easing the anxiety.

In the 20th century many psychologists and analysts became involved with the nature of infantile mental development and the studies revealed that infants were very much involved in the attachment process or bonding. The failure to meet the needs of the early infant brought on psychopathology, and disturbances in development. The notion of separation became a very important focus and the idea of the child needing to believe that they were attached and empathized with brought new depth to the idea of early mental life. Out of these interests came the idea of pre-verbal, or what was called pre-Oedipal, experiences and the difficulty of understanding or decoding them became a serious concern. In psychoanalysis, the interest in this early period of mental life was elaborated by such people as Donald Winnicott and Ronald Fairbairn, as well as Klein. Fairbairn and Winnicott understood and explained that the new infant needed to be fully dependent in order to fully develop. Winnicott stressed that there was no such thing as a baby, but only a mother and a baby. Fairbairn stressed that the internal world was not shaped by infantile powerfulness, but rather by powerlessness and the helplessness of early mental life. One of the major figures who came to understand these early layers of mental life was Wilfred Bion. His talent for probing the non-verbal, sometimes linked with the psychotic, led to deeper familiarity with the formation of disturbances in development, including the formation of psychotic states of mind.

This collection of essays focuses on this trend of appreciating the readiness of the newborn infant to make sense out of their experience, particularly with the primary caretaking one. This in turn led to the notion of prenatal readiness to mark the vicissitudes of prenatal life. Ultrasound studies combined with infant analysis and infant observation made clear how much mental life existed even before birth. The papers that are at the core of this collection follow that trend and also are part of a growth of psychoanalytic theory and infant studies that emphasize the difficulties of resistance and defenses and psychosomatic ailments as a product of trauma or a poor environment for the infant developing his or her outlook. The emphasis on the unruliness or the unfriendliness of the infant's mind has evolved into an understanding that the infant in distress develops obstacles to attaching and to achieving a good, healthy sense of themselves.

Summary of the chapters

James Grotstein's paper is centered around the idea of infantile trauma as mentioned above. He explains in great detail the history of these ideas in psychoanalytic theory and infant studies, for the purpose of revealing the age old confusion between the failure of the environment, trauma and the constitutional difficulties of the infant. He explains that what we call negative therapeutic reactions or somatic difficulties in the infant are not in themselves the problem. He believes that one must understand the psychic reality of the early infantile mind, that this involves fear, traumatic fear (not ruling out entirely constitutional tendencies).

Grotstein's ideas are part of a major movement in Western culture, i.e. the gradual divorce from ideas and theories as the center of one's understanding. Philosophers of the 18th and 19th centuries began to question the certitude of philosophical and religious theories. Their tendency was to develop a new view of the epistemological sources of knowledge and the nature of humankind, which was separated from morality as well as from a priori notions of goodness. The emphasis changed from what was right and proper to a focus on the emotional experience of the individual or the culture. Grotstein's view in this paper, as it develops, takes up the difficulties that come between the analytic couple and/or the familial couple. He emphasizes the notion of the burial of infantile mental life. He explains that the infantile experience is so painful when unattended to reasonably, that part of the personality is buried in a crypt – neither alive nor dead. For all practical purposes the individual is weighed down with the unmet, unaccepted experiences of the baby in the crypt. This important idea applies to society as well and leads to prejudice and hatred of vulnerability.

Antonino Ferro's paper is indicative of the interest in the unconscious as a source of creativity and meaning as well as pain and tragedy. Ferro sees the mind as struggling with the most heightened emotions. He focuses on the unconscious as a source of creativity and passion, but he also sees the evolution of meaning as problematic. He feels that our psychic apparatus and the instruments at our disposal are very recent and rudimentary, as Bion reiterated throughout his work. The precarious nature of our tools also stems from the fact that to develop we need the support of another available psychic apparatus. Ferro explains that he is talking about Bion's idea of alpha function that transforms beta elements as well as proto-emotions into pictograms. These pictograms make up the building blocks that enable us to construct thoughts, emotions and dreams. Ferro takes up in this paper the different ways that deeper emotional life may be avoided or, on the other hand, creatively transformed into new meanings, hopefully the truth. One of the avoidance techniques discussed is the lie, which has to do with how difficult it is to allow the truth to evolve. On the other hand the ability to make myths helps us to move from pictograms to stories or narratives. In this way we can trace the path of our psychic apparatus and find truth, which allows some meaning to evolve. Ferro then compares Greek myths and fairy tales, and takes up the story of Puss in Boots, as one of the most optimistic narratives, comparing it to Andersen's Little Match Girl. Ferro's basic interest is the way that the psychic apparatus handles these proto-emotions. Since they are powerful and strange there is a great temptation to avoid their meaning or message and that can bring on distortion and treachery. Ferro maintains that fairy tales distribute and make known proto-emotions – those without words. He argues that the psychic apparatus seems not able to handle these powerful aspects of emotions, which have not yet been assimilated into the conscious parts of the personality and into some form of symbolic communication.

According to Ferro the proto-emotions are so threatening that avoidance of them is a common aspect to our psychic functioning. However, the avoidance can lead us down a path, which lies and hides the ultimate truth, or as Bion calls it "O", the ultimate emotional experience that has not been tamed or contained. Since "O" arrives from unlimited dimensionality (the unconscious as infinite) the shock of its arrival may lead to distortion and denial, at the same time avoiding aspects of a person's emotional life which could provide meaning and purpose. Ferro continues that one form of avoidance often seen is evacuation, which is the projection of the proto-emotional states to the external world. This may take the form of paranoia, hallucination, delirium, or autism. Clearly this process does not have the conditions needed for thinking. Evacuation can also involve the body, causing psychosomatic illness, or the body social, causing antisocial behavior, delinquency or collective stupidity. Obviously the hope is that these proto-emotions can be kept within the psychic apparatus and be utilized in a way that brings a rich and deep emotional experience, with the ability to reflect and think on the meaning of these basic proto-emotions. Ferro provides us with several clinical examples in which the analysand reflects on his or her emotional story and avoidance or acceptance of these deep proto-mental messages.

Paul Williams is working with some of Klein's ideas about incorporation and identification. In his paper he takes up a particular aspect – the infant's need to adapt to the mothering one. This early incorporation that Williams talks about is felt to be part of the self since it was formed at a time when differentiation was not yet established. However, the incorporated object feels like a foreign body and has some of the characteristics of Freud's and Klein's ideas about an unfriendly super ego. Williams, however, is interested in the effects of early incorporation and/or identification since he believes that it shapes the person's formation of the subject. He also believes that these early incorporations are brought on by an invasive other, the idea being that the mothering one is not able to include the infant's subjectivity in her ministration to him or her, rather she projects and intrudes upon the infant's experience. Williams believes that this particular pattern of incorporation is brought on by several factors; he feels that the formation takes place with a mothering one who has great difficulty resonating with the infant's experience. He suggests that the infant is at risk for allowing the invasive object to become very dominating without the support of the environmental others. Williams also calls our attention to the lack of reciprocity as the invasive object takes on the qualities and characteristics of a dominating and possessive character. The infant subject, or the patient in analysis will find the invasive object in the transference, enabling them to eventually free themselves from this dominant character.

Celia Fix Korbivcher has been interested in specific psychic phenomena in which she believes proto-mental states of mind predominate. In her paper she looks at these processes in patients who may present as neurotic and seem available for analysis but who may have a hidden aspect, which remains unreachable, thereby impeding deep growth in the analysis. Korbivcher states that these aspects are incapable of transformation and undermine the development and growth of thought. Body language and evasion are used to express these states of mind and Korbivcher suggests that if they are able to be touched they will undergo transformation of a very different kind, which she believes is autistic.

Analyst and patient are both engaged in close emotional reciprocity. She explains that the analyst is required to participate in the analysand's experience, but must recover from these states of mind in which action dominates over thinking, and rivalry blocks cooperation and awareness of the absence and value of the primary object. Awareness of the experience of absence of the primary object is eliminated. Absence of affective life is characteristic of these patients and they are left with emptiness and surface auto-sensuality. These autistic pockets are used to shut out other kinds of mental experience. Korbivcher also wants the analyst to be aware of the difference between projective identification and autistic transformation. In autistic transformations there are no separate objects to be projected into, nor are there feelings for that object.

Marianne Robinson's paper investigates psychic territory where vestiges of prenatal states of mind appear in a postnatal analysis. Robinson feels that the perpetuation of these states of mind is caused by a failure of containment, which leads to the dread of falling apart, the formation of a second skin and pseudo independence. Other consequences of the failure of containment of early states of mind are the feeling of falling into a black hole or the creation of a claustrum which successfully keep out psychic experience. These are the creation of various psychic retreats.

Robinson takes us through the journey of an encapsulated woman moving from a stalemate in prenatal fantasies and the use of adhesive identification to block contact and communication to the later acceptance of the difference between "me" and "not me." Robinson states that a binocular vertex develops out of the container–contained relationship and promotes and allows for the two vertices, which are based on pre and postnatal experience – the internal and the external worlds. The search for a containing relationship leads to these capacities and lessens the necessity for exclusive belief in the prenatal and early postnatal phantasies of being and relating. Robinson emphasizes the presence of phantasies and relationships with the umbilicus and placenta as well as those built on the idea of being able to return to mother's body.

Joanna Wilheim's paper introduces us to the idea that the infant has recorded by means of cellular memory the earliest experiences, including prenatal ones. She means by this the whole process of our biological experience from preconception to birth, starting from the formation of each of our basic germative cells and up to the moment of birth itself. These phantasies are memories that correspond to psychic representatives of the infant's early sense impressions. The trauma of conception is well described by Willheim as disruptive to the sperm as he enters into a serious competition with many rivals. The egg experiences great intrusion as the sperm seeks to enter the ovum for fertilization. Thus Willheim believes conception to be the first trauma bringing darkness to the journey into life. Observation of the failure to establish analytic links, which one can see in "attacks on linking" or think about as a "negative therapeutic reaction," are part of the legacy of the painful difficulty of conception.

Jane Van Buren, in her paper, helps us to understand the implications of Bion's departure from the traditional conscious–unconscious interface, and from the Freudian conception of an unconscious which is problematic. She directs our attention to the ways in which Bion's notion of "wild thoughts," or "thoughts without a thinker," presented Western culture with a profound reversal in our understanding of how the mind works at levels beyond the familiar signs and symbols. As she looks at the concepts of mindfulness and significance existing beyond our ordinary reach of realizations, she explores Bion's "language of achievement," the language of emotions before they become represented as concepts, as being in direct contrast to the language of substitution and theories of symbol formation, which have been valorized in psychoanalysis.

Francisco Gonzalez's paper examines the fantasy of a dead or aborted baby as the foundation for a psychic organization of certain negativistic primitive states. He posits that the trauma of birth for these patients is that it has never really happened in a way that inaugurates birth itself as a living process, one that can depict the metaphoric movement from one state into a fundamentally different, higher order of development. He presents clinical material to illustrate the dilemmas of treatment, in which the analyst is required to live out an experience of being evacuated by nothingness in order to create the kind of potential space that might allow psychic birth to take place.

Arnaldo Chuster's paper investigates the difference between the origins of things that are *in* the unconscious and the origins of the unconscious *itself*, through an attempt to understand their characteristic movements, described as movements of expansion and repetition. He emphasizes an inaccessible state of mind in the first movement, and proposes a change of paradigm in our understanding of the unconscious. He uses clinical material to discuss questions relative to the difference between the use of fantasy and the use of imagination. He emphasizes creative imagination, its origin in radical imagination, and its relation to the idea of the expansion of the unconscious, with analytic intuition and the diverse interpretative rhythms of analytical work.

Annie Reiner's paper explores the issues of language and the development of the capacity to think. Using psychoanalytic techniques in the treatment of a mother and baby, Reiner examines the lexical and non-lexical aspects of language (sounds, intonations, gestures) and the means by which the infant "understands" the analyst's verbal interventions. She suggests that while babies cannot be said to understand the words, they nonetheless seem to *gain understanding* from the communication, a less active and more primitive form of mental processing related to projective identification. They gain understanding, that is, *from the understanding of someone who understands*, an identification with the *function* of "understanding," and with thinking, the potential for which is inherent in the human mind.

Johan Norman and Björn Salomonsson respectively, in their papers, present some of their groundbreaking work in which they have adapted psychoanalysis for work with infants. Infants suffer to a considerable degree from disturbances in nursing, sleep, mood, and attachment. Psychotherapeutic methods are increasingly used to help them. According to case reports, psychoanalytic work with infants and mothers has shown deep-reaching and often surprisingly rapid results, both in symptom reduction and in improved relations between mother and child. The clinical urgency of the method makes it important to study its results and theoretical underpinnings. Among the theoretical issues often raised in discussions on this modified form of psychoanalysis, those addressing the nature of communication between analyst, baby, and the mother are the most frequent. For example, how and what does an infant understand when the analyst interprets to her? What does the analyst understand of the infant's communication? Salomonsson addresses these issues by investigating the infant's tools for understanding linguistic and emotional communication, and by providing a semiotic framework for describing the communication between the three participants in the analytic setting. He also investigates problems with the traditional ways of using the concept of symbolization within psychoanalytic theory.

Chapter 1

"Orphans of O"

The negative therapeutic reaction and the longing for the childhood that never was

James S. Grotstein[1]

Introduction

The subject I wish to explore is chronic psychoanalytic resistance, particularly as it occurs in the difficult-to-reach patient (Joseph, 1989). I shall emphasize one particular kind of resistance, however, the negative therapeutic reaction or psychic equilibrium and the problems it creates in regard to interruptions of psychoanalytic progress as well as transference ↔ countertransference enactments. It constitutes a continuation of two previous contributions dealing with infantile catastrophe and its ineluctable consequences, ontological "orphandom" (Grotstein, 1995a, 1995b).

The difficult-to-reach patient

Freud (1926), Riviere (1936), Rosenfeld (1968a) and others described patients suffering from a "negative therapeutic reaction," a clinical situation in which the patient, after achieving recognizable progress in his analysis, subtly begins to compromise or undo that progress. Freud (1916) had prefigured his thoughts on this disorder in his paper "Those Wrecked by Success," in which he described patients who experienced unconscious guilt about their success in analysis as well as in life generally. Betty Joseph (1989) and her colleagues independently categorize this clinical situation as a "psychic equilibrium" that the difficult-to-reach patient attempts to achieve, an equilibrium between his progressive self and his regressively resistant self (Hargreaves and Varchevker, 2004). A universal characteristic of these "difficult patients" is their deep and abiding fear of change (Riviere, 1936; Bion, 1970; Joseph, 1989; Waska, 2006).

A deception was in operation with these patients, and the analyst was subtly being manipulated to collude with it. That the analysts almost universally seemed tempted at times despite knowing better is in itself a subject for inquiry. The analysts in Betty Joseph's Workshop are amongst the finest in training, quality, and experience in the world (Hargreaves and Varchevker, 2004). That is why the phenomenon common to them in regard to their countertransference temptations was so striking to me – as was the common theme that seemed especially to characterize the idiosyncratic, surreptitious resistance. I know it well from my own analytic and supervisory experiences and was grateful to Betty Joseph and the members of her Workshop for their candor as well as for the diligence of their researches.

The problem of transference ↔ countertransference enactments

The transference ↔ countertransference situations these patients evoke are all too frequently able to elicit characteristic enactments both by the analysand and by the analyst, i.e. creating a folie à deux (Mason, 1994) between them – *to arrest the progress of the analysis*. Similarly, a universal characteristic of the analysts treating these patients is their experience of feeling pressured to join them in a compromise, that is, that they, the analysts, should not go deeper and should not question the resistance, which is being put forward as legitimate progress (Sandler, 1976; Joseph, 1989). That the analysts so often were tempted at times despite their knowing better is in itself a subject for inquiry. I shall attempt to shed light on this aberration.

The negative therapeutic reaction as a conflict between internal living systems

I conceive of the mind as a living system consisting of an array of other component unconscious living systems, i.e. *subjects*, each of which possesses its own sense of identity and will (agency) and consequently is capable of pursuing psychic change on the one hand or of inaugurating resistances like the negative therapeutic reaction on the other. This idea is but another way of conceiving of the unconscious as a hologram, a composite of living *subjects*, *preternatural presences*, *intelligences*, *demons*, *homunculi*, or *phantoms*, which uncannily represent as well as interact with each other within the self. *I am reconceptualizing mental mechanisms as interactive subjectivities*, i.e. *living systems*. I introduce this idea because of a clinical experience that made me think in this direction, one that is important in explicating my theme and which I shall present later.

The asymmetry of healing

In analysis, as in therapeusis generally, normal healing or progress occurs asymmetrically. I have noted in a number of cases I have treated and/or supervised that even in high-level cases one could detect "self-envy" (López de Corvo, 1992, 1995, 1999). By this I mean that those aspects of the analyzed personality that *have* made progress seem to inspire envy in those other sub-personalities that have yet to feel liberated. This experience of self-envy seems to be all the more formidable in patients suffering from negative therapeutic reactions. One aspect of the castaway infant or "forgotten self" (López-Corvo, 2006) is the "turncoat self," which enters into a perverse alliance with the "obstructive object" "super" ego (Bion, 1962, p. 97) within the pathological organization of these patients. It thereupon envies the healthier twin all the more because of its own belief (Britton, 1998) that it and its hapless twin, the castaway infant, cannot emerge to make progress.

The clinical stimulus for hearing "a voice from the crypt"

During the analysis of a patient who demonstrated the negative therapeutic reaction, I imagined while in a state of reverie (Bion, 1962, p. 36) that I had heard "a voice from within a crypt," a woeful wail, an ululu, of an erstwhile "castaway infant" or "forgotten self" (López-Corvo, 2006) trapped in a psychic retreat (Steiner, 1993) trying desperately to summon my help by the very intrusiveness and provocativeness of her resistance as well as her wail. This patient had once uttered, "*There's a very little girl in a crumpled heap at the bottom of my mind.*" I remember being deeply moved. Something stirred within me, a desire to comfort the patient (complementary maternal countertransference). Perhaps I had heard not only the mythical voice of the internal patient but also my own (concordant countertransference). I was immediately reminded of Fairbairn's (1943b) concept of the "crypt." I then began to rethink the whole concept of chronic resistances: a need to understand their raison d'être, but from a new perspective: *resistance animated as a phantasmal psychic intelligence*, a homunculus or "daimon" (in the ancient Greek sense: Diamond, 1996), a *subject with agency* and with *legitimacy and reason.*

Background of the negative therapeutic reaction

The negative therapeutic reaction was originally conceived of by Freud (1926), particularly in reference to the unconscious guilt some patients experience when they make progress. It then was described by Abraham (1921) and elaborated upon by Rosenfeld (1964, 1968a, 1968b, 1968c). Riviere's (1936) study of the subject, however, although written long ago, remains one of the defining works on the subject, and I shall list some of her key points: patients have a fear of exposing their love; they have no faith in getting well; they are being forced to face death; the depressive position is stronger in them; their sense of failure, of inability to remedy matters is so great; analysis means unmasking them (p. 312).

Joseph's "psychic equilibrium"

Joseph (1989), as stated above, studied difficult cases whose main characteristic was the development of analytic stalemating, which she termed a "psychic equilibrium" (p. 88) and which, as I interpret it, is identical with the negative therapeutic reaction. This phenomenon is characterized by a balance between that aspect of the analysand that was able to accept his dependent feelings so as to progress, and another which became resistant to analytic progress. *A balance between the effects of these two personalities seems uncannily to develop – as if*, and this is *my* hypothesis, *an unknown force, an ineffable subject or intelligence* (not just mechanism), *is organizing the balancing of the equilibrium by initiating resistance.*

The "paradoxical wisdom" behind analytic enactments

The analyst's vulnerability to participate in these enactments may be due the analysand's unconscious effectiveness in recruiting the analyst's own infantile neurosis in the transference ↔ countertransference – because of two universal invariants within the analyst's make-up: (a) the recruitment of his or her unconscious extra-analytic "maternal" and/or "paternal instinct" that this wayward, fey castaway infant unconsciously beckons (complementary countertransference); and (b) a concordant countertransference (Racker, 1968, p. 135) with the patient's troubled infantile personality. In either case a folie à deux (Mason, 1994, p. 643) with corresponding enactments has taken place. The unconscious motive behind the activation of these enactments may be the castaway personality's need to prevent analytic change so that its welfare is not jeopardized by anticipated imminent fragmentation. Thus, the putative "wisdom" that lies behind enactments by the analysand *and* the analyst may be the castaway infant's desire to:

1 Halt the "engines" of analytic change because of a fear of another and more devastating psychic catastrophe, a massive splitting or fragmentation of the ego, if progress continues – because of the growing disparity between the two "infants," a growing disparity which heralds a massive splitting of the psyche.
2 A desire on the part of the patient to recruit the analyst, first of all, to recognize the cryptic presence of another personality within the former that cannot speak for itself except through gesture and enactments; second, to recruit the analyst to assume the role of a supportive, nurturing mother and/or father (complementary countertransference: Racker, 1968) to make up for that which is believed to have been either absent or not sufficiently present, i.e. to achieve an omnipotent "corrective emotional experience" (Alexander, 1930) in place of regretting that which traumatically happened and mourning that which never

was; third, unconsciously manipulating the analyst into a folie à deux by activating his own infantile neurosis, particularly those aspects which concordantly (Racker, 1968) match those of the analysand (Klein, 1955).

Thesis: the anatomy of chronic resistance – "I am mine own executioner"

The negative therapeutic reaction or psychic equilibrium is a form of *chronic* resistance that issues from a pathological organization ("psychic retreat" [Steiner, 1993], "claustrum" [Meltzer, 1992], "endopsychic structure" [Fairbairn, 1944], "beta-screen" [Bion, 1962], or "enclave" [Baranger and Baranger, 1961–62]) that is split off, i.e. exists extraterritorially to the rest of the personality, and casts a negative spell upon it by behaving like a saboteur to the positive coalition between the cooperative analysand and his analyst. This entity appears to thwart continuing analytic progress. It is my conjecture that the pathological organization itself is an autonomous living system comprised of sub-systems all of which are cut off from regulatory input from the ego and thus develop independently as "rogue organizations" via "alpha-function in reverse" (Bion, 1962, p. 25), i.e. there is "method in its madness."

This pathological enclave consists of what can be termed "scar-tissue" objects (Grotstein, 2000, pp. 167–168), particularly an "obstructive object" or cruel "super" ego (Bion, 1967, p. 97) that has become an arbitrary "protective police force," "protective" by incarcerating the hapless personality in persecutory custody, disallowing any escape – for his own good! One aspect of this hapless castaway self becomes a "kapo" or "turncoat" and enters into a malignant coalition with the obstructive object both to excoriate its split-off hapless, abject, ultra-vulnerable self and to thwart or sabotage the relationship between the cooperative analysand and analyst. The turncoat aspect can be considered to be an example of "identification with the aggressor" (A. Freud, 1936) and, if extreme, the "Stockholm Syndrome," a situation in which the victim changes his loyalty and dependency onto the new cruel but "dependable" object, "dependable" because of its idealized strength to offset the collapsed worldview of the demoralized victim (Bejerot, 1974). In this state the victim may ultimately be incarcerated by his "agoraphobia" since he has contaminated the outside world with his projections. The castaway self corresponds to Girard's (1986) concept of the "*scapegoat*."

Martyrdom as a perverse transformation of the castaway subject

A variation on this theme is the development of the martyr personality, a situation that develops when the castaway infant becomes masochistically belligerent, using its suffering as a sadistic weapon for fear that its analytic progress and/or progress in life augur a foreclosure on its omnipotent prospect to have its lost and incomplete infancy and childhood restored.

"Soul Murder" and its irredeemable aftermath: The forfeiture of the soul

Klein's oeuvre is organized around the infant's unconscious phantasy that he or she had harmed the maternal breast and consequently suffers persecutory anxiety and then depressive guilt in turn (Klein, 1935, 1940). While totally supporting Klein in this regard, I seek to add the hypothesis that what the infantile portion of the personality does to the maternal – and paternal – object, it also does to the most helpless, vulnerable, abject, and shamefully inept portion of its own personality – aside from the object (albeit always identified with it) – which it omnipotently seeks to "repair" through "corrective" blame and excoriation, or, failing that, to ostracize, banish, or finally "murder." *Thus, my ultimate thesis: the negative therapeutic reaction results from a "soul murder" of this self*, and this fateful self reveals itself by haunting the analytic domain, pleading for acknowledgement, rescue, justice, and redemption. This ululu is the "voice from the crypt." "Killing" the infant or "soul murder" actually signifies the "murder" of the connection or link between the self and the object, in this case where the "object" designates the self that is to be disavowed and discarded (Freud, 1923 [1922]; Grotstein, 1979, 1995a, 1995b).

The dilemma for the castaway personality is to dare to foreswear its Faustian Bargain, to foreswear its perverse loyalty and fealty to the obstructive object in the psychic retreat (which, after all, is its own projective creation). The power and omnipotent authority of the obstructive object was the castaway's unconsciously delegated gift to it. Received wisdom tells us the severity of the superego is responsible for the commensurate weakness of the ego. The opposite may also be true: the more weakened and hopeless the castaway personality becomes, the more it needs a commensurately stronger superego to serve as a "hard object" (Tustin, 1981, p. 61) to stanch its vulnerability. It is as if the weakened ego becomes an unconscious ventriloquist as it unwittingly (because of splitting and projective identification) wields the power of the armory it transferred to the superego – and then pretends to be its victim, and all the while it is, in its lamentably submissive state, secretly proud of its complementary identification with its "Frankenstein creation," the "super" ego (Bion, 1962, p. 97).

Alpha-function's rejection of beta-elements considered as a fractal of "soul murder"

Bion (1962) posits "alpha-function" as a receiving, containing, and processing model to account for the transformation of not-yet-mental sensory-emotional stimuli into "alpha-elements" suitable for mental "digestion." Alpha-function functions like a sieve or grating to sort out incoming stimuli that are tolerable and useful for mental digestion from those that are not tolerable, which, according to Bion, are left unprocessed as beta-elements and expelled through projective identification.

In another contribution I depart somewhat from Bion in suggesting that, since alpha-function must first "taste" or sample the incoming sensory stimulus in order to categorize it either for acceptance or rejection – *and since the individual personality that was sensorily and emotionally affected by the stimulus* has already registered and absorbed it into itself – the sensory stimulus can be considered to have been an alpha-element all along, albeit an inchoate one (Grotstein, 2007).

The incoming "beta-element" that is too toxic to be process may consequently be categorized as a *"rejected" or a "rogue alpha-element."* The significance of this idea is as follows: just as we physically "become" the digestive transformation within the limits of the restraints that our body imposes as it accommodates to the metabolism of food, the mind "becomes" the sensory-emotional stimuli that it *does* allow itself to experience, on one hand, but also becomes haunted by the "beta-elements" (I say "rogue alpha-elements") it has rejected – because these beta-elements constitute banished, condemned portions of ourselves that persecute, hound and haunt us, and surround us (Bion's "beta screen" [1962, p. 22]) as they relentlessly seek to be repatriated (the "return of the repressed").

The etiology of chronic resistance[2]

These analysands have probably suffered from an "infantile mental catastrophe" (Bion, 1967, p. 88) or a "failure to go on being" (Winnicott, 1960, pp. 50–54). Winnicott, in regard to the "fear of breakdown," states:

> Not all our patients who have this fear complain of it at the outset of treatment. Some do; but others have their defences so well organized that it is only when a treatment has made considerable progress that the fear of breakdown comes to the fore as a dominating factor . . . [as a result of which] we are examining a reversal of the individual's maturational processes.
>
> (1974, p. 88)

The result is the formation of a split in the ego, corresponding to concurrent splits in the objects and/or part-objects – as detailed by Fairbairn (1940, 1941, 1943a, 1944, 1946) and Klein (1946) – with the establishment of a "true" and "false-self" dichotomy (Winnicott, 1960). There are two separate sub-personalities, one that can be understood as a normal or neurotic personality and which may be readily analyzable, and a second that can be understood as a "castaway infant" (cast away by the more dominant "false-self") – analogous to Bion's (1957) distinction between the neurotic and psychotic personalities within one. This false-self corresponds to Fairbairn's (1944) Central Ego, which is attached to an Ideal Object. As the castaway true-self feels more and more hopeless, one aspect of it, which Fairbairn terms the "internal saboteur" or "antilibidinal ego" (1944, p. 129), identifies with the aggressor, the rejecting object – which Bion (1962, p. 97) terms the "obstructive object" – and it in turn secondarily casts away the helpless and hopeless libidinal self which relates to an exciting object; but this exciting object is but the other side of the diabolical rejecting object.

The castaway self constitutes either a psychotic and/or a post-traumatized personality, one which *presents* itself as unanalyzable, ungrown, stunted, and incapable of development, one which believes that it should never have been born, cannot handle the fact of birth and its consequences, grieves for the infancy and childhood it feels deprived of, and seeks its return. This castaway self either gives up hope or is on the verge of doing so. The castaway self, in its abject hopelessness, seeks protection by identifying itself with the traumatizing object (Bion's "obstructive object", ibid.) in two ways: a fatal split takes place in which one part identifies *concordantly* with the traumatizing object (as a "kapo"[3] or saboteur), and the remaining part identifies *complementarily* in a perverse sado-masochistic bondage with that object. It relates to the tantalizing exciting object, which is but the other side of the demonic, rejecting obstructive object.

Pathological dependency issues in castaway patients

One of the major characteristics of patients suffering from the negative therapeutic reaction is the nature of their dependent relationship to their objects. Whereas the infantile portion of the normal patient *gainfully* depends on the object, i.e. maintains a sense of responsibility for using the object so as to develop and mature, the infantile portion of the other forswears its responsibility for taking care of itself with the help of the object and projects its responsibility as well as its executive ego functions into the object and/or into its more successful personality counterpart. The result is that the castaway personality becomes "irresponsibly dependent" on the object and/or more successful personality but also becomes a mock critic of them by judging the success or failures of their efforts. The result is a further crippling of that personality's potentiality – because it cannot "learn from experience" (Bion, 1962). This type of abnormal dependency is also seen in narcissistic and borderline disorders.

Other factors

Space considerations allow me only to allude to other important factors whose functions are apposite for these pathological transformations. They include: (a) Bion's (1970) concept of "catastrophic change," which can be thought of as the trauma that results from the premature arrival of the future (without the benefit of transitionalization mediating the change); (b) Bion's (1962) conception of the relationship between the "container" and the "contained"; and (c) the status of the bonding (maternal) and attachment (infant) relationship (Bowlby, 1988; Fonagy, 2001).

The fatal bargain for safety: "Selling one's soul to the devil"

The traumatized, stunted, and now contorted personality, in its heightened vulnerability, terror, and aloneness, cut off from its positive self and the help *its* nurturing objects can offer, seeks desperate relief and protection by, in effect, "selling its soul to the devil" – the "obstructive object or "super" ego (Bion, 1962, p. 97) – and thereby surrenders its vitality, its capacity for joy, its power of attorney, i.e. its will or motivation to develop, and finally, its *soul.* Fairbairn states:

> It is to the realm of these bad objects . . . rather than to the realm of the super-ego that the ultimate origin of all psychopathological developments is to be traced; for it may be said of all psychoneurotic psychotic patients that, if a True Mass is being celebrated in the chancel, *a Black Mass is being celebrated in the crypt* [italics added]. It becomes evident that the psychotherapist is the true successor to the exorcist, and that he is concerned, not only with the 'forgiveness of sins', but also with the 'casting out of devils'. . . . [T]he whole point of a pact with the Devil lies in the fact that it involves a relationship with a bad object.
>
> (1943b, pp. 70–71)

Fairbairn goes on to discuss the *Satanic Pact* that the schizoid patient feels constrained to sign (ibid., pp. 70–72) and then discusses his belief that "*the libidinal cathexes of bad objects is the source of resistance*" [italics added] (ibid., p. 72). These patients thereafter become "schizoid" personalities, that is, "existential renegades."

Having forfeited his soul, the castaway is then taken into the arbitrary "protective custody" of the "scar-tissue" bastion or psychic retreat where it is then committed to solitary confinement "for its own protection." Fairbairn (1944) terms this entity "endopsychic structure," but in earlier days it was known as "Hell" or the "Inferno": "Abandon hope, all ye who enter!" (Dante, in *The Inferno*, 2002). The negative therapeutic reaction constitutes a psychic conflict between the healthy personality's bid for psychical growth and mature interdependent relationships on one hand, and the tenacity and will of the remorseless and diabolical "constabulary" of the psychic retreat in collaboration with the collusive turncoat self, and the abject, hapless prisoner, the castaway infant, on the other, to attempt to abrogate change. The crux of the psychopathology and the cure, however, lies fundamentally in the castaway's libidinal cathexis of the bad object (a whole object that *is* originally toxic or unavailable – the "*enemy*," and the castaway's projective construction of a bad part-object, the "*persecutor*"). Together they comprise the "obstructive object (Bion, 1959). The new sado-masochistic organization begins to develop its own life pattern with what Bion (1962) terms "alpha-function-in-reverse." In other words, method, with its own perverse agency, develops in its madness.

A clinical example

MJ was a forty-ish single female attorney who had been in analysis for many years. She was the middle child, situated between an elder and younger brother, the former of whom seemed to have been a problem child since birth, one who became physically as well as emotionally violent and tormenting from the beginning of the patient's life – without adequate family protection. She recalled many times when she had become so frightened of him that she tried psychically to "disappear," to leave her body so as to become numb to her brother's intimidations. Her efforts went too far. Though strikingly poised and beautiful, she had never been able to tolerate intimacy with a man and had consequently never married. When her mother became seriously ill, she all too eagerly quit her law firm to take care of her mother full time. In other words, she "ceased to exist" from an early age.

Early in the analysis she developed an idealizing transference to me, which she needed for protection against bad-brother objects in her current life, including her boss at work. After some time I was able to show her that I, her idealized analyst, also but unconsciously represented her intimidating brother as the one who analytically intimidates her by causing painful memories and emotions to surface. She seemed able to accept that interpretation and attain a higher level of functioning in her analysis – but not her life.

I found myself frustrated by her becoming a virtual hermit and avoiding social engagements and professional relationships. At times she called attention to what she felt was my disappointment with her. I finally realized that she was using passive-aggressive techniques to thwart me. At times she would recall her childhood home life. Her father, a doctor, was away from early morning to late evening, when she went to bed, and consequently had little contact with her and was unaware of her (and her younger brother's) intimidation by the older brother. Her mother was also intimidated but was less than candid in reporting him to her husband.

As the analysis proceeded, it gradually became apparent that the patient was living in a dissociated state, i.e. dissociated from her feelings and her vitality. In my countertransference I initially had begun to feel like a good father who *would* come to her rescue and also began to have feelings which were sympathetic to her plight, although I was also impatient with her. I found myself "lecturing to her for her own good" in an attempt to change her behavior. At other times I found myself being unusually empathic toward and protective of her. At still other times I found myself becoming unaccountably anxious while listening to her.

Meanwhile, the analysis was in a kind of limbo ("psychic equilibrium"). One day I was able to wake from my stuporous folie à deux and realize that I had been on the slippery slope of ultimately becoming a supportive psychotherapist. I was able ultimately to step back from my countertransferences and rectify the analytic situation with appropriate interventions. Apparently, she had been unconsciously manipulating me to become a protective hero–father substitute and at other times, it turned out, she was unconsciously inviting me to "play" her younger brother who was also intimidated by the older brother and who would often huddle with her in mutual terror.

When I interpreted these ideas to her, she suddenly changed – as if she had awakened from a spell. The analysis seemed to have gotten back on track, but there were many regressions on both our parts as time went on. It became evident that she was afraid of leaving her cocoon, which had also become her prison. She felt loyal to and protected by that prison but felt terrified of its turning against her if she ever attempted an escape. She had been confused, in other words, about whether her protective enclave was a protector or a persecutor (both, as analysis revealed).

First dream

Once she dated a man who was shady on many accounts according to her past reporting of him. During one session she reported a dream in which she was parked in her automobile and was necking with an older man. She was sitting in the driver's seat.[4] Suddenly a thief accosted them on her side. He carried a gun. Her partner seemed not to have been involved. The thief asked for her money, and she handed it over to him. Suddenly, she went unconscious from a blow to her head, presumably from the butt of the thief's gun. She awakened in the dream and found the thief still standing by her side outside the car pointing to her boyfriend as the culprit who had struck her.

Her associations to the older man–boyfriend seemed to describe me, including his "not being involved." Her associations to the thief suggested her bullying brother. I interpreted that she had been upset with me for exploring her ambivalence toward the analysis and toward her boyfriend. She had placed the boyfriend in my place in the dream and, "being a double agent," joined up with the dangerous and disingenuous deceiver–thief against me. Alternately, the thief was an aspect of her who was trying to convince her, who was dependent on me, that *I* constituted a danger to her. The thief represented a formidable internal object, patterned after a bullying older brother, who always seemed to threaten, criticize, belittle, and thwart her throughout her life, and she had always been in thrall to him (Stockholm syndrome). Overwhelmed by the evidence from the dream, she agreed with my interpretation.

Second dream

In another dream she had escaped from an armed and guarded mental hospital only to become terrified after she had successfully escaped. She then became even more terrified by attempting to return unobserved so as not to be punished. She became numb and indifferent to the world, disembodied as it were. She lived as a detached person the rest of her life, even up through much of the analysis. She once wondered if she had made a pact with the devil to be safe. The analysis was characterized by long, uneventful plateaus followed by episodic enactments of a self-defeating nature on her part with intimate relationships and with financial matters. These events would privately and characteristically anger and disappoint me. It took me a while to recognize the pattern: she made me into the bully–brother and succeeded in thwarting me and thereby created a stalemate in the treatment.

She finally realized that her masochistic behavior emerged in part from a "contract" she unconsciously believed she entered into to be safe (she was an attorney). She had sold her soul to the devil (which in her case was patterned after her intimidating brother). I interpreted that her having become an attorney may have been the desire of another aspect of her, now with my help, to renege on her contract – that we are together arranging for a "writ of certiorari" to her internal Supreme Court to free her.

One of Riviere's cautions about patients in the negative therapeutic reaction is that they believe that, in effect, the analysis would kill them. This premonition sounds more understandable if we consider that their phantasied Faustian bargain constitutes a concrete "legal" contract with the "devil."[5] Progress by the healthier self amounts to an act of murder – actually, a reminder of a past-self-murder, a forfeiture of their soul. Thus, in analysis the psychic-retreat self, who has an unconscious connection with his or her fey twin in the Inferno, may become a "double agent," disingenuously attempting to pacify both sides.

He may also become a "secret eater" (and therefore a "double agent"), one who pretends not to take in the analyst's interpretations during the session but then goes home and "eats" them privately. The concreteness of the phantasy of soul surrender to the obstructive object (the devil) is so strong that the hapless victim truly believes that he has forfeited his entelechy, i.e. the entirety of his future potential – and, along with it, the capacity to experience joy. He feels forever damned – over the realization of his forsaking his potential self. It is as if he is caught in a self-created agoraphobic bind, desiring to be free and terrified of being free even if he is able to become free.

Third dream

The patient reported another dream shortly after the previous one, in which she was walking down a street alone at night and began to be chased by a band of ominous-looking men. She drove frantically to escape them, but they followed her closely. She found herself approaching a radio broadcast studio, ran inside, and tried to call for help over a microphone. Just as she was about to speak, she was accosted by the dangerous men and frantically shouted, "They've grabbed the microphone!" In the analysis of the dream we were able to conclude that every time her castaway self tries to escape by cooperating with the analysis, her will and speech (the microphone) are taken over by the obstructive object and the psychic retreat.

Another clinical vignette

Once, while treating a very difficult young single patient who had been in a chronic state of resistance in her analysis, I found myself in an unusual state of reverie. While in that state I believed that I experienced visualization: I had caught the briefest glimpse of a curved sheet of glass by the reflection of light from it. In a sudden flash of thought, I developed the notion that I had "seen" a glass capsule containing my patient. I then began a series of inquiries about my "visualization" with her which extended over many months. She and I were able to think of it as a symbol for her state of encapsulation within her internal world. What also emerged from our inquiry was the belief (by both of us) that the capsule was not only a "psychic retreat" (she was also a therapist) but was itself also an internal presence which served not only to protect her by incarcerating her, but also as a "double agent" in so far as it intercepted my interpretations to the patient and the patient's messages to me, censoring and subtly revising each. This mysterious presence gave the patient to believe that I was being critical of her and was consequently a danger to her. To me the presence seemed to be saying that the patient does not wish to cooperate with the analysis. It was with this experience that I first became aware of the consideration that the internal world is better thought of as comprising living subjective presences.

"Hooke's Law," "conatus," and "entelechy"

I hypothesize that every human being is endowed with a mysterious function that corresponds in the physical sciences to *Hooke's Law*, a veritable "thermostatic" calibration that states: the stress on an object equals the strain that it bears times the modulus of its elasticity (flexibility). Some ineffable organization within us *seems* unconsciously to "know the truth" about how much strain we can bear from emotional stress before our resilience gives way to breakdown. I think this ineffable entity may be linked with Freud's (1911) concept of the pleasure–unpleasure principle and with Bion's (1967) concept of "inability to tolerate frustration." "*Conatus*," discovered by Spinoza (in Damasio, 2003, pp. 36–37), is a principle which not only reflects the "will power" of the individual but also helps to guarantee his selfsameness during catastrophic change. Conatus may thus be the operant principle in creating the negative therapeutic reaction.

Aristotle's "*Entelechy*" (in McKeon, 1941; Peters, 1967, p. 57) reflects actuality or realization as opposed to realization. It can be thought of as the actualization of one's inherent potential to become. Its positive side is associated with normal and psychical maturation, including that which takes place in analysis. Its negative side can be associated with "alpha-function-in-reverse" (Bion, 1962) in so far as the obstructive object in the psychic retreat develops its own entelechy and with it, a chimerical mutation of its original state, thereby transforming it into a most complex and redoubtable negative force to contend with.

Proposition 1: "I wish I had never been born!" ("and I pretend that I haven't been!")

The concept of not wanting to have been born seems to have emerged in Bion's treatment of Samuel Beckett. Apparently, Bion and his patient, Beckett, both attended a lecture at the Tavistock Clinic at which Jung was lecturing. In the course of the lecture Jung referred to a patient who wished he had never been born. I recall having presented a puzzling case to Bion when I was in analysis with him. Although it was not a formal supervisory session, Bion did utter the opinion that my analysand had not wished to have been born, that he was not ready for life, that he was more fetal than otherwise.

Proposition 2: "I want to have a chance to relive what I missed when I was little"

I shall now present a very brief excerpt from another case of a patient who had been adopted at birth. After a memorable session the patient seemed together with herself and was very cooperative. Gradually, resistance had again, as frequently in the past, become apparent. She either became cranky or critical of me or indifferent. I was ultimately able to analyze the crankiness as the behavior of a little girl who wanted to be able to be free enough as a child to be cranky with a mother–me. Her indifference was analyzed as her identification with what she experienced in her parents' demeanor towards her. I then became the analyst–parent who had to suffer what she had gone through (Pietà transference–countertransference [Grotstein, 2000]), i.e. I had to "wear" ("become") her indifferent introjected adopting parents *and* her birth parents – and had to experience her pain and the sorrow and contrition that they could not experience or convey, a psychoanalytic "exorcism," if you will.

In a later stage of her analysis I again became aware of her deep ontological anxiety. She became frustrated in her professional career as a photographer. She found that she was making many errors of judgment and was sabotaging herself. She reported a dream:

> She was walking alone down a street in a big city, probably New York (where she was born). As she was walking, she felt herself become gradually smaller and smaller until she was the size of a very young child. She suddenly became very anxious. At the beginning of the dream she knew where she was going. Now she didn't. She was lost! She heard her old wraith-voice calling to her, "Go back, go back! Don't go on! It's dangerous! She awoke in panic from the nightmare.

Her associations led to two books she had been reading recently. One was James Matthew Barrie's *Peter Pan* and the other was about a young man who hated growing up because he felt he had been cheated out of his childhood by having a father who left home when he was born, leaving him with a chronically depressed mother he had to care for. She then began obsessing about the infancy and childhood she felt that *she* hadn't had – and resenting it.

I interpreted that she shrank in the dream because of a powerful regressive force exerted not only by her old friend, the eerie voice (the "protective" "death instinct") but mainly by a long-ago split-off infant her who could not "go-on-being" and went dead – or partly dead. She is now threatened by her analytic progress. If she continues to grow (up), there is another she who will be left behind, forgotten about. "I interpreted that this she" gave her the nightmare to bring her back home, yet to do so is to forfeit all that *we* had accomplished.

The analysand seemed startled by my interpretation at first. Then she reflected on it and began to weep. She then said, "You know, my life has not been a life. I've been an imposter. Now I know why I never had children. I couldn't raise children. I don't know what it's like to be a child, a playful child, and I don't know what mothering is like. I want to have a chance to relive what I missed when I was little."

Proposition 3: An obsession to "return to infancy" or even "the womb"

With the above possible scenario in mind, then, we can consider that from the point of view of the tragically stunted ("failure to thrive") infant-self the analyst is a betrayer by working in collusion with the progressing, dependent infant-self to develop and mature. Development beyond a certain arbitrary point is felt by the stunted infant to herald a disastrous catastrophic change which in turn portends a radical split or dissociation of the psyche, or even a psychotic break. One recalls in Rosenfeld's (1965) description of his work with psychotic patients how he cautioned the analyst to be careful when the patient approached the threshold of the depressive position. Fragmentation of the psyche could then take place. Why? I have already cited Riviere and totally subscribe to her Kleinian explication – as far as it goes. Here is a complementary, equally Kleinian, alternative one:

The plight of this would-be unborn or castaway infant must be analytically addressed by the employment of what Bion (1967) terms "reversible perspective" and/or "binocular vision" – to attend to "both sides now." To put it in other terms, I believe one of the problems many analysts have been dealing with is what I would now call "infancy addiction" for the infancy that never really was or there was not not enough of: This addiction presupposes a primeval pull by a "failure-to-thrive" castaway, a non-developable infant, one who "failed-to-go-on-being" from birth, to seduce or ensorcel the growing, developing twin from progressing for fear of a mental catastrophe.

In addition to "infancy addiction" I should also like to suggest "fantasying addiction." Here I am using "fantasying" as Winnicott (1971) used it – as being a resistance to being in contact with either psychic reality or external reality. It is better known as the "Walter Mitty Syndrome." The patient I last discussed was an example. Her English accent was not just an identification with her English parents. It was her way of entering into a private world of privilege, of being associated with the aristocracy (inside mother's body as the privileged "unborn fetus"), but she ultimately found that her use of it had become addictive. She couldn't give it up, i.e. it had become a psychic retreat. Put another way, the death instinct may be recruited by a powerful regressive force to pull the abject castaway personality ever backwards and ever earlier – so that it can arrive at having a life within death (Tarantelli, 2003), i. e., earliest infancy, the womb, or non-existence.

"This house against this house"

This twinship, which may be as old as Cain and Abel, has been addressed by Winnicott (1960) as the "true-self" and "false-self" dichotomy.[6] Bion (1957) refers to it as the "differentiation of the psychotic from the non-psychotic personalities," Fairbairn (1944) as split endopsychic structures, Thurber (1942) as "Walter Mitty," and I as the analysand and the resistant anti-analysand. I, following Brown (2005a, 2005b), wish to categorize them as traumatized and non-traumatized personalities.

This is the working dialectic for all analyses, in my opinion – i.e. no longer considering resistances a hindrance to progress but rather enfranchising them to legitimate status as signals of an ancient catastrophe, to which they have become the stigmata, sentinels, and guardians. Since this lost enclave may have formed before the dawn of verbal achievement (Stern, 1985) or even before the dawn of primal repression (Freud, 1915; Kinston and Cohen, 1986, 1988), this split-off personality is constrained to make itself known through subtle or even outrageous enactments, gestures, and charades in order to get the attention either of the surviving/thriving personality and/or of the analyst. *Consequently, there really are no bad objects in the internal world, only actors as signifiers of the feared manifestations of O, the unutterable, infinite terror of the ultimate truth about ultimate reality* (Bion, 1967, 1970; Grotstein, 2000).

Technique: "Both sides now"[7]

The approach to the reclamation and restoration of this lost enclave is outlined as follows:

1 Recognition and respect for the raison d'être of its existence, pathos, agony, and futility – with a newfound regard for the justifiably protective aspects of resistance generally and for the negative therapeutic reaction specifically.
2 As the analyst begins to hone in on this enclave and the lost soul encapsulated and incarcerated intestate within his or her "protective" prison, the analyst may at first experience retrospective guilt or dismay for having neglected or impugned this personality as "resistant" or sabotaging and for having garbed him in the "prisoner-clothes" of the "negative therapeutic reaction." The analyst may then begin to feel another kind of guilt, which I think of as the "Pietà transference–countertransference," in which the analyst, like Mary, the "Madonna of Sorrows," exorcistically experiences the guilt and responsibility that the original parents could not fully enough experience (Grotstein, 2000). Mary, the Madonna of Sorrows, is also the "Madonna of Guilt." She is immemorially guilty of agreeing to bring a child into the world that had already been scheduled for martyrdom. All parents, in fact, share, or should share, this guilt – as must every analyst who takes a patient into analysis and causes the psychoanalytic "conveyor belt" to dredge up forgotten sorrows to the surface, irrespective of the consequences.

3 The analyst's experience of sorrow and guilt, via contingent reverie (Bion, 1962) resembles the mystical religious rite of *exorcism*. Since Bion's formulation of container-contained transference became conjoined with the countertransference, one important perspective that emerged was the necessity for the analyst to experience his own inner version of what the analysand is suffering from; to "*become*" the analysand's anguish and agony. Bion (1967, 1970) terms this phenomenon "transformations in O within the analyst."

Whereas the treatment of the healthier personality follows in the typical mode of traditional transference ↔ countertransference analysis, the course of the treatment of the castaway infant self almost certainly involves the indivisibility of the transference ↔ countertransference in the analyst's reverie, his or her capacity to *become* the patient's anguish. The development of the concept of "mirror neurons" goes a long way to substantiate this process.

"The memory of justice"

I should like at this final moment to become the "Judge Advocate General" and "Coroner" at the inquest for that psychic presence known as "resistance" and for the "castaway-cursed-unborn-infant," its precious ward, which it has long and dutifully protected. Yet I know full well that I have a conflict of interest. I also represent his twin, the properly dependent, evolving infant–analysand with whom I have been too long in virtual collusion to make progress. In the former's defense I summon the "Memory of Justice." Once, according to Plato, there was *Justice* on the earth which reigned with *Sophrosyne* (Balance) (Innocence).

As time progressed, our ill-fated infant found himself prematurely exiled into an unknown wilderness of strange and fateful algorithms that were to become his bewildering life trajectory. He grew into his ever developing individual future form as he encountered surprise, rivalry, challenge, predators, abject helplessness, terror, responsibility, and frustration.

Sophrosyne and Justice seem to have deserted him as they faded back into a shadowy domain beyond the horizon of his ever changing being, leaving him to fend for himself and to forfend facing whatever was coming his way. After his murder of his innocence, partially as a consequence of his own initial desire to be a living self but being unaware of its cruel price and of the predators sometimes even pretending to be his mother and father, he made choices he would painfully regret.

Forsaking life and its ineluctable responsibilities, he opted for safety, and his soul all but perished in a self-made redoubtable dungeon where he was protected for a life-death time from the pain of unassisted living. He then had to learn to find survival amongst its ruins and hope against hope that he could be shepherded in analysis someday to redemption where he might again find higher innocence side by side with the terror and the guilt he had earned along the way.

Yet sometimes when the grown up pauses to consider who he has become in analysis and measures it against whom he once was, and if he chances for moments out of time to listen ever so carefully, he may be able to detect an echo of the haunting little voice of someone he once knew, crying out in ancient anguish for Sophrosyne and the Memory of Justice to be restored – for just a brief moment – and have his day in court, in order that that lost little one can then be redeemed, be given a proper burial and departure from that forsaken life that never was, and be mourned. And from his ashes another he, his restored spirit, can rise again, like the phoenix, and rejoin his twin, whom he was all along!

His "death" is only a symbolic token of the end of the fiction of their separation! The putatively successful analytic twin, the one who accepted the fact of his dependency, turns out to have been a "false-self" after all, as with Joseph's brothers in *Scripture*, by selling a portion of himself as a hostage into slavery. Resistance can then depart at last as it is finally being restored to the unjustly deprived honor and respect it has long deserved.

Epilogue: Verdict of coroner's inquest

This was a life that was never lived. It is a case of silent soul-murder by the self in the third degree. The mother and the infant are both found guilty as well as innocent. Reparations are impossible, only the experiencing of the sorrow and the pity of a life unlived, with eternal regret, but with the hope that the soul of the unlived one can be recompensed through its mourning. The mother is remanded to her own recognizance with a commuted sentence because of mercy – for not having had a containing mother herself. The erstwhile infant, the one the analyst recognized as the dependent analysand, is pardoned for having cast away his twin who is now freed from his vicarious stay in *Inferno* but must spend the rest of his lifetime under parole in *Purgatory*, remaining all the while unwavering in his new loyalty to truth and forbearance.

> There was a time when meadow, grove, and stream,
> The earth, and every common sight,
> To me did seem
> Apparelled in celestial light,
> The glory and the freshness of a dream.
> It is not now as it hath been of yore;
> Turn whereso'er I may,
> By night or day,
> The things which I have seen I now can see no more."
>
> William Wordsworth's *Ode on the Intimations of Immortality*

Notes

1 © James S. Grotstein.
2 In this and other sections of this work I shall imbricate my own thinking with that of other contributors.
3 "Kapos" were Jewish policemen in the concentration camps.
4 The transference implications of her being in the driver's seat did not occur to me till much later.
5 The concept of the devil must be understood here as the emergent transformation that the obstructive object (Bion, 1959) undergoes in unconscious phantasy. Emergence theory allows us to understand how in non-linear systems an entirely new and unpredictable or unexpected form can arise that becomes a permanent entity thereafter.
6 I regret that because of space limitations I cannot explicate Fairbairn's (1940, 1944) invaluable and relevant concepts of splitting of the personality and the ultimate splitting of the rejected object into a rejecting and exciting object along with a corresponding splitting of the rejected ego into an anti-libidinal and libidinal ego respectively.
7 With apologies to Joni Mitchell.

References

Abraham, K. (1921). Contributions to the theory of the anal character. In: *Selected Papers of Karl Abraham* (Trans.) Douglas Bryan and Alix Strachey (1949). London: Hogarth Press, pp. 370–392.

Alexander, F. (1930). *Psychoanalysis of the Total Personality*. New York and Washington: Nervous and Mental Disease Publishing Co.

Alighieri, Dante (Revised Edition 2002). *The Divine Comedy: Volume 1: Inferno*. New York: Penguin Classics.

Baranger, M. and Baranger, W. (1961–62). The analytic situation as a dynamic field. *International Journal of Psychoanalysis*, 89: 795–826.

Bejerot, N. (1974). The six-day war in Stockholm. *New Scientist*, 61: 486–487.

Bion, W.R. (1957). Differentiation of the psychotic from the non-psychotic personalities. *International Journal of Psychoanalysis*, 38: 266–275.

Bion, W.R. (1959). Attacks on linking. In: Bion, W.R. (1967) *Second Thoughts*. London: Heinemann, pp. 93–109.

Bion, W.R. (1962). *Learning From Experience*. London: Heinemann.

Bion, W.R. (1967). *Second Thoughts*. London: Heinemann.

Bion, W.R. (1970). *Attention and Interpretation*. London: Tavistock Publications.

Bowlby, J. (1988). *A Secure Base: Clinical Applications of Attachment Theory*. London: Routledge and Kegan Paul.

Britton, R. (1998). *Belief and Imagination: Explorations in Psychoanalysis*. London and New York: Routledge.

Brown, L. (2005a). The cognitive effects of trauma: Reversal of alpha function and the formation of the beta screen. *Psychoanalytic Quarterly*, 64(2): 397–420.

Brown, L. (2005b). Julie's museum: The evolution of thinking, dreaming, and historicization in the treatment of traumatized patients. Paper delivered at the International Psychoanalytic Congress, Rio de Janeiro.

Damasio, A. (2003). *Looking for Spinoza: Joy, Sorrow, and the Feeling Brain*. New York: Harcourt.

Diamond, S.A. (1996). *Anger, Madness and the Daimonic*. Albany, New York: State University of New York Press.

Fairbairn, W.R.D. (1940). Schizoid factors and personality. In: *Psychoanalytic Studies of the Personality*. London: Tavistock, 1952, pp. 3–27.

Fairbairn, W.R.D. (1941). A revised psychopathology of the psychoses and psychoneuroses. *International Journal of Psychoanalysis*, 22: 250–279.

Fairbairn, W.R.D. (1943a). The war neuroses – their nature and significance. *British Medical Journal*, 10: 183–186.

Fairbairn, W.R.D. (1943b). The repression and the return of bad objects (with special reference to the "war neuroses"). In: *Psychoanalytic Studies of the Personality*. London and New York: Tavistock/Routledge, pp. 59–81.

Fairbairn, W.R.D. (1944). Endopsychic structure considered in terms of object-relationships. In: *Psychoanalytic Studies of the Personality*. London: Tavistock, 1952, pp. 82–136.

Fairbairn, W.R.D. (1946). Object-relationships in dynamic structure. *International Journal of Psychoanalysis*, 27: 30–37.

Fonagy, P. (2001). *Attachment Theory and Psychoanalysis*. New York: The Other Press.

Freud, A. (1936). *The Ego and Mechanisms of Defense*. New York: International Universities Press.

Freud, S. (1911). Formulations of the two principles of mental functioning. *Standard Edition*, 12: 213–226. London: Hogarth Press, 1958.

Freud, S. (1915). Repression. *Standard Edition*, 14: 141–158. London: Hogarth Press, 1957.

Freud, S. (1916). Those wrecked by success. *Standard Edition*, 14: 316–331. London: Hogarth Press, 1957.

Freud, S. (1923[1922]). A seventeenth-century demonological neurosis. *Standard Edition*, 19: 69–108. London: Hogarth Press, 1961.

Freud, S. (1926). Inhibitions, symptoms, and anxiety. *Standard Edition*, 20: 77–178. London: Hogarth Press, 1959.

Girard, R. (1986). *The Scapegoat* (Trans.) Y. Freccero. Baltimore: Johns Hopkins University Press.

Grotstein, J. (1979). Demoniacal possession, splitting, and the torment of joy. *Contemporary Psychoanalysis*, 15(3): 407–453.

Grotstein, J. (1995a). Orphans of the "Real": I. Some modern and post-modern perspectives on the neurobiological and psychosocial dimensions of psychosis and primitive mental disorders. *Bulletin of the Menninger Clinic*, 59: 287–311.

Grotstein, J. (1995b). Orphans of the "Real": II. The future of object relations theory in the treatment of psychoses and other primitive mental disorders. *Bulletin of the Menninger Clinic*, 59: 312–332.

Grotstein, J.S. (2000). *Who is the Dreamer Who Dreams the Dream?: A Study of Psychic Presences*. Hillsdale, NJ: The Analytic Press.

Grotstein, J. (2007). *A Beam of Intense Darkness: Wilfred Bion's Legacy to Psychoanalysis*. London and New York: Karnac Books.

Hargreaves, E. and Varchevker, A. (2004). *In Pursuit of Psychic Change: The Betty Joseph Workshop*. London: Brunner-Routledge.

Joseph, B. (1989). *Psychic Equilibrium and Psychic Change*. London: Routledge.

Kinston, W. and Cohen, J. (1986). Primal repression: Clinical and theoretical aspects. *International Journal of Psychoanalysis*, 67: 337–356.

Kinston, W. and Cohen, J. (1988). Primal repression and other states of mind. *Scandinavian Psychoanalytic Review*, 11: 81–105.

Klein, M. (1935). A contribution to the psychogenesis of manic-depressive states. In: *Contributions to Psycho-Analysis, 1921–1945*. London: Hogarth Press, 1950, pp. 282–310.

Klein, M. (1940). Mourning and its relation to manic-depressive states. In *Contributions to Psycho-Analysis, 1921–1945*. London: Hogarth Press, 1950, pp. 311–338.

Klein, M. (1946). Notes on some schizoid mechanisms. In: M. Klein, P. Heimann, S. Isaacs, and J. Riviere (Eds) (1952) *Developments in Psycho-Analysis*. London: Hogarth Press, pp. 292–320.

Klein, M. (1955). On identification. In: M. Klein, P. Heimann, S. Isaacs and J. Riviere. (Eds.) (1952) *Developments in Psycho-Analysis*. London: Hogarth Press, pp. 309–345.

López-Corvo, R.E. (1992). About interpretation of self-envy. *International Journal of Psychoanalysis*, 73: 719–728.

López-Corvo, R.E. (1995). *Self-Envy, Therapy and the Divided Inner World*. New York: Jason Aronson.

López-Corvo, R.E. (1999). Self-envy and intrapsychic interpretation. *Psychoanalytic Quarterly*, 68: 209–219.

López-Corvo. R. (2006). The forgotten self: With the use of Bion's theory of negative links. *Psychoanalytic Review*, 93: 363–377.

McKeon, R. (1941). *The Basic Works of Aristotle*. New York: Random House.

Mason, A. (1994). A psychoanalyst's looks at a hypnotist: A study of folie à deux. *Psychoanalytic Quarterly*, 63(4): 641–679.

Meltzer, D. (1992). *The Claustrum: An Investigation of Claustrophobic Phenomena*. Strath Tay: Clunie Press.

Peters, F.E. (1967). *Greek Philosophical Terms: A Historical Lexicon*. New York: New York Universities Press.

Racker, H. (1968). *Transference and Countertransference*. London: Hogarth.

Riviere, J. (1936). A contribution to the analysis of the negative therapeutic reaction. *International Journal of Psychoanalysis*, 17: 304–320.

Rosenfeld, H. (1964). On the psychopathology of narcissism: A clinical approach. In: H. Rosenfeld (1965) *Psychotic States: A Psychoanalytical Approach*. New York: International Universities Press, pp. 169–179.

Rosenfeld, H. (1965). *Psychotic States: A Psychoanalytical Approach*. New York: International Universities Press.

Rosenfeld, H. (1968a). Notes on the negative therapeutic reaction. Lecture read to the British Psycho-Analytical Society.

Rosenfeld, H. (1968b). Afterthought: Changing theories and changing techniques in psychoanalysis. In: H. Rosenfeld (1968) *Impasse and Interpretation: Therapeutic and Anti-Therapeutic Factors in the Psychoanalytic Treatment of Psychotic, Borderline, and Neurotic Patients*. London: Tavistock, pp. 265–280.

Rosenfeld, H. (1968c). *Impasse and Interpretation: Therapeutic and Anti-Therapeutic*

Factors in the Psychoanalytic Treatment of Psychotic, Borderline, and Neurotic Patients. London: Tavistock.
Sandler, J. (1976). Countertransference and role responsiveness. *International Review of Psychoanalysis*, 3: 43–47.
Steiner, J. (1993). *Psychic Retreats: Pathological Organizations in Psychotic, Neurotic and Borderline Patients*. London: Routledge.
Stern, D. (1985). *The Interpersonal World of the Infant*. New York: Basic Books.
Tarantelli, C. (2003). Life within death: Towards a metapsychology of catastrophic psychic trauma. *International Journal of Psychoanalysis*, 84: 915–928.
Thurber. J. (1942). The Secret Life of Walter Mitty. In: D. Madden (Ed.) (1990) *The World of Fiction*. Fort Worth: Holt, Rinehart &Winston, pp. 977–981.
Tustin, F. (1981). *Autistic States In Children*. London: Routledge and Kegan Paul.
Waska, R. (2006). *The Danger of Change: The Kleinian Approach with Patients Who Experience Progress as Trauma*. London and New York: Routledge.
Winnicott, D.W. (1960). Ego distortion in terms of the true and false self. In: D.W. Winnicott (1960) *The Maturational Processes and the Facilitating Environment: Studies in the Theory of Emotional Development*. New York: International Universities Press, pp. 140–152.
Winnicott, D.W. (1963). Fear of breakdown. In: C. Winnicott, R. Shepard and M. Davis (Eds.) (1989) *Psychoanalytic Explorations: D.W. Winnicott*. Cambridge, MA: Harvard University Press, pp. 87–95.
Winnicott, D.W. (1971). Dreaming, fantasying, and living: A case-history describing a primary dissociation. In: D.W. Winnicott (1971) *Playing and Reality*, London and New York: Tavistock Publications, pp. 26–37.

Chapter 2

Experiencing emotions, avoiding emotions

Between Hercules and Puss-in-Boots

Antonino Ferro

One of the greatest difficulties known to our species consists in managing the proto-emotional and proto-sensorial: we are constantly being "invaded" by all sorts of stimulations from within and without, and the tools and implements at our disposal are only partially capable of transforming these proto-emotions into thoughts, emotions, and dreams.

This weakness in our species derives first from the incomplete evolution of tools assigned to guarantee such transformations: man's psychic apparatus and the instruments at his disposal are very recent and rudimentary, as Wilfred Bion reiterated throughout his work. The precarious nature of the tools also stems from the fact that to develop they need the support of another available psychic apparatus. I refer here, in Bion's language (1962, 1963, 1965, etc.), to the function (the alpha function) that transforms beta elements (all varieties of sensorial appearances as well as proto-emotions) into pictograms. These pictograms make up the "building blocks" that enable us to construct thoughts, emotions, and dreams.

Faced with proto-emotions and proto-sensoriality, we have several choices, of which the simplest – one I would describe as descending – is evacuation. Evacuation allows us to relieve the apparatus enough to permit thought to occur. Evacuations can take place in the body (psychosomatic illnesses) or outside the body (hallucinations) or in behaviors lacking depth of thought (antisocial behavior, delinquency).

The second choice is that of transformation and movement towards thought, emotion, and dream (Ferro, 2002, 2008; Grotstein, 2007; Ogden, 2003), though this, too, once accomplished and the developmental tools are formed, has its difficulties. The first is the constant temptation to lie: thought can be used to distance us from knowledge and avoid the activation of unmanageable emotions. I am no zealot of the truth for either the species, the group, or the individual: there is a degree of tolerable truth beyond which it is impossible to go. Some of the finest pages written on the subject are to be found in Bion's "Fable of the Liars," (1970) which paradoxically praises lying and exalts its usefulness for the species. Besides the formation of the capacity to think, besides the development of thought and its tribulations with the lie, there is the difficulty of experiencing emotions and experiencing them in depth. All this makes me think of the collective dreams we call myths (including alpha functions, alpha elements, and group dreams) that can tell us something or that can be used to tell us something universal about our species.

That Greek mythology is an endless source of suggestions goes without saying. At one point I chose Sisyphus to illustrate that the process leading to "thinking, feeling, dreaming" is an unending chore that must constantly start from square one, because each stimulation implies restarting the system of literacy. On the other hand, I saw Hercules and his feats as representative of the effort that our species, every one of us, must put into making each proto-emotional state literate in a manner not only tragic but also creative if it is to accomplish this apparently impossible task. Certain feats of Hercules are particularly appropriate to describe the metabolization/digestion/mentalization process.

But while myth usually contains a dimension that is collective and tragic and does not provide much cause for hope, the fairy tale contains just enough dishonesty to feed the hope – unreasonable and improbable as it may be – of living "happily ever after," that is, the possibility for man to find a homeostasis outside of time, forever after. It is no accident that we tell our children fairy tales before they go to sleep: the myriad adventures tend to culminate in a soothing happy ending, a fitting entry into the world of dreams.

The story of "Puss-in-Boots" is one of the most optimistic and the exact opposite of, say, Andersen's "Little Match Girl." The hero, a poor orphan, inherits a cat that after a series of adventures leads him to construct a new identity and conquer the most terrible illusions facing him. All this is due to a combination of what we could call defense mechanisms against truth, which run the gamut from seduction to negation by way of omnipotence and falsification and which allow him to overcome all obstacles and in the end marry the king's daughter.

Myth shows us things as they are, but we need fairy tales to show us things as we would like them to be. And if myth leads us to the inevitable fatigue and pain implied by Bion's famous "O," the Truth about ourselves, the fairy tale reminds us that we can do so only indirectly, bit by bit. More often than not we must make the best of things by using approximations, tricks, detours, in short, all the natural defense mechanisms that enable us to accept those doses of the truth – about us and about the world – we are capable of tolerating without experiencing crisis. We are not far from the praise given by Winnicott to the false self as guarantor of the survival of the true self.

Let me now move to clinical work to show how what I have said on the theoretical level is seen and in part transformed during analysis.

Avoiding emotions, experiencing emotions

As I said above, experiencing emotions is an uphill battle presupposing a set of tools able to assimilate, manage and contain them. Creating a "feuilleton" (Luzes, 2000, personal communication), a "human interest column," is what we do best in life, and we can consider the analyst a mender of broken stories, a print setter of sorts or even a papermaker. I see the constant narrative activity, the micro-mythopoeia taking place at the heart of the analytic pair, as a characteristic of our species. Look at pre-historical graffiti. Moving from graffiti (pictograms) to stories, we trace the path our psychic apparatus takes over and over.

The analyst's work can also consist in disentangling masses of fuzzy or fractured proto-emotions to form elementary units that, once transformed, can come back together in new structures and new stories. There is always the risk of the analyst's transference onto the patient or, as I like to put it, the risk that the analyst's psychic apparatus will make transformations in hallucinoses by "seeing" in the patient what he, the analyst, projects onto him in terms of his theories, emotional needs, and personal narratives.

Avoidance

Proto-emotions may be compared to supplies of pin points (I refer to the feelings they are made up of) at various stages of development. Even in the best of conditions, when the psychic mechanisms are functioning well, there is a surplus of them, as is extremely clear in group phenomena. I will not describe here the different degrees of "cushion," combination, or containment among proto-emotional states; I merely wish to show that the avoidance of emotions is an integral activity of our psychic apparatus, be it as patients, analysts, or human beings.

When one form of avoidance takes clear precedence over the others, it becomes a syndrome. Evacuation mechanisms – that is, the projection of the "supplies of pin points" to the external world – may come into play, giving rise to such phenomena as paranoia, hallucination, delirium, and autism. Evacuation may also occur in the body, causing psychosomatic illness, or in the body social, causing antisocial behavior, delinquency, or collective stupidity (Ferro 1996, 2006). If these proto-emotions are not under great pressure or if they can be contained, they can be kept within the space of the psychic apparatus. Accumulations of compact proto-emotions form phobias in the case of an isolation strategy, obsessions in the case of a control strategy, and hypochondria in the case of a strategy designed to confine them to an organ of the body, and so on.

Now let us look at strategies designed to avoid emotions – or, rather, their unmetabolized precursors – in various clinical situations.

Tightrope walkers and ships

A patient with narcissistic tendencies has two dreams. In the first he covers the distance between his house and my office, about two kilometers, in a straight line on a tightrope above the street. From there he can look down on everyone (his intelligence is the be all and end all of his existence), but the real reason he does it, he tells me, is to avoid being run over by the speeding cars; in other words, emotions have a kinetic power capable of running him over. By maintaining a safe distance from any sort of proto-emotion, he can avoid accidents and avoid losing the power of thought (the tightrope or thread).

The second dream is even more obvious. The patient is the captain of a ship. Everything must be shipshape. The crew is constantly making the rounds to ensure that the sails are perfect, the hull has no leaks, etc. As a result, the ship is making good progress. But if the slightest thing goes wrong, catastrophe will ensue – the sails will be torn to bits, a tiny leak will sink the ship – and he will be court-martialed, demoted, even sentenced to death. In Gigi's life everything must be perfect: his work, his children's marks in school, his friends' invitations – the slightest hitch and catastrophe is around the corner. Why?

First and foremost – and this is the response he and I formulated together – because of the active imperfection of unmanageable emotions. Gigi lacks the crew necessary to take care of emergencies, the emotional billows and gales that might come up. The effort he puts into making everything perfect is enormous, but it is nothing compared with what he would have to do should new, unforeseen emotions be activated.

I believe that many autistic behaviors have the same root: the obsession with detail, the identical repetition of gestures, the miniaturization of the emotions serve to avoid emotional impact, which is so hard to manage. By the same token, the reason we steer clear of flaming passions or extinguish them in routine, repetition, exhaustion, boredom, or intellectualization is to stick to a bearable emotional diet. The strategies we invent are highly varied. Take anorexia, for instance, where the split and unbearable parts or proto-emotions, though projected behind oneself, are seen by the anorexic's echographical eye and perceived as heavy and gross.

Although I have always maintained that an analyst and psychoanalytic thought cannot exist outside a patient and a setting, allow me to contradict myself, in the manner of our great novelist Manzoni ("that Capharnaum of the human heart"), because I believe that macro-social phenomena perform the same function, namely, they stymie unbearable emotional states. Think of fanatical political movements, of guaranteed truths and certitudes, of the function of all religion. Viewing ourselves as a "ludus naturae," a game of nature, with no why or wherefore, no before or after, is too agonizing; it activates too many emotions. Religion is indeed an opium of the people, but in the sense that opium has in medicine: a specific antidote for an unbearable pain, the pain of realizing that the only sense in life is living. It is a risk that psychoanalysis itself runs when theory becomes dogma with its attendant heresies.

Rumination

It is likewise important to note that if it is true that one of the activities of our psychic apparatus (a "descending" activity) consists in setting up a defense against the emotions, it is equally true that another activity (this one "ascending") attempts to re-establish contact with what has been banned or isolated or, if nothing else, kept at a distance in connection not only with the return of what has been repressed but also with the continual pressure of what has been split off and banned. Occupational or love-related choices and even whole periods of life frequently have what might be called a ruminatory function, which tries to renew contact with the proto-emotions, with the "supplies of pin points" that have been evacuated, drained, split, doped, isolated, or what have you.

Notary public figure or criminal lawyer

A woman came to see me in connection with a case of constipation so serious that she had been hospitalized several times for intestinal blockage. She reported a family life of "emotional tsunamis," of violent accusations and arguments. She had a sister who suffered from depression and virtually never spoke except for bouts of logorrhea and a father who apparently lived a double life: while leading an irreproachable existence at home, he participated in orgies with high-class prostitutes and took drugs.

Laura's world was clearly divided between two modalities: hyper-containment, which holds all emotion at bay, and total incontinence, which evacuates or drains all emotion. While going through her analysis, Laura decided to give up the idea of becoming a notary public figure like her grandfather and to become a criminal lawyer instead. This professional choice proved to be the "rumination" that enabled her to make contact with a great number of proto-emotions: her work continually brought her together with juvenile delinquents – drug addicts, thieves, blackmailers – and taught her that, even if it came out in different ways, she and they shared a deep despair. The work of the analyst, who must contain, judge, condemn, understand, and defend these "characters," led her to the choice of a profession that became a means for letting what had flown out of the window come in by the back door.

Freeze or melt

There seemed to be no reason why Marta should not enjoy a satisfactory sexual relationship with her husband. Her frigidity was a way of freezing the primitive stage of unleashed proto-emotions; without it she would have to have been abused and "raped" by emotions she could not contain. During her analysis Marta decided to put her long ignored MA in psychology to use. She began working with sexually or otherwise abused children. For Marta as for Laura the choice of a profession served as the "rumination" fostering the recuperation of supplies of frozen feelings.

Laura and lies

Laura entered analysis because of a despair whose origins she could not identify. She also suffered from a compression of the spinal column. She had had two homosexual affairs, one with Licia, the other with Martina. Her relationships with both partners had been extremely affectionate and easy-going but only at the cost of a lie: everything that might have caused friction or conflict she either left unsaid or "fixed" so as to smooth things over. Here is how we might represent her emotional situation:

	♂♂
♀=♀	♂♂
	♂♂

The figures at the left indicate her homosexual relationship and the figures at the right the proto-emotions continually denied and split, a parallel but unconnected universe.

At first the analyst entered into a certain collusion with Laura, writing letters that enabled her to obtain insurance benefits to defray the cost of the analysis: the insurance company would reimburse her only for treatment of her spinal problems, and the analyst ordered a neuropsychiatric course of treatment. In so doing the analyst was guided by Brother Cristoforo's "omnia munda mundis" (to the pure all is pure) in Book One of Manzoni's *Betrothed* (1972). But when Laura's professional situation permitted her to pay for the analysis herself, the analyst decided to refuse the patient's request that he continue writing the letters.

This was the moment of truth: now that there was a breach in the wall of negations and lies, would the emotions that irrupted in the field destroy her former ability to contain them? Or would the joint action of analyst and patient (thanks in part to the apparent complicity of the analyst – I say "apparent" because the analyst believed that by writing a document linking pain and psychiatric care he was saying metaphorically that Laura was suffering from despair and pain and that the analysis was thus a "psychiatric treatment") succeed in containing the emotions activated by the analyst's refusal to keep the collusion going?

The analysis went back and forth; the explosions of anger, rage, jealousy, and revenge were fierce. Laura went so far as to threaten to denounce the analyst for issuing false documents. In the end, however, the analysis held its own and with her analyst's help Laura was able to take charge of the proto-emotional states she had theretofore kept at bay by means of her lies. It was not until the analysis was over that the analyst realized that the psychoanalytic field (Baranger and Baranger, 1961–62; Ferro and Basile, 2009) had to catch Laura's disease of lies and connivance to see whether the analytic work would allow her to emerge from the lies and confront greater and greater degrees of emotional truth. And in fact it did just that.

I might add that biological sex was of no importance here and was merely a way to speak of the passage from the initial behavior to the behavior ♀ and ♂. In this instance the analysis seems to have promoted the construction of a digestive apparatus to facilitate the digestion of split pre-emotional states.

A point I never tire of making is that it is wrong to confuse violence, explosions, and the inability to contain the emotions with aggressivity. Aggressivity is a given of the species, and as such, I feel, never a matter of surplus. What is surplus is the pressing need of proto-emotional states to be accepted, contained, and transformed.

Another important aspect of Laura's story is that it shows that the urgency of proto-emotional states underlies many types of behavior which look aggressive on the surface. Emotional or proto-emotional forces often look like destructive tsunamis, but they are not aggressive or even, to my mind, destructive. Their effects result from the impossibility of containing the forces at work and sometimes from insufficient dikes or run-off canals or breakwaters. If the emotional horde is welcomed to the field, it tends to move in the direction of rationality, which tames wild thoughts (Bion, 1997).

Experiencing emotions

Experiencing one's emotions, which I understand to include dreaming one's dreams and thinking one's thoughts, is the destination of a series of operations. Sometimes the first stage is a story beginning to form in the psychic apparatus of the analyst, who then creates more extensive scenarios in which behaviors that have been split can come back to life, at least in the field. In fact, the field is highly sensitive to contagion: no place in the field fails to contaminate the others.

There is no gazelle without a tiger: Timidity and persecution

Luisa was a nice if somewhat colorless young woman. She worked as a librarian and was also doing a degree in literature. She liked detective novels, especially the Agatha Christie kind, where the guilty party gets his comeuppance. For years she suffered from agoraphobia and other social phobias. She refused to appear in a bathing suit in public and wore two pairs of panties; she sweated immoderately and had a dislocated jaw; she was subject to panic attacks; she had a number of obsessions, including checking over and over to make sure doors and windows were shut for fear that strangers would intrude; she took several baths or showers a day, washed her hair once a day, and used deodorants all the time; she preferred vegetarian dishes and never ate "meat with bones or the entrails of any animal"; she always slept alone because she feared her mouth would "come open strangely."

There was enough evidence to make me think she had a split part, which I imagined as a panther, a tiger, or a wolf. I recalled the 1944 film *The Tiger Woman* and Verga's story *The She-Wolf* (1982). At our first session I started making hypotheses: Luisa was persecuted by her split part or, rather, by the emotions accumulating in the beast, where they were unmanageable, and because she feared her "secret" might be discovered she kept washing to cleanse herself of the constantly recurring emotions. But keeping the emotions at bay was not enough: though dispersed and "evaporated" externally, they made themselves known by polluting her external appearance, which took on "tiger-like" features and grew dangerous, threatening. The gazelle must keep running to get away from the tiger, but much as it tries to appear perfect, it sweats. I could hardly believe my ears when she told me the name of a boy she liked but who was giving her trouble: Leo!

At this point Christie's Poirot would have considered himself lucky: the case was resolved, at least in cognitive terms. But another task presented itself: I had to undo the threads with which Leo was woven and braid them into the threads with which Luisa was woven. In Luisa's story Leo had a little dog with sharp teeth that she learned to trust and not fear.

I shall stop here, except to say that the work with Luisa that lay ahead consisted in integrating the genetic inheritance of a gazelle with the genetic inheritance of a lioness. It could happen when a lion-tamer came to life in the field in the form of an analytic function capable of metabolizing the jungle emotions the patient feared. She would then integrate tenderness and passion under the watchful eyes of the "tamer," that is, the weaving and story-telling function of the psychic apparatus of analyst and patient.

The doctor's panties

Nicola had been in analysis for years. He was going on about something when I felt myself drifting off. When I awoke, I was conscious of having missed a portion of his story. I tried to make up for it by referring to something I had heard earlier, but I did not fool him. "You seemed to be breathing very regularly, too regularly," he said. I did not know how to respond, because I had in fact fallen asleep. I said he might have been worrying about a lack of attention on my part, about whether I had forgotten the points we had been working on, so I went through all the major subjects of the most recent sessions. I had the feeling Nicola's thoughts were elsewhere.

As the session drew to an end, I was annoyed with myself for being dishonest, yet I realized that the reason I had fallen asleep – as if given a shot of pentothal – was that I was facing something painful. I was like a circuit breaker that goes off when the tension gets too high. Then I made things even worse by suggesting a far-fetched interpretation, and I saw Nicola withdraw. I told myself it was more the intensity of the emotions (jealously, rage, envy) than their negative quality that was the problem.

The next day Nicola said with a certain reticence that during the previous session he had had a fantasy that distressed him: a man, an exhibitionist, was showing him his genitals and he was trying to withdraw. I replied that that was clearly what had happened during the session: I had gone too far towards the end; I had been exhibitionistic spilling out everything I had told him. I added that I had in fact drifted off for a moment as if I had been given a shot of pentothal. Perhaps the same thing happened to him when I went overboard in my remarks: he withdrew. Perhaps the two of us had withdrawn owing to an excess of emotion. Nicola was relieved. He said that when he sensed that I was not with him, that I had fallen asleep, he was telling me about the extremely intense emotion he had felt (we had just resumed our sessions after a week's break) when he ran into his former fiancée: he had nearly run away and blushed bright red. So that was what I had missed. It had taken place on an ice rink but at a place where the ice seemed to be boiling. I asked him why he had not asked me whether I was awake when he heard me breathing regularly. He said he did not want to upset me and felt responsible for what had happened. I told him it was as if his girlfriend had fallen asleep beside him and instead of getting angry he had thought he must be boring. We went on like that – speaking freely and explicitly about what had happened to both of us when confronted with emotions too strong to handle – until the ice seemed to break in the heat of it all.

The day after that he told me two dreams. In the first he experienced a strong sense of exclusion. In the second a woman doctor spoke to him very openly and sincerely. He caught a glimpse of her red panties. Then she laid him down on a bed, examined him with great objectivity, and even gave him something for his fever.

The girl with the curls

I opened the door expecting Francesco, a handsome 30-year-old, and what did I see but a tall young woman with curly hair and the face of an angel. Refocusing my personal lens, I immediately saw the Francesco of old, but I was surprised, even flabbergasted by my sensorial misapprehension. Nor did it help for me to tell myself it must have been a daydream: I could find nothing to link it to.

During the previous day's session I had made some daring interpretations about certain aspects of Francesco's love life or, to be more precise, about certain fantasies connected with his sexuality. In one dream he was piloting an F14; in another he was Briatore, the well-known Italian magnate, running an offshore drilling operation. Somewhat maniacal though they were, these images gave Francesco, who had always thought of himself as respectful and even obsequious, a new picture of himself. He was a very decent person, but like everyone he was more than that. During that day's session he told me about a dream in which he played a video game and then came to my office, which is room 360. I said he seemed to see the analysis as a game with no nooks or crannies off limits, a 360-degree video game. Laughing, he said he was surprised he had so many things in him he was unaware of. He went on to relate another dream, of a male nurse going up to a sweet young girl with what seemed to be evil intent: he may have wanted to abuse her. That brought me back to my earlier daydream, the sweet girl with the curls, and I told him that what I had said the day before about his sexual fantasies had certainly opened some formerly inaccessible nooks and crannies but had probably scandalized him a bit. He confirmed my suspicion by saying it was hard to discover that, unlike what he had always thought, he was more like Gérard Depardieu than one of the seven dwarfs. I responded that there was no way of knowing whether any of the seven dwarfs had sexual fantasies about Snow White. He burst out laughing. It was a sonorous, liberating laugh.

But if it is true that the "transformational" space moving through the conversational style of analysis is one of its main driving forces, it is also true that daring interpretations are sometimes the key to opening new horizons. Clearly I place the issue of proto-emotions/emotions at the forefront of my thoughts, and I see the link between avoiding and experiencing them in the possibility of the transference of the proto-emotions.

Several further thoughts on the psychic apparatus

Man is usually thought of as the product of an evolution: thanks to the development of the psychic apparatus he has learned to deal with the instincts and drives that make him related to the other primates. I concur with Bion's statement that the mentalization typical of our species is a highly disruptive factor with respect to an instinctual behavior that functions well in and of itself. Only when the psychic apparatus has developed under optimum conditions do we have enrichment and maturation; otherwise there are many reasons for the psychic apparatus to malfunction and become a disruptive factor even with respect to the basic instinctual behaviors that could have functioned well.

The psychic apparatus represents the best and the worst of our species, a gift of evolution as well as its difficult, dangerous legacy. Extrapolating from Bion's theories, I have spoken (Ferro, 2002) of the imperfections the psychic apparatus may have and how they may interfere with its behavior, the behavior of the body and of the "body social." If we accept the idea that the behavior of the psychic apparatus is specific to our species, we must face a number of consequences we do not understand very clearly. To put it differently, we could say that if there is a continuum between the species that preceded us along the ladder of evolution then there can be no major problems or gaps; if, however, there is a leap – the appearance of the mental side of things – then there is something truly special and specific: the psyche. But if that is so, then the mental side of things should not only regulate or deregulate the rest of the human apparatus, it should also stand over it.

Let us take sexuality as an example. If we think of it as the sexuality of bodies, we can easily define what is heterosexual and what is masculine homosexual and feminine homosexual. But everything changes once we regard sexuality as the means of the coupling of and between psychic apparatuses. From this standpoint the masculine homosexual would be ♂♂, something contained trying to couple with something else contained so as to subjugate or help it, while the feminine homosexual would be ♀♀, a relationship of pacified homogeneities where the proto-emotions are split (Ferro, 2008). The true heterosexual relationship would be only ♂♀, that is, something contained coupling fertilely with something containing, which fosters the development of the thing contained by itself developing. That would mean, however, that homosexual and heterosexual are essentially concerned with the behavior of psychic apparatuses. A couple made up of men could have a heterosexual behavior if their psychic apparatuses coupled creatively, or they could have a masculine or a feminine homosexual behavior ♂♂. The same would hold for a phenotypically heterosexual couple: they could have a homosexual behavior ♂♂ of the psychic apparatuses with continual clashes or a fusion-like ♀♀ behavior, and so on.

Another often repeated consequence of the mental side of things is the consciousness of and frequently intolerable nature of our end, the fact that we do not know and can therefore have no responses: we are at a point in evolution that brooks no questions. The fact that we cannot bear the absence of responses leads us to a form of anesthesia, of necessary lies, as Bion reminds us in the "Fable of the Liars" (1970), an apologia for lying which points out in all modesty that we have no choice but to be tolerant of ourselves and others and must give up the idea of being "champions of Truth" and be content with doing everything in our power to help ourselves and our patients to attain the highest degree of mental development possible.

> Liars show courage and precision in their opposition to scholars . . . they succeeded in postponing if not preventing the spread of doctrines

that could only provoke a feeling of despair and emptiness in their beneficiaries.

(Bion, 1970, p. 100)

Conclusions

The concept of fatigue – physical and mental fatigue – is inherent in our nature at every level. The Italian poet and novelist Cesare Pavese (1936) called a volume of his verse *Lavorare stanca*, which literally means "to work tired." Even when everything is going well, when we have managed to produce thoughts and experience emotions within the bounds of the possible, to escape the Sirens' deceitful flattery and the Lotophagi's eschewal of feeling, we still have one inescapable task: we still must face up to the void behind all things and the void par excellence represented by the idea of our death. At that stage the psychic apparatus must confront a new trial: it must handle the pain of our own dissolution. The antidotes man has come up with are legion, from Goethe's *Faust* to the erotomania of Heinrich Mann's *Professor Unrat* (1905). "Puss-in-Boots" tells us we can gobble up any ogre-anxiety, but to do so we must go on telling our tale – as in the *Thousand and One Nights* – forever.

What I mean is that we need new myths, because if on the one hand myth is the concentrate of a group dream meant to introduce order into a nodal point of our emotional life, on the other it may also become a brake, a quagmire in relation to other unforeseen paths not contained in it. We must therefore constantly attempt to create new analysis-based myths, private myths belonging to each pair but also collective myths capable of serving as tellable concentrates of lived life and opening an unending succession of new perspectives.

A modern myth

Let me now say in a different way what I have been saying all along by placing myself in row C of Bion's grid – the row of dream, myth, and stories – which I often find superior to psychoanalytic theorizing and even clinical descriptions. I shall use Thomas Harris's trilogy *Red Dragon* (1981), *Silence of the Lambs* (1988), and *Hannibal* (1999), which constitutes a kind of modern myth about the absence of primary treatment and its consequences. I am not concerned with its literary quality, which is not for me to judge, but I feel the author has a keen sense of the psychological.

The first volume is about a serial killer, Francis Dolarhyde, who murders whole families on each third full moon using rituals that involve the mortification of the victims, such as breaking mirrors and placing the corpses so they will look into the mirrors. The hero's childhood was tragic: he was abandoned by his mother and his face was so deformed that he did not dare look into a mirror. The massacres begin after he tries in vain to rejoin his mother and become part of the new family she has made for herself and after his grandmother's death. They go on until he meets a young woman who, blind, is not horrified by his face and accepts him fully and lovingly. The result is a schism between the part of him that refuses to give up the "red dragon" vengeance and the part of him that wants to preserve the relationship he now has with the young woman.

The second volume is about another serial killer, Jame Gumb, who murders buxom women. He, too, has a past full of violence and abuse. He kills because he wishes to make a garment out of women's skins to serve him as a "new skin and identity."

Both novels have a character by the name of Dr. Lecter, a psychiatrist who is also a serial killer and is kept in a cage in a high-security prison. A woman police officer by the name of Starling, who appears in the second volume, is aided in her pursuit of the killer by Dr. Lecter, whose relationship to her is almost one of protection. This becomes clear in the third volume, the title of which, *Hannibal*, is Lecter's first name. It deals with Starling's attempts to arrest Hannibal, who has escaped from prison. He is the novel's protagonist, and more important than the cops-and-robbers adventures is the story of his childhood: he lost a younger sister whom he loved; she was the victim of an act of cannibalism perpetrated by two starving criminals who broke into the farmhouse where the children lived and having found nothing to eat but a skin-and-bones deer devoured her. The trauma Lecter experienced drives him to repeat the scene: as an adult, hoping to turn back time (he would make time non-linear) and bring back his sister, he himself turns cannibal. Starling would seem to be a partial substitute for the sister, a kind of "receptacle" in case time should in fact move backwards and she return to the living. His bouts of cannibalism continue until a horrible situation in which a man, whom Lecter sees as guilty because he has not been able to save his sister, has a brain operation and partakes, fully conscious, in a meal consisting of the frontal lobes of his own brain sliced into strips and cooked, much as Lecter gnaws at his own brain for failing to have saved his sister.

Is this not what happens when there is no "food" for the psychic apparatus, when there are no dreams? The gentle, loving parts (the sister, the alpha function, the ♀ capacity) are destroyed by the violent parts, which then cannibalize the psychic apparatus itself. What is experienced is then imposed on others, who become victims. The same thing happens with violent projective identifications, which are in fact a desperate attempt to communicate and find relief. Had there been such food – a dream, a day-dream – the emotions would have found their place and Dr. Lecter would not have become a victim and a murderer ravaged by guilt.

Police officer Starling may be seen as the relatively sane part of the personality, which tries to "arrest" the psychotic part even if temporarily fascinated and paralyzed by it, forced into a kind of connivance in the crime, suckling the psychotic part, subjugated by it. As for the criminals at the beginning of the story, they can be seen as beta elements who, lacking in the capacity for dreams and transformation (of an alpha formula), cannibalize the psychic apparatus. The serial killer in the first volume represents the need to evacuate trauma-tinged emotions by means of action: the evil persecuting object drives him to vengeance until he meets the gentle girl and the schism between the psychotic part and the "part capable of sustaining a relationship" develops. What is neither accepted nor transformed causes madness and persecution. The second volume also contains an attempt to find a psychic "skin," a container, a mother capable of "taking in" (a ♀ capable of making space for a ♂). The last volume features the most disturbing character, the actual force behind all the stories, the mad psychiatrist, a veritable archaic superego, who together with his intolerable guilt feelings – leading to desperate, destructive, and self-destructive action of the type Bion (1965) would call ♀♂ – devours the most desperately psychotic part of the personality. In my opinion these three books constitute an admirable modern myth about the absence of primary treatment and its consequences: the killer, the attempt at self-treatment (the skin), the archaic superego, and the seduction of the healthy part.

They or, rather, their contents should in my dream be coupled with another work, John Katzenbach's captivating novel *The Analyst* (2002), which can be read as a thriller, a trenchant critique of the psychoanalytic world, or any number of other ways. For me it immediately called forth the difficult process an analyst much go through within himself if he is to succeed in effecting a true "cure." It is the story of Dr. Ricky Starks, an analyst getting on in years, tired of life and tired of his profession. One day during the last session he hears someone knocking and entering the outer office. Who is it? he wonders. A patient's parent? A patient in crisis? After the session is over, he goes into the outer office but, finding no one, is about to leave when he sees a note on a chair. The note is anonymous and says he will have to commit suicide in a month if he fails to find the person who wrote the note because if he does not, all the members of his family – their addresses are attached – will be murdered. The story that ensues is one of growing pathos laced with incredulity and persecution. All his certitudes are undermined, shattered – his credit card is blocked, his bank accounts emptied, his houses destroyed; he is hounded out of his psychoanalytic society – until he wakes up, takes charge, revamps his mental organization, starts to search for his persecutor, comes closer and closer to him . . . almost nabs him . . . and in the end, totally transformed, stops practicing the same old routine therapy and decides to be himself above all and give his all to his patients once he has found his persecutor, who turns out to be the patient he was seeing when the knock came at the door.

Thus, if people who have never had a psychic apparatus capable of dreaming, people like Dolarhyde and Gumb, find a therapist who understands the problem, they can truly be transformed. Hannibal Lecter, the mad psychiatrist, would then be able to find succor in Dr. Starks, now able to take charge of madness, narrate it and re-narrate it with all the possible transformations starting from our childhood's "once upon a time." What I am proposing as a therapeutic factor, therefore, is the quality of the analyst's mental behavior during the session, in particular, his receptivity and flexibility and his capacity for transformation, tolerance, and patience. When part of the field, these qualities help to make transformations. Beta elements – proto-mental, emotional or sensorial contents – that were not transformed into pictograms (alpha elements) and were impossible to contain will no longer need to be "camouflaged," "stored," split, projected, or evacuated and instead become thinkable. After all, analysis should be able to swing back and forth between Hercules and Puss-in-Boots.

References

Baranger, W. and Baranger, M. (1961–1962). La Situacion Analitica como Campo Dinamico. *Revista Uruguaya de Psicoanalisis* 4: 3–54.

Bion, W.R. (1962). *Learning from Experience*. London: Heinemann. Reprinted London: Karnac Books (1984).

—— (1963). *Elements of Psycho-Analysis*. London: Heinemann. Reprinted London: Karnac Books (1984).

—— (1965). *Transformations*. London: Heinemann. Reprinted London: Karnac Books (1984).

—— (1970). Fable of the Liars. In *Attention and Interpretation*. London: Heinemann. Reprinted London: Karnac Books (1984).

—— (1997). *Taming Wild Thoughts*. London: Karnac.

Ferro, A. (1996). *In the Analyst's Consulting Room*. London/New York: Psychology Press.

—— (2002). *Seeds of Illness Seeds of Recovery*. London/New York: Routledge.

—— (2006). Clinical Implication of Bion's Work. *International Journal of Psychoanalysis* 87: 980–1003.

—— (2008). *The Mind Works: Technique and Crativity in Psychoanalysis*. London/New York: Routledge.

Ferro, A. and Basile, R. (Eds.) (2009). *The Analytic Field*. London: Karnac.

Goethe (1935). *Faust*. London: Camden House. Originally published 1935.

Grotstein, J. (2007). *A Beam of Intense Darkness*. London: Karnac Books.

Harris, T. (1981). *Red Dragon*. London: Arrow Books.

—— (1988). *Silence of the Lambs*. London: Mandarin.

—— (1999). *Hannibal*. London: Arrow Books.

Katzenbach, J. (2002). *The Analyst*. London: Ballantine Books.

Mann, H. (1905). *Professor Unrat*. Anflage.

Manzoni, A. (1972). *Betrothed*. London: Penguin Books. First published 1827.

Ogden, T.H. (2003). On Not Being Able To Dream. *International Journal of Psychoanalysis*. 85: 17–30.
Pavese, C. (1936). *Lavorare Stanca*. Florence: Solaria Edizioni.
Verga, G. (1982). *The She Wolf*. Berkeley: University of California Press. First published 1883.

Chapter 3

Incorporation of an invasive object

Paul Williams

Under normal circumstances, incorporation is the earliest mode of relating in which the infant feels himself to be at one with the other and is unaware of separation between the two personalities (Fenichel, 1945; Searles, 1951; Sterba, 1957). This experience decreases if development proceeds relatively unimpeded. If development is impeded the experience can persist leading to an equation between relatedness and engulfment, in which one personality is felt to be devouring the other (Searles, 1951, p. 39). The impulse to unite incorporatively with the other as a defense against separation anxiety has been discussed by Freud (1900, 1933), Klein (1935), Heimann (1942), Fenichel (1945), Searles (1951), Federn (1952), Greenacre (1958), Segal (1981), Rey (1994) and others. Laplanche and Pontalis (1972) note how physical experiences are a feature of incorporation, in contrast to the fantasy dimension of introjection into the ego, which assumed importance in Klein's (1935) thinking and which she discusses in the context of incorporative activity and the genesis of psychosis.

The patients I shall describe manifested incorporative self-states in the form of bodily and psychological symptoms. I shall suggest that they probably underwent traumatic disruption to the psyche–soma at a time when the sense of self was barely formed and the psyche–soma had yet to undergo differentiation. A primitive introject appears to have been installed in their minds and bodies that was held by them to belong to their own self-representational system. At the same time, it was experienced as the concrete presence of a 'foreign body' inside. The experience of something that is not a part of the self yet is confused with the self can create not only psychic conflict but also incompatible or 'heterogeneous' states of mind (D. Quinodoz, 2001). 'Heterogeneity' is denoted by D. Quinodoz, following Green, as the product of a 'heterogeneous constitution of the ego' (Green, 1993). This description reflects Bion's observation that 'there is a psychotic personality concealed by neurosis as the psychotic personality is screened by psychosis in the psychotic, that has to be laid bare and dealt with' (1967, p. 63). D. Quinodoz argues that heterogeneous patients present for help because they suffer from their heterogeneity, unlike the majority.

This heterogeneous condition underlies the intrapsychic confusion of the patients I shall describe and seems to have had implications not only for the way in which my patients related, but also for how their thinking developed.

Clinical example 1: James

James, 27, entered analysis after a series of failed relationships culminating in depressive attacks with suicidal ideation. He possessed an exceptionally high IQ and was capable of abstract levels of thought beyond his years, and of grasping the nub of ideas and arguments. There was a paranoid tinge to many of his observations and his attention to others' motivation seemed compulsive. James was a quintessentially self-made man. He had failed at school but as an adult had become successful in business. James' father, an addict, died in his forties of a drugs overdose. James was a replacement child; a previous son had died, apparently unmourned, 10 months before James' birth, his mother having been advised by her doctor to get pregnant again straight away. James' mother seems to have been an unstable woman preoccupied by grievances. He said that his parents fought during the marriage over affairs each accused the other of having. He recalled as a child sitting in fear in his pajamas on the stairs while his parents brawled. He left home at 16 and remained unreconciled to them. He only saw his mother again once, when she was unconscious on her deathbed in hospital.

I was struck from the outset by the speed with which James seemed to reach the meaning of his fantasies and dreams. He would often get there before me, sometimes with impressive intuitions, without making me feel excluded. I felt that he strove to be a 'model' analysand. It became apparent that he needed to control the analysis, subtly and diplomatically, and that he suffered intense anxiety when he did not feel in control. He revealed that his controls were, in fantasy, controls over my thoughts. Why he needed to feel in control of my thoughts was not clear. His dream life provided evidence of a serious disturbance of the self. He dreamed repeatedly that he had murdered someone. The body, a male, lay buried under a road; it was a secret but the police were piecing together clues and were on his trail. He developed insomnia to avoid these nightmares.

James' compliant, controlling behavior decreased as he became more depressed and nihilistic during the second year of analysis. In one session he lay contemplating suicide and said, with piercing dejection, 'I came into analysis to find consolation, as I knew nothing could ever come of my life.'

I was affected by this comment, which was said with no trace of defensiveness, and my response – an intense, lonely sadness – persisted after the session. I realized that I had been struck by, to paraphrase Marion Milner, a 'thought too big for its concept.'[1] I wondered whether 'analysis-as-consolation' masked, for James, the site of an experience of annihilation anxiety. This phenomenon has been referred to as 'a memorial space for psychic death' (Grand, 2000), in which unspeakable traumatic events are always felt to be present, yet by definition must always be absent. Metabolisation through language is the means we possess of approaching such catastrophe, yet this is disbarred, as language is experienced as being unable to approximate the scale of the events involved.

I shall pass to a period in the third year during which James decided he wanted to quit analysis and his suicidal feelings took a psychotic turn. He had become disillusioned and was prone to long, angry silences. 'Is this all there is?' he would complain bitterly, following stretches of withdrawal. He could be abusive, accusing me of keeping him in analysis to maintain the vain illusion that I could help him. If he felt I might be close to understanding what he was feeling, he would lash out contemptuously – for example, 'This [analysis] is hypocrisy. It deceives, it lies, it's wanking. It's a middle-class fix: you haven't got the first idea about me or what people like me go through.'

He told me he felt burned out, disgusted by himself and hopeless. The nightmare of having killed someone preoccupied him, including during the day, making it increasingly difficult for him to function. As his condition worsened, I became anxious for his safety, as he was immersed in what appeared to be a developing transference psychosis. This situation continued for some weeks. I interpreted his disillusion with me and the feelings of unmanageable rage this engendered.

An event occurred in which James communicated his rage in a way that I felt revealed his having incorporated an object characterized by invasiveness. James had spent most of this particular Wednesday session in tormented distraction at his inability to control his feelings of hatred towards his female partner, who he was afraid would leave him. He described unpleasant scenes between them that left him confused and suicidal. The idea that there might be no change appalled him. He twisted and turned on the couch, as though in bodily pain.

I interpreted how afraid I thought he was of becoming more and more like his parents, at home and here, and how feelings of growing resentment and hatred of his partner and of me pushed him into a terrible sense of fear and failure: hating destroyed his power and hope, he felt, turning him into a desperately needy child. The only way out he could imagine was to kill himself but even this didn't work as he still felt no one understood what he was going through.

James' writhing stopped and his body relaxed visibly. He appeared to be relieved at having his confusion and fear acknowledged. He then became gradually more restless and what appeared to be a more thoughtful silence turned out to be not the case. He slowly and purposefully got off the couch, stared at me – or rather through me – and shouted with unbridled hatred: 'Keep your platitudes to yourself, you stupid fucking moron.'

This outburst of violent narcissistic rage seemed also to embody a desperate effort to try to rid himself of an alien presence or state of mind, of which I appeared to have become an incarnation. He fell silent, walked unsteadily round the room, distracted, and eventually sat on the edge of the couch, trembling. I felt assaulted by the attack – fear and anger welled up inside me. I could not think of anything appropriate to say, only a wish to protect myself. I felt stripped of a capacity to contain the situation. James sat for some time holding his head in his hands. I recall the session ended with me asking him whether he felt able to manage getting home.

The next day James was in a distressed, confused state. 'I don't understand. I can't remember it clearly . . . it is like a fog . . . something just came over me. I don't know how to explain it . . . I'm sorry. I feel a bit like it now, kind of stunned. My head feels full . . . there is so much going on that I can't think and my legs feel like lead . . . like my body wants to collapse. I don't quite know where I am in this. I don't know why I should scream at you like that . . .'

He continued in this bewildered, anxious way that seemed to combine guilt about what he felt he had done to me and confused feelings of dread and relief at having lost control. I said to him that, although he felt a need to apologize, what was striking to me was that he had allowed me to see some of his deepest feelings, including those about me, without camouflage. We discussed his anxieties further and he said,

> I don't think I had a choice; it doesn't feel like I did . . . it wasn't taking a risk. Something exploded. It was anger but there's something not right about that . . . it's not the whole feeling. Something in me could have killed you. I wasn't thinking this when it happened but it makes me think that something in me wanted to smash and smash you and shut you up so I didn't have to listen any more. As I say this it reminds me of my mother and how I couldn't stand the shouting but I couldn't do anything about it. Maybe I was fighting her . . . maybe even being her – or being like her somehow – but in another way I was outside it, watching it going on.

He talked about a 'blizzard' having descended, pains in his head and a heavy sensation in his body. I was led to think that he had been in a psychotic transference. During ensuing weeks, James experienced much confusion and worsening bouts of withdrawal. Further attacks occurred, usually when I least expected them. They seemed to be precipitated by contact with James' infantile self that he despised – that is, when he felt a childlike need for me or when I said something that touched him. His withdrawals at times took on what I thought was a psychopathic quality: it was as though I could suddenly cease to exist for him. Although, in the beginning, each attack had seemed to free something in him, I noticed that his rages could be accompanied by a malignant, anti-life attitude that destroyed opportunities for his infantile needs to be met. What had been a form of letting go could come to resemble a sadistic, narcissistic defense. James' responses to his attacks varied from obliviousness to persecutory anxiety to acute paranoia. Yet, after one outburst he commented, 'I feel bad about what just happened. I hate you and you make me furious with the things you say, but I think it was out of proportion – my reaction, that is.'

I queried his feelings and he said,

> I don't know how real my hatred of you is sometimes. It wells up . . . it is true. But it can feel like an automatic thing . . . a gut reaction . . . sometimes it doesn't really matter what you're saying: it erupts without me having any control over it, as though I just have to silence you.

I felt that James was experiencing anxiety possibly over feelings of frustration and rage towards me, but was also confused by a psychotic identification that precipitated attacks in order to try to annihilate our relationship. Non-psychotic and psychotic aspects of his personality seemed to vie for expression. James' behavior outside the session reflected his confusion, as seen in this example: at home one Sunday he heard a dog squealing in the street. He dashed out to find a large dog belonging to some drunken youths pinning down a small dog by the throat. He dived between them, prising open the jaws of the larger dog until the smaller one was freed. The youths turned on James but his unassailable resolve caused them to back off. In his session, he could not account for his impulsive behavior, was not proud of it and yet felt oddly better. He showed little indication of overwhelming guilt or confusion. He had to separate the dogs, he said, and he could see that many people would think that what he did was crazy. He wanted to know why he had been compelled to act. Later in the session, he remarked, 'The thing with the dogs has made something clearer to me: it sounds obvious but it isn't. Although it does sound mad, I think I thought that the fight that was going on was my fault, but it wasn't.'

This insight permitted work on feelings of 'being intrinsically wrong,' as he put it, in the eyes of his mother. He conceived of this as:

> Nothing I did was right. It wasn't only about making mistakes or doing things that annoyed her. It was like I got everything wrong as a matter of principle . . . when I was small I thought I could please her and I tried to but by the time I went to school I think I felt defeated. Nothing worked . . . she couldn't bear to look at me . . . not disapproval exactly, although there was a lot of that . . . more that I was some terrible burden she'd had forced on her and couldn't stand. It was bewildering . . . there were times when she would suddenly be incredibly nice but these would only last for a few minutes. I stayed out of her way, but I

often forgot and got screamed at. It took years for me to realize that the whole thing was impossible . . . she was on a different planet. I know that by the time I was seven or eight I had thoughts that I'd be better off dead. I would feel relieved when I went to bed that I'd got through another day and pray that I wouldn't wake up. For years I went to bed early to blot things out.

A: You feel you died as a child.

P: I do [cries] . . . everything went wrong and I have been stuck with it all my life. I think my childhood was ruined . . . now I am like her and I ruin it myself.

A: You feel you died and yet somehow you managed to go on; not only go on but do well eventually.

P: I can't explain it. The only thing that comes to mind is that I realized a few years ago talking to my grandmother that my mother must have been delighted that I was born healthy and lived. She must have been desperate not to lose another child. My grandmother said I was doted on – given special orange juice and supplements to build me up. But she told me that the marriage was in trouble and my mother started having affairs when I was born. I do recall different men came to the house from as far back as I can remember. I don't know . . . maybe I was made to feel special in some way and that gave me a kind of good start. What I've always felt is that my life wasn't my life. I felt I was somebody because of what I did for others.

The analysis focused, in the transference, on the feelings of his having died as a child and how his attacks and withdrawals defended him from the painful experience that his attempts to live felt like a lie, so confused was his sense of his own self. Gradually, he became more able to work at understanding the relationship between feelings of love and hate and a welling up of psychotic rage against me that expressed his destructive narcissism. These eruptions were preceded by a visceral sensation, blood coursing through his veins, he said, or tinnitus-like ringing; then outbursts that bore a resemblance to accounts of his mother's aggression. As they came under more control (they ceased in the seventh year) he told me he had always had a 'wild side' to him of which he was ashamed. He felt the same hatred of people that his mother had shown, with no justification. He did not evade responsibility for this, but was concerned that it did not represent the complexity of his feelings, even at his angriest. He described it as 'default extremism' or a 'scorched-earth policy.' James had indicated how frightened he had been of his parents, but his intimidation at his own and his mother's mood changes only now became apparent. These had left him disoriented as a child. He said that his mother's attacks had occurred from as early as he could remember and he had been convinced he had provoked them. He began similar attacks from the age of about seven, he thought, including on his mother's dog, which he had tormented. The need to attack others 'when they got too close' was lifelong and compulsive.

After much work on the defacement of his personality, his primitive identification with invasiveness receded and he acquired greater tolerance for his emotions and limitations. He also began a more articulated grieving process that was paralleled by a reluctance to comply with others' demands. His relationship with his female partner improved and they began a family. The love between him and his baby daughter, though sometimes painful, afforded him awareness of his value to another person, something he had not previously been able to experience. This helped to offset his sense of loss at what he had missed in his life because of his behaviour. In the eighth year of his analysis he said, 'I feel I have to pay attention every day to that child I was. It's like visiting someone in hospital or a grave. If I don't think of him or hold his hand, I can feel lost. I will never let him go again.'

I felt that James had buried his childhood identity and evolved an impenetrable, seamless second skin that afforded him a false sense of integration (cf. Winnicott, 1960; Symington, 1985). Within this illusory maturity lay an experience of being unrecognized for himself and uncontained in his feelings. When James' true, alive self stirred, he was susceptible to fears of abandonment and disintegration, triggering, among other things, a defensive, imitative introjection of an object that could not bear loss (and, hence, life) and which reacted invasively, generating narcissistic rage and masochistic compliance in an attempt to preserve a sense of coherent selfhood (P. Williams, 2001).

Clinical example 2: Ms B

Ms B, 49, was diagnosed in her thirties with a paranoid psychosis although I came to think she suffered from a borderline personality disorder. She came into analysis 13 years ago (cf. P. Williams, 1998). The middle child of a working-class family, Ms B complained she had had no relationship with her mother, who passed her from birth on to her father because she favored the first child, a boy (Ms B's other sibling is also male). Her rage at her mother's rejection of her was unremitting – 'she never showed any sign of wanting me – never' was her refrain. The father appears to have been paranoid and periodically incapacitated by his difficulties. Ms B said that at around two or three years of age she had retreated into a fantasy world, becoming friendly with creatures from outer space who promised to take her away. She also came to believe that she was a famous actress. She maintained that she and her father had had an incestuous relationship up to her 14th year. She told me she had acquired a manager, a pimp-like figure called the 'Director,' who controlled many of her actions, feelings and thoughts. 'He' was to emerge in the analysis as a pseudo-hallucination.

After four months of analysis, Ms B reported the following dream: 'I am being fed. A hand slaps me across the face hard. Then I am on a terrorist exercise, rolling down a hill clutching a male officer. We fall off a cliff or shelf.'

I interpreted that she was letting me know of a catastrophe, a loss in her life that she felt could never be made up, and that she had turned to men and sex to try to compensate. I rapidly became an object of idealization, while her violent, perverse pathology was acted out, mainly sexually. By the second year Ms B had begun to cut herself; she took a non-fatal overdose and jumped from a moving train, injuring herself. A psychosis asserted itself. This is a dream from that time:

> A minibus crashes through the front of a food store. There is a huge explosion. My older brother helpfully leads people away. There are many dead pregnant women. I touch the stomach of one but there is no life. Tins of food are embedded in people's faces. They are missing arms and legs. The manager says, 'We carry on, we stay open.' I try to stop him I but can't.

She was unable to consider the themes of murder or dead mothers and babies in this or other dreams. Her behavior became more disturbed and she was hospitalized following attempts to swallow a lethal dose of lithium medication. After a two-year period in which there was a good deal of extreme disturbance (which I do not have space to describe here), the direction of the analysis began to shift towards a more verbalized, transference-oriented hatred of her dependence on me. The patient moved from a predominantly paranoid position and acting out to one of sadistic, abusive attacks. From having complained of abuse, she became an abuser, of me and the analysis. For the purposes of this paper, I want to illustrate how the patient seems to have incorporated an invasive object that combines characteristics of the patient's projective activity with features of both parents.

In a Monday session during the second year of her analysis, Ms B complained at length that she was no good because girls don't get love. Love from mothers is 'lesbian,' she said, and this is the most awful thing in the world. The way to get love was to be a boy like her older brother, or like her father. She was a boy, really, she said: she could do anything boys could. She recounted how when she masturbated she fantasized that she was a man and that women queued up to have sex with her. She sometimes strapped a dildo to her waist when she went out to make her feel like a man. She talked further about childhood fantasies of being a powerful boy and that she had changed her sex (although the patient was talking about fantasies, I was unsure whether she actually believed she was male as she spoke).

A: I can see what you mean about the advantages you felt boys had, but I'm wondering about and remembering that you were born a girl; where is she? What has happened to the longing for love you wanted from your mother that you have told me about? You often tell me how lonely you feel and how much you want to talk to me, especially during weekends. That person seems to me like a little girl who feels her needs are being ignored.

P: [becoming agitated and shouting]: Keep out! Lock the doors . . . the walls are moving. Lock the doors, shut up, lock them! Keep them out!

A: Something I have said has alarmed you. Can you tell me what's happening?

P: It's the Director . . . he's telling me somebody is coming in. They're coming in and they're going to get me . . . they're going to kill me!

This intrusion of the psychotic 'Director' figure was to happen frequently and exerted enormous influence over the patient. The technical problems associated with interpreting these paradoxical 'influencing machines,' which purportedly protect but in practice deny the patient any good object-relating experiences, are obviously considerable. What I wish to stress here is that these paranoid outbursts revealed, in my view, not only Ms B's deep-seated fears of her own destructiveness and invasiveness, but also evidence of miscarriage of early introjective processes. The invasive narrative of Ms B's 'Director' (which always involved accusations of people getting in, breaking in, stealing and attacking, when not manically advocating sex) displayed certain elements of concordance with the patient's accounts of her father's powerful paranoid anxieties and of the rejections and indifference she attributed to her mother (and which she herself exhibited). Observations by her about her father over several years of analysis, often inadvertent and spontaneous, were paralleled by ways in which she herself could think compulsively when in the grip of a psychotic transference characterized by invasive fantasies and feelings of fragmentation. The 'Director' seemed to afford her a sense of identity when in crisis. 'His' underlying objective was, as I have suggested, to influence the patient's ego to reject human contact and pursue a course of pathological, narcissistic withdrawal, reflecting her primary narcissistic crisis.

Invasive experiences and the self

To avoid misunderstanding, I want to stress that I am not suggesting a simple concordance between this patient's and her father's or mother's personalities or a linear causality between the external object's influence and the patient's fantasies. There is no direct equivalence between her father's projective activity and her identification with invasiveness – or for that matter between the patient's narcissism and the mother's psychopathology.

The same applies to James, I suggest, or to any patient with this kind of disorder. The intra-psychic situation I refer to is likely to be extremely complex, involving pathological aspects of the patient's infantile self becoming confused and amalgamated with sequelae of uncontained projections and with the projective activity of the object. Identification with the aggressor is evident, but the process also has a primitive, fragmented quality linked, in my view, to threats to the core sense of self. Inadequately contained objects and part-objects become installed in the psyche of the infant, generating confusion and anxiety. Gaddini (1992, p. 4) provides an account of how this early crisis might evolve. He studied how normal imitation or mimicry – an oral introjective activity which takes place prior to identification – can develop pathologically. Precocious conditions of oral frustration may cause disturbances in the psycho-oral area and in introjective mechanisms. Imitative introjections, instead of acting as precursors to normal introjections, may substitute for true introjections and, as a consequence, cause internalization processes to fail. Imitation may then be used defensively to avoid introjective conflicts. The child's fragmented personality and thinking will then develop on the basis of this failed identification process, imitation being substituted for genuine object relating. Weiss (1960), in distinguishing imitation from identification, stressed that 'no simple imitation' takes place in the mind of the infant. There is, he suggests, a form of 'reproduction' or 'autoplastic duplication' (following Ferenczi, 1919) in which the organism acquires and modifies its shape and functional parts. In my view, it is probably a defensive use of autoplastic duplication that gives rise to the concordance between certain primitive elements of the patient's disturbed personality and invasive projections.

Prior failure of containment and breach of the 'contact barrier' (Bion, 1962) in the mother–infant relationship probably renders the individual vulnerable to excessive permeability, and development of the self is then impaired at the stage of mimetic introjection. This disturbed early attachment process seems to have created, in my patients, a backcloth against which a pathological amalgam of projections arose and expressed itself corporeally as well as mentally. Although there is no space in this paper to discuss the relationships between phantasy, projection and introjection in these states, especially the influence of unconscious sexual phantasies, the organizing roles of unconscious phantasy and memory, the impact of deferred action (après-coup) in their aetiology and evolution and the re-elaboration of psychic reality that follows would need to be taken into account to clarify the resulting amalgam of projected and introjected elements. My aim in this paper is to emphasize the complexity of these early object-relations experiences – what might be termed metaphorically as encounters with 'fractal objects'[2] – and to indicate how, through attention to a range of transference communications, it may be possible to identify, a posteriori, introjective patterns that underlie failures in identification formation. Such investigation is analogous to identifying the 'sensitivity to initial conditions' in deterministic chaos theory, through which one or more variables can come to have an enduring, disproportionately perturbing effect on a complex system.[3]

If we think of the self as a developmental achievement deriving from the infant's need to mentally represent internal states, using the mind of another, then recognition of the intentionality of the caregiver's mind permits the infant to establish an internal representation of himself as a truly separate, intentional being. The quality of the caregiver's image of the infant as an intentional being is critical for the formation of this representation. If caregiving fails to contain and reflect the infant's experiences and anxieties, a misrepresentation of the infant will be internalized corresponding to the partial or distorted representational capacity of the other. The patients I have described, I believe, experienced during this early developmental phase failure to have their projections contained and metabolized leading to an experience of emotional violence. If assailed by invasive projective activity, the trauma would be an amalgam of inchoate experiences, the residuum or precipitate of which may correspond to the 'foreign body' which is experienced as lodged in the unconscious and in the body and which lacks mental representational status.

Attempts to repel invasiveness through the counter-use of projective identification are likely to heighten the intensity of the pathological interaction, as it is the identification with invasiveness (associated with projections by infant and object) that is employed defensively. The infant's body is implicated in the trauma in that it carries the status of a primary object to which the infant relates and which can become installed as an internal object. Laufer (2002) has discussed how uncontained bodily states due to poor handling of the infant by the caregiver can create adverse developmental conditions. I think that such deprived conditions could pertain to incidences of invasiveness. Indeed, extremely deprived infants may 'invite' invasion or at least incorporate avidly powerful projections as a consequence of extreme need.

Those who are compelled to expel unbearable mental states force the mind of the other to deal with what the invasive object's mind cannot. I became aware that, in my patients, once an offending mental state has been expelled, an invasive object ceases to have use for the subject as an object and reverts to a position of narcissism. Perhaps it is more accurate to say that the invasive object returns to a narcissistic state of unconscious fusion with an idealized internal object. Developmentally, managing a foreign body inside destroys mental space allocated to the symbolizing activity by the ego. Identification with characteristics of invasiveness disrupts processes of integration of experiences necessary for secondary-process thinking. The individual who has incorporated an invasive object is likely to feel unstable, depleted of personal meaning and occupied or haunted by unidentifiable bodily perceptions. Complaints of feeling controlled, alienated, possessed, ill or diseased may accompany these self-states. During analysis, the transference neurosis can come to resemble a psychosis, with the patient able to think only intermittently and prone to interaction that reflects the dynamics of invasion. The patient may employ stereotypical ideas and language displaying power without conviction, and if pressed may become disorganized. Identity diffusion can occur and there may be acting out. Such patients are unsure of who they are, and under stress can communicate by proxy through their bodies.

Intrusion and invasion

Although by definition invasive objects intrude, I have found it useful in my clinical work to distinguish between intrusive and invasive objects. Intrusive objects, at least in my experience, tend to be motivated by a need to occupy or become a feature of the subject for reasons that can include parasitism and sadism. Invasive objects seek primarily to expel unbearable, infantile conflicts using, for the most part, excessive projective mechanisms. Expulsion is compulsive and violent and they do not appear to strive to colonize or become a feature of the subject in the same way, as their aim is to mould a repository for evacuation prior to a retreat to a position of pathological narcissism. The identity of the recipient of the projected state is less important than securing a mind into which the state can be jammed. I think of invasive projections as akin to 'psychosomatic missiles' that are expelled or 'fired' into the other. The dream of Ms B, in which tins of food are embedded in faces and unborn fetuses are killed, seems to be a vivid image that reflects oral invasiveness. Ms B's failure to internalize benign representations of her mother probably induced a developmental crisis of critical proportions at the oral stage, exposing her to uncontrolled envy and murderous feelings towards her mother and brother. Perhaps her gender confusion contained a wish to be her brother as a way, in phantasy, of attempting to resolve her identity problems. She seems to have violently rejected her mother, incorporated aspects of her mother's rejecting attitude and become consumed by fantasies of invasion echoing themes evident in her father's paranoid personality. I thought that a claustro-agoraphobic dilemma in relation to her mother (Rey, 1994) had forced her to turn to her father and assume a phallic omnipotent stance in relation to her objects. Her abnormal superego (O'Shaughnessy, 1999) usurped central ego functions, directing her thinking predominantly around the theme of invasiveness via the psychotic figure of the 'Director'. The fluidity and confusion of identificatory processes in Ms B's early life seem to have rendered her vulnerable to feeling inundated and overwhelmed, and subsequently she experienced herself as having little or no core personality of her own. Fonagy and Target (1998a) have discussed how violence in certain patients may be employed in an attempt to establish a sense of who they are, and I think the advent of Ms B's 'Director' probably reflects such a process. Interestingly, after 12 years of treatment, Ms B reported that she was no longer sure whether sexual intercourse had occurred between her and her father. How true this statement is I do not know, but it made me wonder whether it is possible that incorporation of aggressive, sexualized part-objects of the type I have described may lead a disturbed infant's mind to phantasize, via the somatic dimension of the incorporative process and confusion between inner and outer reality, that sexual contact has, in fact, taken place.

James, in contrast to Ms B, incorporated the impact of a refusal to acknowledge his very identity. This derived from what appears to have been projections by a narcissistically disordered mother unable to mourn the death of her first child and who became 'centrally phobic' to experiences of loss (Green, 2000). James' feelings of authenticity were destroyed and he consigned himself to living out a counterfeit, shame-filled life in identification with this denial of his separate existence and his brother's death. It is possible that there are different forms of incorporation of invasive objects. For example, the impact of a projectively invasive mother as experienced by bulimic patients may point to how projected 'missiles' can later be reprojected physically as well as mentally (G. Williams, 1997). Invasion fantasies also feature in the psychodynamics of anorexia (Lawrence, 2002). In certain psychoses, auditory or command hallucinations can reflect incorporated aspects of objects, drawing on unsymbolized sexual and aggressive impulses (cf. Jackson and Williams, 1994). Perhaps the dynamics of rape and their implications for the types of personalities involved merit study from the perspective of experiences of invasion by an object. It seems that invasive experiences can occur under a variety of circumstances and are linked to faulty or over-fluid identificatory processes. What they appear to have in common is the production of pathological internal part-objects that disrupt ego functioning and the evolution of a sense of self. The confusion with which the subject lives reflects multiple axes of relatedness (projective and introjective) to these part-objects – a subject about which we currently still know relatively little.

The literature on early object-relations conflicts touches on issues raised in this paper from different perspectives. Richard Sterba (1957) and Anna Freud (1951) studied the impact of oral invasion that leads to overwhelming identification with a rejecting object. Heimann (1942) described miscarriages of sublimation linked to experiences of intrusiveness. Rosenfeld (1975) depicted vividly the clinical consequences of introjected part-objects, particularly their 'mafia-like' qualities that 'protect' the ego through intimidation while countermanding any opportunity for recovery and development. Sohn (1985) identified in sudden, unprovoked assaults a form of primitive identification with a violent, uncontaining object he calls the 'identificate.' Gaddini (1992) made the observation that the primitive self of the infant that reverts to a pathological use of mimesis can experience subsequent attempts at integration as a threat to the fragile sense of self, if a fragmented identity has come to be relied upon defensively. This defense can perpetuate developmental arrest. Winnicott's (1960) concept of the false self is a detailed portrayal of one of the ego's principal, radical responses to such infantile crises. Bion (1962, 1963, 1977), above all, identified the consequences of failure to contain an infant's projections and how this can give rise to states of terrifying persecution. There is considerable consensus, irrespective of theoretical persuasion, that, without the establishment of a 'third' position based on a capacity to incorporate the 'mother-as-environment' (Winnicott, 1967) leading to the acquisition of 'reflective function' (Fonagy and Target, 1998b), 'binocularity' (Bion, 1967) or 'intersubjectivity' (Trevarthen, 1993), ego capacity is consigned to managing psychic trauma and development is impaired. The examples I have given indicate that no 'third' position had been established. If characterological disturbances within the parents are projected into the offspring throughout their development, leaving no stage of childhood untouched, a third position is probably unattainable. From this point of view, object-relations disturbances are lifelong, starting in infancy and impacting on each unfolding developmental stage (Martindale, 2004, personal communication).

The appearance of invasive objects in treatment is often seen as unpredictable and based on disorganized patterns of attachment (cf. Fonagy, 2000). I think that these invasive assaults, on examination, may be more predictable than they appear, being patterned according to the ego's phobic responses to particular constellations of primitive affect (Green, 2000). Recent developments in neuroscience suggest that assaults on the psyche–soma of infants during the first year of life can indicate loss of cortical function in the fronto-temporal areas (Perry, 1997). The long-term neurological and psychological impact of invasive experiences may be significant in understanding serious disturbance in infant development.

To conclude, incorporated aspects of an invasive object can become confused with the nascent infant self and are subject to idealization. In analysis, the prospect of relinquishment of a mimetically constructed, incorporative relationship for one with an ambivalently cathected, separate object can be experienced as catastrophe, as this is equated with loss of the ongoing sense of self. It may be necessary for the patient to endure a period of psychotic confusion as the process of un-incorporation and dis-identification takes place. Without this, the invasive object remains active in the unconscious. The patient may attack the therapeutic process in order to prevent the experience of catastrophic change (Bion, 1965). This defensive activity is, in my view, a response to the confusion that derives from the 'foreign body' inside, which must be got rid of if disruption to psychic functioning is to be halted and personality development restored, but which the patient feels cannot be forsaken as it is experienced as a part of the self.

Notes

1 The title of an abstract picture painted by Marion Milner.

2 A 'fractal object' is a structure that repeats itself infinitely and remains identical whatever its scale.

3 I am grateful to Jean-Michel Quinodoz for the observation that 'sensitivity to initial conditions' refers to one variable among many being responsible for modifying an entire course of events. It is possible to predict only the short-term evolution of such a system; however, it is also possible, a posteriori, to go back to initial events and to determine one or more factors that may have triggered the perturbation of the system. Quinodoz (1997) has discussed this analogical model in the context of psychic change.

Acknowledgement

Incorporation of an Invasive Object, Paul Williams, Copyright © 2004 *International Journal of Psychoanalysis*, Reproduced with Permission of Blackwell Publishing Ltd.

References

Bion, W.R. (1962). The psycho-analytic study of thinking. II – A theory of thinking. *International Journal of Psychoanalysis* 43: 306–10. Reprinted in Bion, W.R. (1967) *Second Thoughts: Selected Papers on Psycho-Analysis*. London: Karnac.

Bion, W.R. (1963). *Elements of Psycho-Analysis*. London: William Heinemann. Reprinted in Bion, W.R. (1977) *Seven Servants*. New York: Jason Aronson.

Bion, W.R. (1965). *Transformations*. London: Karnac Books, 1984.

Bion, W.R. (1967). *Second Thoughts: Selected Papers on Psycho-Analysis*. London: Karnac Books, 1993.

Bion, W.R. (1977). *Seven Servants*. New York: Jason Aronson.

Federn, P. (1952). *Ego Psychology and The Psychoses*. London: Imago, 1953.

Fenichel, O. (1945). *The Psychoanalytic Theory Of Neurosis*. London: Routledge & Kegan Paul.

Ferenczi, S. (1919). *Further Contributions to the Theory and Technique of Psychoanalysis*. London: Karnac Books.

Fonagy, P. (2000). Attachment and borderline personality disorder. *Journal of the American Psychoanalytic Association* 48: 1129–46.

Fonagy, P. and Target, M. (1998a). Towards understanding violence: The use of the body and the role of the father. In: Perelberg, R. (ed.) *Psychoanalytic Understanding Of Violence And Suicide*. London: Routledge.

Fonagy, P. and Target, M. (1998b). Mentalization and the changing aims of child psychoanalysis. *Psychoanalytic Dialogues* 8: 87–114.

Freud, A. (1951). Negativism and emotional surrender. Paper presented at the Congress of the International Psychoanalytic Association, Amsterdam.

Freud, S. (1900). The interpretation of dreams. *SE 4–5*. London: The Hogarth Press and The Institute of Psychoanalysis.

Freud, S. (1933). New introductory lectures on psycho-analysis. *SE 22*. London: The Hogarth Press and The Institute of Psychoanalysis.

Gaddini, E. (1992). *A Psychoanalytic Theory of Infantile Experience*. London: New Library of Psychoanalysis.

Grand, S. (2000). *The Reproduction Of Evil: A Clinical And Cultural Perspective*. Hillsdale: The Analytic Press.

Green, A. (1993). *The Work Of The Negative*. Andrew Weller, translator. London: Free Association Books, 1999. [Le travail du négatif. Paris: Editions de Minuit.]

Green, A. (2000). The central phobic position: A new formulation of the free association method. *International Journal of Psychoanalysis* 81: 429–51.

Greenacre, P. (1958). Early psychical determinants in the development of the sense of identity. *Journal of the American Psychoanalytic Association* 6: 612–27.

Heimann, P. (1942). A contribution to the problem of sublimation and its relation to processes of internalization. *International Journal of Psychoanalysis* 23: 8–17.

Jackson, M. and Williams, P. (1994). *Unimaginable Storms: A Search for Meaning in Psychosis*. London: Karnac.

Klein, M. (1935). A contribution to the psychogenesis of manic-depressive states. In: Klein, M. *Love, Guilt and Reparation and Other Works 1921–1945*. London: The Hogarth Press and the Institute of Psychoanalysis.

Laplanche, J. and Pontalis, J.-B. (1972). *Dictionary of Psychoanalysis*. London: Hogarth Press.

Lawrence, M. (2002). Body, mother, mind, anorexia, femininity and the intrusive object. *International Journal of Psychoanalysis* 83: 837–50.

Laufer, E. (2002). The body as an internal object. Presented as the Spring Lecture for the Centre for the Advancement of Psychoanalytic Studies, London, 15 February.

O'Shaughnessy, E. (1999). Relating to the superego. *International Journal of Psychoanalysis* 80: 861–70.

Perry, B. (1997). Incubated in terror: neuro-developmental factors in the cycle of violence. In: Osofsky, J. (ed.) *Children in a Violent Society*, New York: Guilford Press, pp. 124–49.

Quinodoz, D. (2001). The psychoanalyst of the future: Wise enough to dare to be mad at times. *International Journal of Psychoanalysis* 82: 235–48.

Quinodoz, J.-M. (1997). Transitions in psychic structures in the light of deterministic chaos theory. *International Journal of Psychoanalysis* 78: 699–718.

Rey, H. (1994). *Universals of Psychoanalysis in the Treatment of Psychotic and Borderline States*. London: Free Association Books.

Rosenfeld, H. (1975). *Impasse and Interpretation*. London: Tavistock.

Searles, H. (1951). Data concerning certain manifestations of incorporation. In: Searles, H. (1965) *Collected Papers on Schizophrenia and Related Subjects*. New York: International University Press.

Segal, H. (1981). *The Work of Hanna Segal: A Kleinian Approach To Clinical Practice*. New Jersey: Jason Aronson.

Sohn, L. (1985). Narcissistic organization, projective identification, and the formation of the identificate. *International Journal of Psychoanalysis* 66: 201–13. [Reprinted in Spillius, E.B. (ed.) (1988) *Melanie Klein Today: Developments in Theory And Practice. Vol. 1: Mainly Theory*. London: Tavistock Routledge (The New Library of Psychoanalysis), pp. 271–92.]

Sterba, R. (1957). Oral invasion and self defence. *International Journal of Psychoanalysis* 38: 204–8.

Symington, J. (1985). The survival function of primitive omnipotence. *International Journal of Psychoanalysis* 66: 481–7.
Trevarthen, C. (1993). The self born in intersubjectivity: The psychology of an infant communicating. In: Neisser, U. (ed.) (1993) *The Perceived Self*. Cambridge University Press.
Weiss, E. (1960). *The Structure and Dynamics Of The Human Mind*. New York and London: Grune and Stratton.
Williams, G. (1997). Reflections on some dynamics of eating disorders: 'No entry' defences and foreign bodies. *International Journal of Psychoanalysis* 78: 927–41.
Williams, P. (1998). Psychotic developments in a sexually abused borderline patient. *Psychoanalytic Dialogues* 8: 459–91.
Williams, P. (2001). Some difficulties in the analysis of a withdrawn patient. *International Journal of Psychoanalysis* 82: 727–46.
Winnicott, D.W. (1960). Ego distortion in terms of true and false self. In: Winnicott, D.W. (1964) *The Maturational Processes And The Facilitating Environment*. London: Hogarth, pp. 140–52.
Winnicott, D.W. (1967). The location of cultural experience. *International Journal of Psychoanalysis* 48: 368–72.

Chapter 4

The theory of transformations and autistic states

Autistic transformations: A proposal[1]

Celia Fix Korbivcher

Introduction

Beginning with my clinical experience, I have been interested in researching specific psychic phenomena where primitive, protomental states of mind predominate and are often inaccessible to analysts. Some patients, even though they communicate predominantly on a neurotic level, hide a part of their personality in which certain impenetrable encapsulated nuclei prevail. By impeding access to these aspects of their minds, they make it difficult for real changes to take place in the course of their analyses (S. Klein, 1980; Tustin, 1986). Frequently, in these situations, my experience has been that the relationship established between the analyst and analysand is kept within prescribed 'repetitive patterns' of communication that conceal perception of the unknown by the analyst and bring about a crystallization of the analytic process and the acceptance of this situation by both analyst and patient. Specific manifestations of this phenomenon elude analysts and are left out of their field of observation. I am referring, in particular, to sensorial manifestations in which protomental phenomena prevail and where there is no discrimination between physical and mental stimuli. The impact of these stimuli on the analyst's mind is considerable and, according to the mental phenomena's degree of primitivism, they are not brought out, thus rendering them incapable of transformation. An analyst's reactions to such stimuli should be observed and included in his field of endeavor as an essential part of his work. Often these reactions take the place of thought. Body language and evasion are expressions of these states.

Adopting Bion's (1965) theory of transformations as an observation method in analytic sessions, I hypothesize a new group of transformations, namely, autistic transformations, where autistic phenomena prevail. This concept may contribute to a better understanding of these phenomena in neurotic patients who, when confronted with situations in which mental pain is intolerable, resort to 'maneuvers' of an autistic type to avoid the pain. Fluctuations in mental states entailing phenomena of this sort occur in all human beings.

Do I dare disturb the universe?

The same phenomenon can have different interpretations depending on an observer's theoretical viewpoint. In psychoanalysis, it can be said that the apprehension of a psychic phenomenon and the meaning attributed to it are related, among other variables, to the analyst's theoretical orientation. Thus, an analyst's interpretations can vary according to his theoretical standpoint. All interpretations will be pertinent provided they are based on a particular reference frame; otherwise, there is a risk of committing errors of judgment.

At the beginning of the 20th century, discoveries in modern physics completely changed perspectives in many fields of intellectual endeavor. Concepts of space, time, matter, and cause and effect were altered. The influence of this way of perceiving phenomena can be found in different fields: in all science, in literature and in the plastic arts. I consider Bion's (1965) transformations theory to be part of this new way of perceiving phenomena. Although I cannot make a direct connection, there are, in fact, many points in common.

Grotstein (1981), when editing a collection of papers by various authors on Bion's ideas, very appropriately chose the title 'Do I Dare Disturb the Universe?' Bion's theory (1962a, 1965, 1970) has often created great turmoil and polemic within the scientific community, inducing a state of anxiety. His principal theoretical theme is connected to the development of thought which is, in itself, quite unsettling, since 'thinking' as I understand it would work against the human tendency for 'non-thought.' Individuals, moved by the need to avoid the pain that comes from the inherent helplessness in their own impotent and limited condition in the face of an unknown universe, are impelled to create an illusory or even hallucinatory world to ensure a reasonable equilibrium.

The analyst's field of work, Bion (1962a) maintains, is 'to learn from the emotional experience' shared by the analytic pair, and transformations theory (1965) is proposed as the observational standpoint for phenomena in that field. By adopting that standpoint, an analyst can make his observations knowing that 'the facts to be observed are distorted by the very act of observation' (ibid., p. 45), since the tool he possesses for his work is his own mind, which is susceptible to psychic movements equal to those of his clients. Beginning with his contact with these movements, the analyst formulates his version of a particular emotional experience. In this way, the analyst abandons his position as authority, as possessor of knowledge and as the vehicle of an absolutist vision of mental phenomena.

In my opinion, this was how Bion (1965) 'dared disturb' what had been established. He inserted into the analytic field the notion of the analyst in movement, active, at the mercy of the dynamism imposed by all live contact. In transformations theory, any movement, whether the analyst's or the analysand's, is considered to be the link in a chain of successive movements resulting from the interaction established by the analytic pair since the beginning of the session. The analyst's transformations come about in this field when it is no longer possible to assign a definitive meaning to a particular phenomenon experienced in the relationship. What he can do is offer the analysand his personal transformation as 'one' of many possibilities to be considered in his dealing with the material. An analyst's participation in the session is pregnant with elements from his own personality and with baggage he has accumulated through his lifelong experiences. It is influenced by his intuition, acquired during his psychoanalytic training, and by his own analyses.

As Bion (1965) points out, the concept of transformation contains the idea of invariance. To bring about a transformation of an emotional experience, some elements in that transformation should vary; if not, the experience is no longer a transformation, just another experience. I am not speaking about a random transformation, but about one to which the very invariants of the theory the analyst has adopted are conjoined. His theoretical system will partially determine how he apprehends the material. Bion (1965), as far as I can see, by proposing transformations theory as a method of observing mental phenomena, reproduces in the analytic situation an experience somewhat closer to a meeting of two people: two minds in movement, interacting, one modifying the other with each movement that occurs. Within this approach, each analytic pair is a specific pair, each with its own movements resulting from the emotional situation at hand.

The analyst's mind, like his patient's, is susceptible to the vicissitudes peculiar to human beings, and this requires the analyst to be in a constant state of self-awareness. This is what makes him different from the analysand. Why not imagine, then, that the analyst, subject to strong emotions in these experiences, would not also proceed in states of non-thought in which –K links (Bion, 1962a, 1962b, 1965) abound? The transformations of such an experience will depend on the conditions at that time and on the internal and external pressures under which he may find himself. What one hopes for, however, is that the analyst's mental development will be different from the analysand's, that the analyst would be in better shape for recovery once in a –K mental state so as to save his ability to think. Often, in such circumstances, the analyst, trying to avoid the upsetting experiences to which he is exposed, falls back on theories and on concepts he uses as anchors, which gives him the appearance of having a modicum of organization within the chaos of the situation.

A transformations theory perspective

The analyst using the transformations theory perspective can only access the emotional transformations going on during a particular session, since contact with the emotion itself, O, as Bion (1965) called it, is not accessible. Bion proposes several groups of transformations: in rigid motion, via projectives, in hallucinosis, in K and –K, as well as O transformations. I shall discuss only the first three groups.

In transformations in rigid motion, the field of observed phenomena includes the classical transference described by Freud, where situations from a patient's past are transferred to the analyst without being 'deformed' (Symington and Symington, 1996). In projective transformations, the mechanisms of cleavage and projective identification that M. Klein (1946) proposed prevails. One's mind projects undesirable parts of one's self on to the object so as to obtain relief. It is the analyst's role to take on the patient's projections, receive them and transform them, and make sense of them, so as to inform the patient and make it possible for him to keep that content in his mind and no longer expel it. In transformations in hallucinosis, the emotional relationship experienced with the analyst, who is a real object, is transformed in such a way that the real person is replaced by another figure created by the patient. This group of transformations, as Bion postulated, can be detected by the presence of phenomena in which:

> . . . 'actions speak louder than words' with . . . rivalry as an essential feature of the relationship. The general picture the patient presents is that of a person anxious to demonstrate his independence of anything other than his own creations. These creations are the results of his supposed ability to use his senses as organs of evacuation which are able to surround him with a universe that has been generated by himself: the function of the senses and their mental counterpart is to create the patient's perfect world. Evidence of imperfection is ipso facto evidence for the intervention of hostile envious forces. Thanks to the patient's capacity for satisfying all his needs from his own creations he is entirely independent of anyone or anything other than his products . . .
>
> (1965, pp. 136–7)

Bion points out that, in any group of transformations, to a greater or lesser extent, the hallucinatory phenomenon is always present, since he considers this one of the mind's functions. He also maintains that, 'Rivalry, envy, greed, thieving, together with his sense of being blameless, deserve consideration as invariants under hallucinosis' (ibid., pp. 132–3). By introducing the notion of transformations in hallucinosis, Bion widens the psychoanalytic field of observation, with this concept shedding light on psychic phenomena with qualities that are different from those previously considered, mainly concerning projective identification as M. Klein (1946) described. Bion (1965), by including hallucinosis among the various types of transformations, points out that the presence of this mechanism in neurotic patients is more frequent than we suppose. When subjected to great levels of pressure, patients such as these operate with the psychotic part of their personality (Bion, 1957).

By accepting transformations theory, one admits the possibility that other groups of transformations can be observed. Is it possible to include another group of transformations in this theory, a group in which the preponderant phenomenon might include characteristics different from those described by Bion (1965)? I am referring specifically to the autistic phenomenon observed in autistic states.

Autistic transformations

Tustin (see also Meltzer, 1975; Bick, 1986; Ogden, 1989) has contributed greatly to the study of autistic states. Beginning with analyses of autistic children, Tustin puts us in contact with these patients' idiosyncratic behavior, which she describes acutely. Tustin (1986) and S. Klein (1980) assert that behind the neurotic part of one's personality lies a part where encapsulated, impenetrable nuclei prevail. These nuclei are resistant to change and are responsible for patients' lack of emotional contact. These emotional states produce phenomena similar to autistic defenses, whose purpose is to protect the primordial self from intolerable states of non-integration.

According to Tustin (1981, 1984, 1986, 1990), autistic phenomena are characterized by a subject's 'emotional withdrawal' into a self-generated 'protective shell.' The individual flees from affective contact with the object in order to avoid painful experiences likely to trigger feelings of dissociation and intolerable vulnerability. Such phenomena occur mainly among people who manifest extreme sensitivity and exacerbated autosensuality. For these people, awareness of separation from the object occurred abruptly, without their having any way to bear it. Separation is experienced as if parts of their own body have been wrenched from them, making them feel annihilated. The notion of the object in the neurotic part of the personality is quite different from the notion of the object in states in which the autistic phenomenon predominates. The relationship between 'me' and 'not-me' occurs, mainly, through relations with 'sensation objects.' 'Autistic objects' and 'autistic forms' are both laden with sensations. Sensorial contact with the objects is essential, not because they represent another object or because of the phantasy they may release, but because they become the actual object. Awareness of the missing object is shrouded by the autistic object, such that the terror felt in its absence is eliminated. The relationships that are established through autistic forms are sensorial experiences that acquire form. Their form, which is entirely personal, is peculiar to each individual; they are created from bodily substances or from objects experienced as such. It is not a matter of forms shared with other people, they are 'sensed forms' which acquire rudimentary notions of limits and perform a pacifying function. They contain a space.

Often, in clinical work, analysts come across configurations such as the ones considered here. Through my experience with some patients, I have discovered that, over time, in my efforts to apprehend their mental states I have failed to notice some preverbal communication expressed by body language. Later, I discovered in the analytic relationship that these idiosyncratic communications revealed deep experiences which the patient lacked sufficient verbal resources to express. Given these manifestations' degree of non-integration, the analyst is often overwhelmed by the situation and uses evasion as a means of maintaining himself psychically balanced in a cohesive state.

The analyst's recognition and inclusion of such phenomena in his practice can considerably widen his field of observation concerning mental states and allow him to plumb primordial stages of his patient's emotional development. Awareness of these states of mind and access to them permit and encourage the separation between the 'me' and 'not-me' and allow an analysis to go on so as to promote the elaboration of these states and avoid merely repeating them.

If transformations theory is used as a reference point, this will modify the apprehension of autistic phenomena. One can abandon the description of an isolated phenomenon where the analyst, as an outside observer, is prone to interpret it according to theoretical concepts. The analyst becomes involved in the context of the emotional experience shared with the patient, and his observations emerge as a link in a chain of successive movements deriving from the pair's interaction. Thus, the analyst's work is circumscribed to experiencing the emotion present in the analytic encounter with the analysand. He can then try to transform the experience and give it meaning. If this is not possible, the analyst can let the patient know about his ignorance. Both possibilities – conferring meaning or pleading ignorance – will allow the patient to approach his own mental world. The patient caught up in states in which autistic phenomena prevail will neither include nor exclude the analyst in the session. Rather, he will ignore him and often remain absorbed in activities having to do with his own body and through which he gains pleasure and comfort, as well as a feeling of self-sufficiency.

In this state of affairs, the analyst experiences an 'absence of affective life,' which calls forth in his mind a high level of suffering tending toward evasion and which makes it difficult to keep in contact with the situation and communicate. Such situations require that the analyst engage in constant, strict self-observation, which is essential to rescue his mind and keep abreast of the circumstances. In this case, it behooves the analyst to attempt to let his patient know that his autistic maneuvers are resulting from the terror of seeing themselves as psychically separate human beings. Admittedly, however, it is not always possible to penetrate the autistic barrier. In the case of autistic transformations, rather than actual autism, one hopes, as Tustin (1990) suggests, that fluctuations of consciousness and some contact can be established. In the event the patient can become aware of his terror, he may feel accompanied by his analyst and become sufficiently confident to regain contact with his mind and, in an attempt at elaborating what is going on, momentarily experience his true condition. Ana's clinical material, which I present below, will illustrate this point.

By viewing the elements described up to now from the standpoint of transformations theory, it can be said that this new group of transformations, which I call autistic transformations, must be confronted. It is necessary to point out, however, that, by proposing autistic transformations, I am dealing with mental configurations with autistic characteristics rather than with pathological autism. Similarly to how Bion (1965) emphasizes hallucinatory phenomena by positing transformations in hallucinosis, which are not hallucinations, I posit autistic transformations and distinguish between autistic phenomena and pathological autism. In addition, it should be emphasized that the prevailing phenomena in autistic transformations, even though they may share some similarity with hallucinatory phenomena, are diverse in nature. The analyst's emotional experience in autistic transformations is one of emptiness, lack of emotion, whereas transformations in hallucinosis are intense and full of life. 'Absence of affective life,' 'emptiness' and autosensual activity can be considered invariants in 'autistic transformations.' These invariants imply the absence of the notion of internal and external objects. In transformations in hallucinosis, the notion of the external object is present.

There is another significant feature: Bion (1957) distinguishes between the neurotic and the psychotic parts of the personality. When he proposed transformations in hallucinosis, he made it possible to access psychotic parts of the patient's personality, which broadened observation of mental phenomena to include psychotic areas. Tustin (1986), by introducing the notion that there are 'autistic parts of the personality,' widens the field even more. The autistic transformations proposed here likewise facilitate access to autistic phenomena in neurotic patients by extending the observation of mental phenomena into the autistic realm.

Clinical examples

I will now present clinical vignettes from two patients: Mariana and Ana. Mariana is a child who, in my opinion, functions primarily through transformations in hallucinosis, even though there is also evidence for projective transformations. Ana is an adult patient who functions mainly with the neurotic part of her personality (Bion, 1957), but also presents notable autistic nuclei. I hope to demonstrate what I mean by 'autistic transformations' by contrasting Ana's material with Mariana's. It is necessary to make a clinical distinction between autistic transformations and transformations in hallucinosis because, as will be seen, both share a series of characteristics, and failure to distinguish them can give rise to errors.

Mariana, an 8-year-old girl, arrives at the analyst's office carrying a huge bag full of paper, folders and notebooks. While she is still outside the analyst's consulting room, in the doorway, she begins a conversation with her students: 'Hi there, class! Auntie has just arrived.' She throws everyone kisses. Paying no attention to the analyst and in the midst of great satisfaction and importance, she spreads everything out on the table and begins to talk, addressing herself to imaginary listeners. With her finger pointed to the sky and an authoritative air, she begins to interact with her students. The analyst gets caught up in this situation like one more student. Soon the room seems full of all those beings Mariana has created, and these beings begin to exist, with a life of their own. Mariana's superiority, her triumphant air, is immense!

The analyst, when trying to communicate with her, is immediately interrupted by Mariana, who says, 'You there, be quiet, not a word!' She slaps the table with her ruler and, addressing the other students, says, 'Look how stupid she is, she doesn't know a thing! She's the worst of all of you!' In this situation, the analyst is immobilized, unable to think, react or work. All she can do is wait! The analyst feels impotent, unable to act, she can't even blink. For a few moments, she assumes the personality Mariana has assigned her: the worst of all her students. The session goes on like this. When the time is up, Mariana gathers all her possessions and, from the door, says 'bye-bye' to everyone, adding, 'Everybody be quiet, Auntie is going away and when she comes back, she wants to find everything in order.'

In this clinical vignette, the analyst finds herself in the presence, predominantly, of transformations in hallucinosis, even though there are some projective transformations as well. The patient, with great skill and shrewdness, creates a scenario in which her 'characters' acquire a life of their own. The analyst, as a separate entity, does not belong in this scenario, except as one more student who performs the very role reserved for her among the patient's students: the worst of all! The predominant atmosphere in this experience betrays rivalry and superiority of the analysand over the analyst. Her goal is to maintain this relationship regardless of cost, so she reacts violently to any possible threat to her dominance. The emotional climate of the session is intense and vivid. Mariana's action can be characterized as evacuatory; its function is to try to maintain control over the analyst, so as to make her an object she created, allowing her to avoid contact with the analyst's real-life, dynamic presence. She uses hallucinatory mechanisms to this end; had she not, she would need to face her own helplessness owing to her true fragile and powerless condition. Her triumph over the analyst when she confirms the superiority of her methods (Bion, 1965) is significant. All these elements together indicate that transformations in hallucinosis prevail.

The analyst experiences a state of helplessness in the face of the session's intensity. She has to wait patiently until some break in the situation can occur, a break during which an interlocutor might emerge and to whom the analyst can communicate that all the emotion in which the patient is wrapped up is a product of her own mind. Awareness of that fact on the part of the patient might help her attenuate her hallucinatory state and allow her to establish communication on a different level within the analytic pair.

In this clinical fragment, transformations in hallucinosis prevail, but some of the patient's movements can be characterized as projective transformations. The patient massively projects her undesirable internal content on to the analyst, who feels what it is like to be a small child subjected to violence coming from an authoritative adult. The intensity of this projection overwhelms the analyst and incorporates her into the scenario the child had set up, so much that the analyst momentarily loses her perspective concerning the separation between patient and analyst and forgets that her patient's hallucinosis really has nothing to do with her. These elements point toward the presence of phenomena characterizing projective transformations. In circumstances such as this one, the analyst should take in the analysand's projections, and, using her capacity for reverie, as well as the α-function, transform them and assign them some meaning. Communicating that meaning perhaps could allow the projected content to resurface in such a way as to become more bearable and likely to be kept in mind.

As Bion (1965) points out, phenomena related to projective identification and transformations in hallucinosis permeate all communication to some extent. For the analyst, it is important to determine, according to his point of view, what the prevailing phenomenon is at a particular moment. This is important because the clinical approach will be different according to the type of transformation presented.

Ana, aged 35, has been in analysis for several years, coming to sessions four times a week. She is a competent professional. When the analyst meets her in the waiting room, she can see a blank look on Ana's face denoting a certain 'absence of emotion.' When Ana comes into the consulting room, she slowly and carefully puts her purse on the couch. She lies down, straightens out her skirt on both sides and crosses her legs. A few minutes later, she presents matters related to timetables, honoraria, coming vacations. She gives the impression of being concerned about some practical aspect of the situation. The analyst answers her questions, even though she is aware that Ana's vacation is still far in the future and that there is no evidence that such matters have anything to do with separation anxiety. This subject wears out quickly and Ana withdraws once again, diving into a state of retraction. The analyst notices that, besides the gum Ana is chewing, she is also using one hand to fiddle with an earlobe. Little by little, the analyst reviews some of the patterns she has shared in Ana's universe.

She realizes that Ana's ritual of entering the consulting room, her questions, her chewing gum and fiddling with her earlobe are all she can do, since, apparently, she has no other resources at that moment for sharing anything real with another person. This 'repetitive pattern' makes the analyst feel discouraged and helpless because she knows from other sessions that pointing this out to her will not help. She decides to wait. Ana keeps quiet for a long time, as if she were under the effect of some strong anesthetic. With no one to talk to, the analyst feels isolated. She notices that she needs to make a conscious effort to stay in contact and not evade all this.

After some time, Ana comes to, stretches slowly, seeming to awaken from that anesthetized state and, in a tone of voice as if she were talking to herself, she says, 'I need to say something.' The analyst replies that it seems as though Ana may have momentarily become aware of her presence in the room and may want to tell her something, but then she sees that Ana has not listened to her. Ana begins a long narrative full of minute descriptions of things that have happened. She recounts this with such a richness of detail and elaboration that it is impossible for the analyst to figure out what Ana is trying to tell her. The analyst tries to take up a point and offer an interpretation based on what Ana is saying, but realizes that nothing she is saying makes an impression. From what Ana is saying, the analyst perceives that she seems to be totally immersed in the enjoyment of the 'speech act' rather than in its content. She appears indifferent to what the analyst is saying to her and goes on piling detail on detail, as if, by doing this, she were trying to avoid some feeling of emptiness. The analyst notices that her mental state is now attentive so that she will not be overwhelmed by the situation and can remain in contact. Then she realizes that there is no connection between her comments on the content of Ana's utterances and the emotion being felt. Ana seems as absorbed with her speaking as she was with her gum and her earlobe.

Keeping some distance from the situation, the analyst tries to find some way of telling Ana that what is happening in the session shows how she experiences situations in her life and that perhaps this is the core of her mental life. The analyst tells Ana that she has seen that she is terrified whenever she becomes aware that she is a separate individual. She mentions that the long time in which Ana remains withdrawn and isolated, as well as the entire narrative she becomes so wrapped up in, and the gum are stratagems she has found to try to protect herself from terrifying experiences and to maintain a state of continuity with the analyst.

She listens attentively. The analyst sees a change in her mental state, and the atmosphere of isolation present in the room has diminished. She says she understands what the analyst is saying. Then she adds that she withdraws in this manner whenever she fears that the situation in which she finds herself will not suit her expectations. She says, 'That's the way I am when I'm in any situation, real or imaginary. I think I'll never change. I need to feel totally safe, and that is only possible if the person I'm with is inside of me, but I know that will never happen.' The analyst understands Ana's suffering. She tells her that she is seeing things from a totally different perspective now and that perhaps she can feel 'being separate.' After this, the analyst can tell that they have become closer to one another and that Ana seems capable of gradually giving up her defenses. She seems to be a little closer to her own emotions and perhaps now she can tolerate her vulnerability.

Being with this patient makes the analyst oscillate between feeling intense emotion and paralysis. Were the analyst incapable of maintaining herself in a self-observation state, her tendency would be to disconnect, distance herself and abandon the patient. Also, her staying in contact with the patient's 'emptiness or void state of affairs' is not stable, depending on the amount of suffering involved, in addition to other imponderable factors. When contact is possible, the analyst is able to rescue her thought capacity and to step back somewhat from the situation so as to see that such manifestations are maneuvers that Ana has developed to protect herself from her extreme internal vulnerability. In this circumstance, the analyst's emotions can be changed and made to see that Ana's detailed narration, prolonged silence, her gum, her manipulating her earlobe, and her body language take on another dimension: they express her experiencing terror owing to her knowledge that she is psychically separate from the object. She withdraws from contact and, through sensations in her own body, creates a state of corporeal continuity with the external object, thus avoiding the intolerable mental pain brought on by the awareness of the physical separation from the object. In this way, she manages to preserve some cohesion of her self.

From my point of view, this clinical material shows how one can understand autistic phenomena from the standpoint of transformations theory. I will now examine some of the movements in the session and identify autistic transformations.

The analyst, when she meets the patient in the waiting room, sees a person with a 'blank look' and 'lacking emotion.' She notices non-verbal manifestations: the gum, the fiddling with her earlobe and her ritualistic body movements when she lies down on the couch. The analyst observes that the patient attempts to communicate with what words she has available and, to do this, she asks questions about practical matters related to her analysis. On examining this cycle of transformations, it is evident that the emotional experience shared in the session becomes the key element directing the analyst toward what Bion (1965, 1970) called O. The analyst's theoretical invariants are part of what she sees. The patient's speech in this sequence did not seem to be related to her content, but she makes a maneuver that, together with her autosensual activity, protects her from the pain deriving from her awareness of being separate from the object, and, thus, protects her from the threat of annihilation. These maneuvers are an attempt at maintaining continuity with the object. In this chain of movements, the patient's transformations are what I call autistic transformations.

In the next cycle of transformations, the patient is still absorbed in her autistic maneuvers. The analyst, not able to penetrate the patient's mental world, is overtaken with a discouraged feeling as she remembers similar sessions from the past. She decides to wait. In the next chain of movements, the patient's transformations are 'autistic transformations.' One still might ask if the analyst's transformations might not have been in hallucinosis.

After a long period of withdrawal, the patient realizes that she must say something and begins a long narrative. The analyst feels isolated and empty. She has the impression that the patient's pleasure coming from her sensation of making a 'speech act' prevails over her interest in the content she is communicating. The analyst becomes aware that the patient's speech, her gum and her fiddling with her earlobe are means of maintaining a state of continuity with the object. To her way of thinking, this is how the patient avoids feelings of disassociation brought on by the terror of the awareness of separation from the object. The analyst stays in the situation and tries to find a way of letting the patient know what she is seeing. In this cycle of transformation, the patient's transformations will be autistic, the analyst's in K (i.e. knowledge) transformations. The analyst's communication of these perceptions to the patient make her autistic barrier more permeable. The atmosphere in the session changes. The emptiness disappears, and contact between them becomes more vivid. With this new cycle of transformations, we can see that the analyst performs a splitting in her mind, she is able to keep herself in the situation, and, in such a way, recovers her analytic function. She observes that her state of discouragement disappears and she can communicate her findings in a more precise manner. The patient shows an interest in what the analyst says. The protective armor the patient constructs in the beginning of the session becomes more permeable. She seems to have developed some confidence in relation to the analyst and lets herself reveal her vulnerability without feeling so threatened. She says, 'That is only possible if the person I'm with is inside me, but I know that will never happen.' In this sequence, we see that the patient can experience being separate from the object. In this particular cycle, I suggest that the analyst's transformations are in K and the patient's, in K→O.

It is important to point out that the transformations presented in this session are peculiar to that particular analyst. Another analyst, with different personality traits, who uses a different theoretical framework, would address this material from a different, yet equally valid, standpoint. I acknowledge that this session could have unfolded in other ways.

Discussion

I begin this discussion by characterizing, through the two clinical vignettes, what I call autistic transformations. To this end, I shall contrast some of Ana's material with Mariana's. Then I shall try to share some misgivings that arise from the ideas I have developed here. It is easy to see that the emotional atmosphere of Ana's session is quite different from what went on in Mariana's. Both patients live immersed in their own worlds, worlds in which the presence of the 'other' is disregarded. It is, nonetheless, evident that the quality of the phenomenon in each of the situations is quite different and, thus, the way to approach them is different. In the relationship with Mariana, the analyst shares an experience in which emotion prevails. The environment is intense, lively, full of impact. Finding herself without a means of reaching the client, who keeps herself wrapped in a hallucinatory state of mind, the analyst feels, above all, helpless.

In the relationship with Ana, the analyst experiences a 'state of affective emptiness.' The contact here is with an object physically present, but psychically absent, 'with no affective life' available to relate to other people. During Ana's session, the analyst experiences an accentuated unfamiliarity as far as the analysand's inner world is concerned. The analyst needs to develop some means of maintaining her analytic footing to figure out what is going on. Ana's relationships are achieved through autosensual activities or with objects that she takes to be physical. She tends to hold on to these sensations to feel protected. Any attempt by the analyst to approach her mental world exacerbates the threat she feels. And the analysand fears that her entire structure might abruptly crack and that her vulnerability would be exposed. This collection of phenomena points toward what I call 'autistic transformations.'

I will now explore some important points. The first is the apparent paradox contained in the term 'autistic transformation.' Tustin (1981, 1984, 1986, 1990) tells us that the working of the autistic mind is characterized by the individual's living in a world dominated by sensation and that his dealing with people derives from the sensations people arouse. These are protomental phenomena whose degree of primitivism stops them from being represented in the mind, and this makes them immune to transformation. Yet, we can suppose that any manifestation, even one on the protomental level, as well as its apprehension, would be a transformation, since we have no access to the experience itself, however primitive it may be. As long as these phenomena may be concretely expressed on a sensorial level, they are transformations. With this fact in mind, and in spite of the idea that an 'autistic transformation' may seem paradoxical, the notion is extremely useful because it gathers autistic phenomena and makes them identifiable. The merit of this distinction is related to the possibility of including such phenomena within our observational methodology –

transformations theory. We then will be better able to define the phenomena in question. If vigilance can be maintained, it will be possible to shed more light on our day-to-day clinical practice, where recognizing these phenomena is not always possible, mainly because it is hard for the analyst to stay in contact with the situation, given the strength of these stimuli.

It is important to emphasize that not every autosensual activity in the session is associated with autistic transformations. What determines the nature of a particular transformation is the emotional experience the analyst identifies within the session. There are autosensual activities that produce intense emotion in the analyst, and they are of a different nature from those found in autistic transformations as I have formulated them.

A further point for consideration is the need not to confuse the impact on the analyst's mind in the face of autistic phenomena with phenomena coming from projective identification. The degree of primitivism present in protomental states causes intense reactions in the observer. These reactions are likewise disorganized, which may lead one to consider them a phenomenon of successful projective identification. I believe this is a mistake because, in the states where autistic phenomena prevail, the object is not considered a separate object. In these cases, there is no possibility of a patient's release of undesirable content by projecting it on to the analyst. The patient in this state is wrapped up in himself and in the sensation he creates, and for him there is no difference between 'me' and the 'not-me.' Having the analyst face the patient's level of emotional development is a fundamental distinction to make. In view of these mental states, for the analyst as well as the analysand, it is preferable that both be aware of the unknown brought on by these situations, as well as of the limits in understanding. It would be worse to propose some inappropriate approach and create a static situation (Fix Korbivcher, 1999).

I will now return to those transformations brought on by the analyst when confronted with 'autistic transformations.' Mental stimuli are powerful in this area, where the absence of emotion prevails. For the analyst, it can be intolerable to stay put when faced with a mental state of affective emptiness. The way the analyst will respond to what the patient is relating will vary according to the interplay of movements shared by the pair.

The analyst often creates in his mind a 'different analysand' with whom he communicates, ignoring, in this manner, the patient's mental condition. In an attempt to reach his patient, he advances interpretations based on specific theories and does not realize the error he has committed. The analyst uses this mechanism to free himself from a situation as it is, replacing it with one of his own making. In these cases, the analyst experiences transformations in hallucinosis.

There are also situations in which the analyst, overwhelmed by anguish in not finding an interlocutor with whom he can communicate, cannot contain the feelings these situations bring about, so he tends to avoid the discomfort he feels. He often expels and projects his own hostile impulses coming from that experience on to the analysand's mind and pressures his patient to operate with resources that are not available at that time. When this happens, the phenomenon of projective identification prevails. Can the analyst's transformations be considered as projective? Other times, depending on the degree of suffering in the particular situation, an abyss is created within the analytic pair. Each member remains self-absorbed, in a private universe, with no connection to the other. To deal with these situations, the analyst can be caught up in activities related to his own body, with his own mental goings-on, totally unrelated to the client. He can also be carried away by the pleasure in the act of speaking and producing long speeches that clearly address his own needs, rather than those of the patient. This analyst can be said to be undergoing 'autistic transformations.'

It is also possible for the analyst to maintain some distance in relation to the experience the client presents. In this case, he can perform a split in his mind, without this split overwhelming him, and make it possible to discern the nature of the transformation of the particular emotional experience. In this case, the analyst recovers his thought capacity and stays with the patient in his isolated universe. In the event the analyst can transform this experience into some communication and offer it to the patient, some contact may be established between the two of them. A patient's experience of sharing with the analyst his state of mental emptiness, his lack of affective life, and of being informed about the workings of his inner world can be extremely valuable. This would be a rare opportunity for these patients to feel close to someone. In these circumstances, the analyst would be operating under K transformations.

The ideas I have developed in this paper proposing 'autistic' transformations are designed to unite a particular group of mental phenomena with specific characteristics, to limit them, name them and fit them into an established theoretical framework so that, perhaps, they can acquire a life of their own. I am fully aware, however, that, in spite of the effort involved in this attempt to unite these phenomena, 'this model will not entirely describe the totality of the actual situation' (Capra, 1975, p. 39).

Note

1 Paper presented at: Marcas Identificatorias del Psicoanálisis en Latinoamérica [Identifying markers of Latin American Psychoanalysis], Rio de Janeiro, Brazil, 18–19 June 2004. Translated by Arthur Brekel.

Acknowledgement

The Theory of Transformations and Autistic States. Autistic Transformations: A Proposal, Celia Fix Korbivcher, Copyright © 2005 *International*

Journal of Psychoanalysis, Reproduced with Permission of Blackwell Publishing Ltd.

References

Bick, E. (1986). Further considerations on the function of the skin in early object relations: Findings from infant observation integrated into child and adult analysis. *British Journal of Psychotherapy* 2: 292–9.

Bion, W. R. (1957). Differentiation of the psychotic from the non-psychotic personalities. *International Journal of Psychoanalysis* 38: 266–75.

Bion, W. R. (1962a). *Learning From Experience*. London: Heinemann, p. 128 [(1991). *Aprender com a experiência*. Rio de Janeiro: Imago.]

Bion, W. R. (1962b). The psycho-analytic study of thinking. II A theory of thinking. *International Journal of Psychoanalysis* 43: 306–10.

Bion, W. R. (1965). *Transformations: Change from learning to growth*. London: Heinemann. [(1983). *Transformações: Mudança do aprendizado ao arescimento*. Rio de Janeiro: Imago.]

Bion, W. R. (1970). *Attention and Interpretation*. London: Tavistock.

Capra, C. F. (1975). *The Tao of Physics*. Boston, MA: Shambhala. [(1983). *O tao da física*. São Paulo: Cultrix.]

Fix Korbivcher, C. (1999). Mente primitiva e pensamento (Primitive mind and thought). *Revista Brasileira de Psicanálise* 33: 687–706.

Grotstein, J. S. (1981). *Do I Dare Disturb the Universe? A Memorial to Wilfred R Bion*. Beverly Hills, CA: Caesura.

Klein, M. (1946). Notes on some schizoid mechanisms. *International Journal of Psychoanalysis* 27: 99–110.

Klein, S. (1980). Autistic phenomena in neurotic patients. *International Journal of Psychoanalysis* 61: 395–402.

Meltzer, D. (1975). *Explorations in Autism*. Strath Tay: Clunie.

Ogden, T. H. (1989). On the concept of an autistic–contiguous position. *International Journal of Psychoanalysis* 70: 127–40.

Symington, J. and Symington, N. (1996). *The Clinical Thinking of Wilfred Bion*. London: Routledge. (Makers of Modern Psychotherapy series.)

Tustin, F. (1981). *Autistic States in Children*. London: Routledge. [(1984). *Estados Autísticos em Crianças*. Rio de Janeiro: Imago.

Tustin, F. (1984). Autistic shapes. *International Review of Psychoanalysis* 11: 279–90.

Tustin, F. (1986). *Autistic Barriers in Neurotic Patients*. London: Karnac. [(1990). *Barreiras autistas em pacientes neuróticos*. Porto Alegre: Artes Médicas.]

Tustin, F. (1990). *The Protective Shell in Children and Adults*. London: Karnac.

Chapter 5

A binocular view of adhesion

From prenatal contiguity to postnatal appetite

Marianne Robinson

Introduction

The passage in development that spans the movement from intrauterine life through physical to psychic birth involves development of the capacity to become aware, and within that awareness to differentiate between the internal world and external reality. Over the history of psychoanalysis there has been an expanding awareness of the psychic territory that can be perceived, understood, and analyzed. This has yielded new theories and techniques both in terms of depth (more primitive/elemental aspects of experience) and in terms of level of pathology (more severe illness).

Freud explored and chartered the territory of 'the child within the adult,' and Melanie Klein and her followers elaborated the area of 'the infant within the child.' Both Freud and Klein anticipated the investigation of an even earlier territory of experience, that of the prenatal. Freud (1926) wrote about the continuity between intrauterine life and earliest infancy and Melanie Klein (1952) stated that the young baby's experience of the pain during birth is felt by him as persecution, attack by a hostile force. This describes the infant's reaction to discomfort and loss in terms of the paranoid schizoid and depressive positions (theories of postnatal development) leaving to others the investigation of what is actually continued between the physical act of birth and the complex body/mind work of psychic emergence. Such investigations into prenatal territory have been faced with the need to develop new concepts or extend and/or redefine old concepts in order to accommodate new knowledge gained from clinical observation of prenatal states in the analytic setting.

A well-known example of such an extension, albeit in the postnatal area is Bion's (1962) expansion of Melanie Klein's (1952) concept of projective identification, which she regarded as a pathological defense and which Bion, using the concept of container/contained, expanded and deepened to include an early aspect of object relations where projective identification is the main currency of experiential exchange within the mother–infant bond and as such is vital for the health and psychic growth of the infant.

There is a need to continue to investigate other concepts in order to explore their potential for expanding our understanding of the prenatal domain of experience. In the process, we may need to consider that what has been regarded as a pathological defense against a postnatal object link may now profitably be understood as a way of relating (physically and sensually) that belongs in the prenatal world, where it may have been adaptive and in the service of life but, for reasons to be investigated in each individual analysis, has persisted, relatively unmodified, as a way of coping in the postnatal world.

In this paper I confine myself to the psychic territory where vestiges of prenatal states of mind appear in postnatal behavior and for the purpose of this discussion I suggest the following definition of prenatal states of mind. They consist of the use of postnatal mental and physical capacities as concrete prenatal equivalents for the purpose of expressing an aversion to the experience of pain and intolerance of change, also to achieve a timeless unconsciousness about postnatal reality which contact with the object world stirs up. One can infer here underlying unconscious fantasies of existing in an intrauterine state.

Within this prenatal territory, my specific focus in this paper is adhesion, the kind of stickiness Meltzer and Bick (Meltzer, 1975) called adhesive identification and Ogden (1988, 1989) described as related to efforts to organize a contiguous experience. Using the developmental paradigm of psychic emergence, I propose a prenatal extension of Ogden's postnatal concept of contiguity (1988, 1989) and I suggest the view that adhesion is evidence of the patient's unconscious search for a prenatal containing relationship. This applies Bion's concept of binocularity (1962) to the simultaneous presence of prenatal fantasy and postnatal action and suggests a binocular attitude when listening to clinical material.

Psychic containers, healthy and pathological

The theme of the human need to live and orient within a containing physical or psychic space is ever present in the literature on prenatal states. Bick (1968) first presented the idea of a psychic skin, the prototype of which is the nipple in mouth. It holds parts of the self together and is at first undifferentiated, but with development evolves to have physical and psychic components. Mancia (1981) hypothesizes a prenatal development of this psychic skin which flows from un-differentiation to alpha function using sensory information transmitted via the intrauterine skin connection during active sleep.

Bion's concept of container/contained expanded and deepened our understanding of the infantile experience of reverie, alpha function and meaning-making that fosters capacity for thought within the mother–infant bond. In normal development the experience of the containing relationship is internalized, resulting in the capacity for internal whole object relationships and the ability to orient oneself within such a containing internal world. There are situations, however, in which the containing function of the object world fails, leading to development in a different direction. There are also internal forces that pull for discontinuity, or mobilize to stop forward psychic movement, inviting regression to the unchanging familiar, however painful that may be.

Bion (1963, 1970) wrote about the stopping of psychic movement as a rupture into psychosis when a container is taxed beyond its capacity and there is no conception of a containment nor the ability for visual thought, which might serve as coordinates for reference. It is a violent expulsion of elements of the personality, the outcome of which is a situation where time and psychic distance are expressions of intensity of pain and where frustration and intense pain are equated. He goes on to point out that the dangers to the containing relationship lie in the ruptured boundary when the container is devoured by the contained or when the contained succeeds in puncturing the container.

There is an urgent need to survive psychically after an actual rupture or in the face of a threat to the integrity of an existing container. Such survival consists of the creation of a 'new' alternative container constructed on the basis of a fantasized ability to keep safe the wounded and threatened parts of the personality from exposure to contact with reality and to the painful turmoil of further transformation. Various writers have named, described, and defined different aspects of such defensive containers. Bick (1968) stated that the uncontained baby will frantically search for an object to hold parts of its personality together – and, if a good-enough maternal relationship is not available, disturbances in the primal skin function can lead to the development of a second-skin through which dependence on the object is replaced by pseudo-independence. This second skin is related to anxieties in the unintegrated, not limited to specific persecutory or depressive fears. Grotstein (1990) has written about the black hole as a simultaneous painful hell and a savior from feared infernal pain. Meltzer (1992) writes about the Claustrum, relating it to intrusive identification into the mother's body, Steiner (1993) refers to psychic retreats as interlocking defensive systems, and Paul (1997) mentions autistic barriers that are connected to a fantasy of prenatal existence. Maiello (1995) postulates a containing function of a prenatal 'sound-object' which if disrupted has postnatal relationship consequences. Tustin (1986), in addition to her well-known work on autism, elaborated on non-autistic neurotic encapsulations. Mitrani (1992, 1995) has written about autistic barriers within which the unborn aspects of the personality are protected and preserved.

All describe pathological containers and, although they elaborate on different aspects of them, it is the function of stopping psychic movement in order to find protection from the psychic pain of emergence that I will refer to in this paper, with the terms pathological container and encapsulation used interchangeably.

Adhesion

The psychoanalytic meaning of adhesion is the subject of ongoing discussion between representatives of two main ways of conceptualizing its place in object relations theory. One is represented by Bick (1968), Meltzer (1975), Tustin (1988) and Mitrani (1994, 1995a, 1995), and uses the term 'adhesive identification' to describe a pathological maneuver and an aspect of autistic defenses. The other is represented by Thomas Ogden (1988, 1989), who relates it to an 'autistic/contiguous position' along a normal developmental continuum. I will briefly discuss both views and suggest a summarizing formulation that expresses my binocular attitude on which I base my discussion of adhesion in this paper.

Bick and Meltzer (Meltzer, 1975), observing adhesion in their patients, understood it as a pathological resistance to the development of psychic space. Further, they observed that these patients were subject to states of disintegration much like infants. They had dreams of body parts falling away (teeth and arms) and a sense that their skin was too tight. Their attitude toward life was of muscularity, non-thinking and always involving doing and action. Something seemed wrong with their ability to identify; they were intolerant of separation and had a fluctuating relationship to time. Ogden (1988) proposed a more comprehensive idea of adhesion with the concept of an autistic-contiguous position that he places in dialectic relationship to Melanie Klein's paranoid-schizoid and depressive positions. It is a sensory-dominated, pre-symbolic mode of generating experience where surfaces touching one another is the main mode of relating. It provides a sense of a 'place' where experience occurs. Outlining an idea of a continuum, Ogden (1988) suggested that human experience is the outcome of a dialectical relationship between the three positions. The autistic-contiguous mode, as he names it, provides the sensory continuity and containment of experience, the paranoid-schizoid mode is the expression of the timeless, concretely expressed experience, and the depressive mode is the medium through which the experience of time and symbolic linkages is generated.

Explaining the dialectic action, Ogden states that the potential for pathology in the paranoid-schizoid position is given a sensory floor 'from below' by the autistic-contiguous and a realistic ceiling 'from above' by the depressive awareness of time and symbolic linkages. He (1989) also addresses the pathology related to the autistic-contiguous position and writes that inability to organize the primitive experiences of rhythm and touching surfaces into containing experiences result in unspeakable terror of leaking, dissolving, or falling endlessly. He holds that the defenses against these unbearable states are second skin formations as described by Bick (1968).

Ogden also outlines countertransference responses specific to the autistic-contiguous mode. They involve bodily experiences, including a state of drowsiness, which he believes is not boredom but more closely connected with Bion's (1962) idea of 'reverie'.

Mitrani (1995a) describes adhesive identification as appendancy rather than a dependency, writing that there may be a mode of pseudo-object relating that results in a seamless clinging to the surface of an undifferentiated-object.

Grotstein (1980) initially described adhesive identification as a stage prior to the stage of projective identification within the paranoid-schizoid position (symbiosis) and stated that it is the earliest quest of the infant for mindless definition against the mother's body. He referred to 'patients who are striving for definition, not explanation (to be felt, not to be found)' (1980, p. 500). Currently he believes (personal communication) neither in linking adhesive identification with autism, nor in a new position that antedates the paranoid-schizoid position.

Within these diverse ways of conceptualizing adhesion, I find it useful to formulate and outline adhesion to accommodate my own binocular vertex. In order to retain the broadest meaning of adhesion, I will drop the reference to autism and retain 'contiguous,' which refers to the mode of relating described by Ogden (1989) (surfaces touching). My suggested prenatal extension to the continuum of adhesive activity can then be seen to range from prenatal contiguity to postnatal molding.

I believe that, in the area between Bion's container/contained and pathological encapsulation, there is a maneuver that can be understood as an effort to resist a containing relationship on the one hand while not succumbing, either to the agonies of separateness or to a pathological container, on the other. That is adhesion in its appearance as postnatal resistance. Paradoxically, using the binocular attitude, I suggest that adhesion is also the prenatal expression of contiguity. In terms of the developmental struggle to build structure between the different positions, keeping in mind the points in the preceding discussion on prenatal vestiges, it might then be said that anxieties of the depressive position may find regressive comfort in the fantasized certainties of splitting in the paranoid-schizoid position, and that anxieties of that phase may find regressive comfort in the fantasized familiarity of prenatal contiguity.

In order to demonstrate the underlying unconscious fantasy behind adhesion in the case to be presented, I will briefly describe my patient's rigid encapsulation, the dismantling of which ushered in adhesion. I will proceed to demonstrate that a binocular vertex allowed for understanding this adhesion and its resolution in terms of prenatal contiguity transforming into postnatal appetite for life. I will organize the relevant clinical material chronologically, paying attention to the transformations along the way – a sequence I call a transformational continuum. First an explanation of how the idea and the term of transformational continuum came about.

During the many years of my patient Mary's treatment I found it helpful to keep in mind Bion's statement that, in the treatment of psychosis, time and psychic distance do not reflect conventional time and psychic connection but instead are statements of the magnitude of frustration and pain that gave velocity to the ejection of the personality at the moment of the psychotic break. My experience during this analytic process was one of being on a journey through shattered and widely dispersed psychic territory. It was only after I had catalogued my noted captions of each session over a period of years that, at that level of perspective, patterns emerged which allowed me to conceptualize the whole in terms of themes, or transformational continua, one of which is adhesion.[1]

Before presenting the clinical material, I will give a very brief history and allow the relevant elaborations to emerge as they did in the treatment. In my opinion, this illustrates how those events are connected in Mary's internal world, thus giving the reader a more thorough view of the gradual movement and working through which I will also discuss in context.

History

Mary is a middle-aged woman who married for the first time at the age of 45. She was in analysis with me for over 14 years. She is the second of two daughters, her sister being three years her senior. She described her family as dysfunctional and her mother as explosive, ranting, unpredictable and so intrusive that she reached in and robbed Mary of her insides. She described her father as ineffectual and unable to protect her from mother. Maternal grandmother, who lived with the family, she described as insane and evil.

Mary became psychotic during her late teens and early twenties and, at one point, was hospitalized for a number of weeks. A feature of her struggle was a fear that she would tear her eyes out. She had been in some kind of treatment ever since her breakdown. While in treatment with me she discovered that her mother had a psychotic break involving an extended hospitalization during Mary's first year. She and her sister were cared for by an aunt and uncle during that time. Mary felt she had been lost and depressed since then and that, over the years, she 'catapulted' and developed an outgoing, energetic and engaging persona that successfully disguised her vulnerability.

In the first few weeks of treatment Mary's then boyfriend abruptly broke off their relationship and Mary reacted by unthinkingly, and without telling anyone, running away to another state, holing up for several days before returning.

Clinical material

From the beginning of treatment I noted that Mary used speech as a defense. She spoke in a way that fascinated and compelled her listener to idealize her intellect and hang on her every word. I understood that this adhesive speech had a dual function. It served as her pathological container, holding her safe from being found and touched by relationships in the outside world. It also created a prenatal indivisibility with me that defied consideration of psychic space and separate-minded thinking. In combination they were a barrier against meaningful contact between us in the analysis.

For a long period, Mary's speech was the main evidence of her adhesive tie to me. However, looking back, an early dream foretold the very primitive level of Mary's object relationships. Returning after our first two-week break, Mary declared, 'I did not miss you at all, but I had a dream. There was a baby in a crib all alone in a room. You came in and the baby *flew* from the crib, through the air into you.'

It seemed our break threatened a fantasy that Mary had intruded into me. Noticing my absence with feelings of missing me would then have been experienced as my revengeful engulfment, something she could not bear to experience. Her reaction was the dream of violently going back inside and I felt the force of that reunion during that session. This suggested an internal relationship with ruptured container/contained boundaries as Bion described (1963).

I also came to recognize other components of Mary's pathological container. Her muscles formed a painfully tight shell. She had a tight back and her chest was constricted so she could not breathe fully. She described her muscles as protectively wrapping around her and 'beating' her while also providing structure so her insides would not collapse in a mess. She also used her muscles to act in situations when thinking was called for, so they protected her in two ways. They constricted and gave 'holding pain' and they discharged in action and gave 'evacuative relief.'

In addition to her speech and the muscular action, Mary's sensual capacity seemed to have been appropriated in order to help maintain her pathological container. She continuously reinforced its walls by cutting the link to her psychic capacities for sight, sound and touch and thus to the reality of the postnatal object world.

The first few years of Mary's analysis consisted of working to soften her rigid encapsulation and over time that work presented an increasing threat to her status quo. After one break, she said that 'separation was like being torn and having my intestines hanging out and my eyes are tired from paying attention.' She reacted to this softening with increased efforts to hold her muscles tight and to use her eyes to hallucinate 'so the inside and the outside will be the same,' her ears to limit what she heard or she 'would explode' and her voice to have outbursts, all for the purpose of denying reality and holding the capsule intact.

She experienced flesh tearing and repeatedly dreamed that she was feasting on cut-up strawberries (attacked nipples), which soon turned into bugged grapes (vengefully eavesdropping persecutors). She said that there was a lot of killing going on. I heard and interpreted these as subjective experiences of her pathological container tearing and a description of the simultaneous violent attack on her objects as she cut the link to reality.

Over time Mary began to realize that her efforts to keep her pathological container intact were failing and I believed that the painful process of realizing her dependency was at hand. However, in the sixth year of analysis, Mary became increasingly silent in the sessions, and the next several months were puzzling to me as I tried to experience contact with her. Stillness seemed to invade the space that had been filled with our dialogue. When I attempted to name what was between us, Mary begged me repeatedly to do my own thing and just let her be there, 'don't pay attention to me. I'll be here very still and quiet.' She remembered wishing for that with her mother. If she could only hang on without her mother knowing, things would be OK.

During the silences, I began to have a sensation on the surface of the side of my body, as if something was stuck on there. It seemed that by trying to be so silent and lie so still that I would not notice her, Mary, in her fantasy, was making our connection one of physical contact. I felt as if she wished to be glued to me, permanently immobilizing us both and the analysis.

Aided by my countertransference and past descriptions of Mary's early relationships I formulated interpretations. I said that she might now be afraid of being attacked and having her insides plundered by me as she had feared with her mother. I said that if she moved, there would be space between us, which she might experience as confirmation of the growing psychic space in her internal world that she feared becoming aware of.

The silent period extended over many months and during that time there was evidence of incremental movements. Mary became increasingly aware of her reaction to our weekend separations. She dreamed that her hated grandmother fell from a train and her arms fell off. I understood that Mary experienced moving away from the 'protection' of her old psychotic internal objects as a falling apart of the familiar, the physical, and the crazy. The dream was also a symbolic transformation of the earlier description of separation as her intestines hanging out.

The following week Mary brought a dream that she was leaving her mother for an analyst/woman. During that session, I was overcome by intense, almost unbearable fury in the countertransference. When some perspective on that experience was possible, I thought of this state as Mary having deposited an aspect of her personality into me (Bion, 1962). I understood it to mean that her hatred of separate-mindedness had resonated 'wholesale' in me and revealed that I unconsciously identified with a murderous maternal attitude toward her emerging aliveness. I felt the impact of the hatred Mary had experienced when attempting to separate from her internal mother. This was a convergence between Mary's and my unmentalized internal worlds that invited self analysis on my part.

However, the hatred of emerging life reverberated between us in complex ways for a period of time. Mary reported a dream that her face was a hard ball that had receded into her head. This described her efforts to harden her protective second skin and to 'pull in', thus reversing the direction of movement in order to avoid 'facing' and 'seeing' our couple ship. This is consonant with Paul's (1981) description of the physical and psychic interweaving during the disturbing pressures which culminate in the face-first exposure to the external world and to the experience of intermittent physical contact with a feeding breast that replaced the constant prenatal contiguity.

By this time, however, the analytic process had taken hold and Mary dreamed that she was in an old small house where she had lived for a long time. She was told there was no job for her there. I said that she seemed to realize that her wish to lay so still next to me, in an effort to be very small, was not working and that left her feeling unemployed, ejected and in need of a new job. This interpretation prompted Mary to recall that when she first came home after her hospitalization, she was totally vulnerable and 'regressed to infancy.' However, she left within a couple of months and, thinking about that now, she realized that she must have recognized that if she had stayed she would have been 'trapped by mother and never gotten away.' She was sure that mother couldn't bear her helplessness and would have taken over, 'if I had become psychotic, hallucinating and in another reality, unable to function and not in touch with this reality mother would have done me in.' She had been very aware that she couldn't let herself go insane and thought she must have felt that way as a baby, too. In the session, she realized that she connected being insane with people coming and taking over her life. She remembered that, during that same period, she tried hard to get to another reality, 'another planet' as she put it.

These statements eloquently describe the mind-saving function of her encapsulation. It protected her by cutting the link to the object world in order to preserve her vulnerable unformed mind for possible future enlivening. Under these circumstances the pathological container becomes equated with health/life while connecting to the object world is equated with insanity/death. Mary's world turned upside down to save her then. Now the analysis threatened that equation and while becoming healthy she felt like she was going insane.

After ten years of treatment, Mary married her boyfriend of five years and experienced increased intimacy with, and commitment to her husband. This was followed by confusion in our sessions and a time of an intensely troubling, sickening countertransference reaction in me that finally surfaced into my understanding with the words 'this life has got to stop.' I believe that the previously mentioned experience of the hostile-to-life mother in Mary's internal world again reverberated between us. It was a convergence of similar levels in our unconscious and Mary's experience reverberated with aspect in my internal world that needed work on my part in order to become conscious. Lombardi (2008) refers to this as bodily counter-transference citing Williams' (2007) definition of it as 'phenomena that involve the analyst's deep unconscious and capacity to absorb and contain in his own body the patient's massive projections' (pp. 403–4).

The life-hating relationship again continued to reverberate between us, giving increased clarity as the following interchange illustrates. Later that year Mary and her husband took a long vacation overseas. We had arranged for twice weekly telephone contact during the break, but I soon received a call in which Mary told me that she needed an unscheduled session. When we connected, Mary was in panic, crying 'IT HAS TO DO WITH DISTANCE! I'm afraid I'm going to disappear, like I'll go foop! and just not be. I'm too far away from my safety.' She said she was holding her breath and gripping her gut into a ball so that she wouldn't dissipate and float away. She felt out of control saying, 'something inside me is playing its own game.' She heard a voice yelling 'GET ME OUT OF HERE' and she wanted to run away.

I told her that her body seemed to be trying to stop her experience of separateness by reacting to physical distance as if it were emotional distance and pointed out that we were having a connection right now. She seemed to calm and the rest of the vacation went well.

While receiving the force of her upset over the phone, I also noted that she was putting words to what she had expressed in action many years earlier when her boyfriend broke up with her and she ran away to another state. She was verbally, albeit forcefully, describing and communicating her pain to me and did not act it out, thus containing her wish to stop the present and go back to her old protective shell of muscular actions.

Upon returning from that vacation Mary had a dream that she was on a boat and waved 'hi' to somebody. Then she caught a halibut/stingray in the eye. She released it, hoping it would live and decided to find me. At that point she saw her husband and his brother bashing each other in the face. They were mad because she had said 'hi' to another person.

I said that perceiving nourishment (the fish) was experienced by Mary as a stinging attack on the eyes. She immediately recalled her teenage fear of tearing her eyes out while sleeping. She remembered lying in bed with her hands under her body so she wouldn't pull her eyes out. I said I thought the dream related to her old wish to punish her internal eyes for becoming aware of the nourishing experience of our relationship which she now hopes will survive. Keeping in mind the fact that her hatred of her mother often functioned as an attack that held her together, I added that this dream may also suggest that saying 'hi', acknowledging me, may feel like letting mother off the hook and that may be hard to face even though it was the direction she wanted to take.

I believe her saying 'hi' to another person meant she was facing the painful realization of her dependency on me and it resulted in slapping birth pains on her face in the process of feeling pushed out. Physical experiences involving the face during psychic movement are familiar to me (Paul, 1981) and in this instance they confirmed that Mary's direction of movement was toward increasing outside psychic space.

The next day Mary described a hallucination while in the session. She had a horrible picture of mother coming toward her and attacking her. She remembered that being with mother felt physically like they were magnets being attached to each other. She didn't know why the word 'magnetic' worked because there wasn't much attraction between them. She went on to recall something she had never told me. When she went to play school as a three-year-old, she had a hard time leaving mother and 'screamed and shouted and carried on' for a number of weeks. The woman who ran the school told her mother to leave because Mary had to work it out.

I silently recalled the early dream of the baby in the crib flying into me after our break. It seems that her current adhesive (magnetic) transference, together with this historical fact, confirmed an early pathological stickiness in Mary's relationship with her mother. It was a stickiness that could now be recalled in tandem with her adhesive transference.

At the time, I described my countertransference in my session notes. While I felt Mary was emerging, adhesion still reverberated between us and I experienced it as an unbreakable umbilicus that would never yield to allow for psychic space and psychic emergence. In retrospect, I understand that statement to be an expression of my postnatal vertex in which adhesion is seen as a wish to concretely stick in order to deny a premature separation in the past or prevent a present one. However, as I had come to realize, Mary's concrete adhesion could also be seen from a prenatal vertex to contain an acknowledgement of that premature separation and a simultaneous search for a relationship that reverberates on prenatal levels thus making emotional reconnection and conditional resumption of healthy development possible.

After the halibut/stingray dream and subsequent exchange, Mary had two dreams. In the first she was afraid while watching a wild, hungry and dangerous native tribe. In the second she was working for a foundation assisting a Native community to rediscover their traditional food after they forgot how to eat it. She needed to find a Native person and to figure out what their native foods were. The foundation was being very difficult and she needed to call me at my extra private office number.

I said I thought that she wanted to connect with me on a very early forgotten level but that she may be afraid that there will be a repetition of her past experience with her mother so she wants to appeal to an extra private, personal aspect of me. I silently wondered if the aboriginal food in question was her forgotten, prenatal contiguous experience or the postnatal intermittent maternal breast that she had not allowed herself to see. However, as time passed I came to understand that the early (native) nourishment of her analysis was no longer felt to be an unbearably humiliating assault on the survival of her formerly encapsulated prenatal vulnerability.

The adhesion now seemed to be resolving and in its place emerged issues around appetite. I will describe how Mary's continued analysis reveals the connection between adhesion and appetite and shows the usefulness of the binocular attitude to simultaneous presence of pre- and postnatal states.

In reaction to the emotional pain of separation that she experienced as pain to her eyes in the halibut/stingray dream, Mary began to use her voice in an effort to deal with and re-align her understanding of a world where there are two different realities, the internal and the external. An example of this occurred when returning after a one-week break (my vacation), Mary said that she was sad when I was gone and she wanted to say something about that. She stated that if it were a song it would be a very low note and she would have to go down really low where it is 'emotionally gravelly and rasp along there.' She thought she wanted to experience the physical body vibration as she sang. I said she was describing something that resonates between us very deeply and has to do with coming together after the break. She agreed emphatically and said it was like how elephants communicate – below human hearing.

I believe this exchange puts words to a psychic reconnecting inside Mary. Using sound, she was joining the body memory of prenatal touch/sound vibrations with the postnatal experience of a containing relationship where the singing communicated both the concrete and symbolic repair of a broken connection, the symptom of which had been the encapsulation and, when that failed, the adhesion. Expressing her experience in a sad song about separation that vibrated her physically showed her re-joining a previously broken prenatal link and making space for an intermittent postnatal relationship with me while at the same time holding onto an internal experience of contiguity.

The unconscious meaning of this reconnection was revealed in a romantic dream about being unfaithful. She and a friend were kissing quickly and secretly but it felt like a delicious secret between the two of them and it was against the rules 'in many ways.' I suggested that she was grappling with an accusing voice from an old part of her that feels left out when she accepts the nourishing aspects of our relationship, so it accuses her of being unfaithful – breaking the old rules. She recalled that when she went to college and had her breakdown, there seemed to be no boundaries and that's how she felt now. In her house there were boundaries everywhere. I believe that Mary here confirmed my interpretation that the old contiguous object connection became an envious accusing persecutor. In that way feeding by mouth was experienced as betrayal of her prenatal contiguous connection. She was expressing her reluctance to expand her boundaries to include the postnatal intermittency.

Further transformation of adhesion into psychic space was symbolized in a dream where Mary was swimming in the midst of a pod of orcas. She could feel their bodies against her on either side and air bubbles between their skins were bubbling up against her. She feared they were killer whales and would eat her but then thought that the air bubbles were their echolocation. I believe that this dream illustrated how adhesion yielded to allow space for echolocation (Mary's creative description of projective identification in a containing relationship) and stirred up fear of being attacked by ravenous appetite from inside and, in its projected form, murderous hunger from outside. She could now endure the experience of separate bodies within whose skin there was internal space and capacity to reverberate together in a nourishing exchange.

After additional work there was confirmation of Mary's unconscious fantasy about the meaning of postnatal connecting that explained her inability to separate at important levels of development during her life and was at the core of her need to stop everything. The last event in the transformational continuum of adhesion in Mary's analysis was a dream of her dogs running around in an immense amount of poop. She noticed that the poop had unusual properties and realized it was 'carnivore poop.' While analyzing the dream, it emerged that Mary's unconscious fantasy of her appetite was of oral destruction, and, if she engaged in a nourishing connection with me, I would be eaten and killed and there would be evidence of this in our exchange. From this point Mary's previously encapsulated, healthy appetite for life could be seen to exhort a powerful pull toward facing the reality of her object world and dealing with her need to take in and digest as well as to evacuate what was not needed or indigestible.

She went through a period of deep sadness and found meaning in literary descriptions of people who had suffered great losses, saying they 'were the coal that was turned into a diamond.' She read about a woman who ended up on an aboriginal walkabout that she hadn't planned and said that ever since her mental breakdown, she had been on a mental walkabout. She had had no choice. Her next thought was that there would be a time when she would finish analysis but she didn't want to listen to that thought yet.

This, for the most part, ends the transformational continuum of adhesion in Mary's analysis. Much work still remained but that belongs under other headings.

Discussion

In order to illustrate how using a binocular attitude can shed light on the dynamics of adhesion in this fourteen-year analysis, I approached the large amount of clinical material using the concept of transformational continua which I explained to be transformational themes that emerge when viewing clinical material gathered over a long period of time.

Other aspects of my approach included defining prenatal phenomena as revealing underlying unconscious fantasies of existing in a timeless intrauterine state by using postnatal mental and physical capacities as concrete prenatal equivalents for the purpose of avoiding pain and psychic change, also to achieve a timeless unconsciousness about postnatal reality of object relationships.

Regarding adhesion, I relied on accepted aspects of the diverse literature, retaining the broadest meaning of adhesion as contiguity, which refers to the surface touching as described by Ogden (1988). I also outlined psychic development in terms of Bick's concept of psychic skin with particular emphasis on second skin formations referred to as encapsulations or pathological containers. This view suggests a possible continuum of prenatal contiguity to postnatal appetite where being-in-touch transformed from concrete surfaces touching to being in emotional touch with internal and external reality.

The above frame allowed me to demonstrate how Mary's initial state of encapsulation over some years of analysis evolved to show a connection between adhesion and appetite.

In presenting clinical material from the analysis of Mary, I showed that her encapsulation had three facets. The first was her adhesive speech, which served as a barrier to contact. The second was her muscular action when thinking was called for. The third was Mary's concrete use of her senses, equating in-sight with her actual vision and equating food for thought with concrete matter which led her to close her hearing for fear of exploding.

The material showed that the analytic work slowly eroded and threatened the integrity of Mary's encapsulation, giving rise to renewed unconscious efforts to hold it together. To that end she hallucinated to 'make the inside and outside the same' and dreamed of her face being a hard, pulled-in ball showing a muscular effort to change direction. She had verbal outbursts to rid herself of unwelcome experiences.

When these unconscious efforts failed to reinforce the walls of her encapsulations, there were increasing signs of disintegration and she said that without it her 'intestines hang out.' Her dreams of attacking the breast (cut up strawberries and bugged grapes) showed her increasingly clear view of a nurturing object. Her statement that there was a lot of killing going on can be seen to refer to both internal and external destruction.

At the height of this turmoil, with the increasing awareness of dependency, a transformation into depressive anxieties would have been expected. Instead the adhesion appeared evidenced by statements that she just wanted to be with me without my knowledge and by my simultaneous physical sense of her being stuck to me. I interpreted this from a prenatal vertex as a wish for a seamless relationship approximating an intrauterine contiguity for fear of realizing our separateness and in doing so recalling her past overwhelming pain as well as a fear that it would mean the concrete repetition of her past.

As a result some psychic movement could be observed and her dream that she no longer had a job in the old small house showed a sense of being pushed out of her old pathological container. As a consequence, turmoil erupted as Mary experienced convergence of her senses of sight and hearing (Meltzer, 1975; Paul and Carson, 1980). This can be seen as a process of her developing binocular capacity of her own.

In terms of seeing and being seen, she felt the pain of seeing her dependency on a maternal object for her nourishment (the dream of a stingray hooked in the eye). This was followed by fear of the intensity of her hunger (aboriginal voraciousness) which transformed into curiosity and a wish to investigate and find this nourishment (the dream of working for the difficult foundation). In terms of being in touch Mary's song connected physical internal reverberations with emotional resonance between us.

With these transformations Mary's adhesive fantasies of concrete physical connection (no distance) opened into conflicts related to the other two senses involved; vision and audition, both involving distance. Further transformations showed how her resistance to change became an accusation that using her mouth to find emotional pleasure was being unfaithful to the old umbilical way of being attached (the dream of kissing). It also showed the reason for her resistance to be a fantasy that taking nourishment destroys the object (association to carnivore poop).

These realizations ushered in the depressive period where she felt herself transform from coal to a diamond. I believe that the dream of the echolocation bubbles between skins (the orca dream) was Mary's realization of deep emotional reverberations between us. It seems to illustrate the experience of catastrophic change in the transformation between pre- and postnatal states where the currency of exchange is prenatal visceral reverberations between analyst and patient that accumulate over time to be digested by the analyst's alpha function. With Mary, adhesion was embedded in the analytic sequence and I believe that adopting a binocular attitude during the analysis facilitated its resolution. Viewing the transformational continuum of adhesion in Mary's analysis as an escape from the annihilation of ruptured boundaries, the following transformational links are revealed:

adhesion ↔ rupturing/engulfment ↔ recovered appetite.

Summary

The clinical sequence presented in order to illustrate the binocular view of adhesion supports my proposal of a prenatal extension of Ogden's postnatal concept of contiguity that ranges from prenatal contiguity to postnatal molding. From a postnatal vertex adhesion can be seen as a maneuver to resist a containing relationship while not succumbing either to the agonies of separateness or to a pathological container. It is viewed as a wish to deny a premature separation in the past or prevent a present one. From a prenatal vertex adhesion can be viewed as evidence of the patient's unconscious search for a prenatal containing relationship that reverberates on prenatal levels thus making emotional reconnection and conditional resumption of healthy development possible.

Note

1 This paper is a part of a larger work (2007, unpublished), investigating prenatal relationships in terms of a number of parameters, adhesion being one.

References

Bick, E. (1968). The Experience of the Skin in Early Object-Relations. *International Journal of Psychoanalysis*, 49: 484–86.

Bion, W. R. (1962). *Learning from experience*. London: Karnac Books.

—— (1963). *Elements of Psycho-Analysis*. London: Karnac Books.

—— (1970). *Attention and interpretation*. London: Karnac Books.

Freud, S. (1926). Inhibitions, symptoms and anxiety. *SE 20* London: Hogarth Press.

Grotstein, J. (1980). A proposed revision of the psychoanalytic concept of primitive mental states – Part I. Introduction to a newer psychoanalytic metapsychology. *Contemporary Psychoanalysis*, 16: 479–546.

—— (1990). Nothingness, meaninglessness, chaos, and the 'black hole' II – The black hole. *Contemporary Psychoanalysis*, 26: 377–407.

Klein, M. (1952). Notes on some schizoid mechanisms. In M. Klein, P. Heimann, S. Isaac and J. Riviere (eds.) *Developments of Psycho-Analysis* (1952). London: Hogarth Press, pp. 292–320.

Lombardi, R. (2008). The body in the analytic session: Focusing on the mind-body link. *International Journal of Psychoanalysis*, 89: 89–110.

Maiello, S. (1995). The sound-object: a hypothesis about prenatal auditory experience and memory. *Journal of Child Psychotherapy*, 21: 23–41.

Mancia, M. (1981). On the beginning of mental life in the foetus. *International Journal of Psychoanalysis*, 62: 351–57.

Meltzer, D. (1975). Adhesive Identification. *Contemporary Psychoanalysis*, 11: 289–310.

—— (1992). *The Claustrum: An Investigation of Claustrophobic Phenomena*. Perthshire: Clunie Press.

Mitrani, J. (1992). On the survival function of autistic manoeuvres in adult patients. *International Journal of Psychoanalysis*, 73: 549–59.

—— (1994). On adhesive pseudo-object relations – Part I: Theory. *Contemporary Psychoanalysis*, 30: 348–66.

—— (1995). On adhesive pseudo-object relations – Part II: Illustration. *Contemporary Psychoanalysis*, 31: 140.
—— (1995a). Toward an understanding of unmentalized experience. *Psychoanalytic Quarterly*, 64: 68–112.
Ogden, T. H. (1988). On the dialectical structure of experience – some clinical and theoretical implications. *Contemporary Psychoanalysis*, 24: 17–45.
—— (1989). On the concept of an autistic-contiguous position. *International Journal of Psychoanalysis*, 70: 127–40.
Paul, M. I. (1981). A mental atlas of the process of psychological birth. In: J. Grotstein (ed.) (1981) *Do I Dare Disturb the Universe? A Memorial to W. R. Bion*. London: Maresfield Library, pp. 551–70.
—— (1997). On the imitation of human speech. *Journal of Melanie Klein and Object Relations*, 15(1): 51–76.
—— and Carson, I. M. (1980). A contribution to the study of dimension. *International Review of Psychoanalysis*, 7: 101–12.
Steiner, J. (1993). *Psychic Retreats*. London: Routledge.
Tustin, F. (1986). *Autistic Barriers in Neurotic Patients*. London: Karnac Books.
—— (1988). Psychotherapy with Children who Cannot Play. *International Review of Psychoanalysis*, 15: 93–106.
Williams, P. (2007). The body and the mind (including of the analyst) in treatment of a psychotic state: Some reflections. Commentary on paper by Ricardo Lombardi. *Psychoanalytic Dialogues*, 17: 401–9.

Chapter 6

The trauma of conception[1]

Cellular memory

Joanna Wilheim

> Masters of subversion, human sperm cells seek to penetrate an ovum. Foreigners in a hostile body, they employ several strategies to survive their mission, including a fluid coating that may hide their antigens. If conception occurs, the egg has an even harder job, since it is marked as foreign and targeted for destruction throughout its nine months of development. The placenta allows the passage of vital oxygen and nutrients, but not blood, which is laden with immune cells. Understanding how sperm and fetus elude attack may help scientists develop new contraceptives and treat infertility.
>
> (Peter Jaret, 1986)

> We now have increasingly convincing evidence that there is mental receptivity noted in the first month of embryonic development . . . Just as there are vestiges of primitive embryological structures such as notochordomas and branchial clefts in the adult human being which express themselves in adult life as pathological forms, there can also be psychical states which are remnants or vestiges of the foetal state of mind or elements of the maternal environment laid down as engrams or mnemic residues which have varying degrees of expressivity . . . These stages of mental development can dominate the mind of an adult, and these memories and possible "interpretations" arrived at by the foetal mind can find expression.
>
> (Michael Paul, 1992)

I have been dealing with the issue of the existence of early traumatic imprints in the human mind since 1983. It was brought home to me through an analytical experience which I shall briefly summarize.

The patient, in her early thirties, had sought analysis because she felt unable to conceive a child. She already had a child but was unable to have another one. Whenever she conceived, she would lose the concept through a miscarriage. She also spoke about difficulties in maintaining interpersonal links. She observed having disruptive movements which led her to sudden ruptures with people and group work situations. She used to behave in a way that would end up in a disaster.

After some time, during our analytical work, I realized that in our relationship she was repeating the same movements which she had described. They were threatening our link and the continuation of our work. Every time she progressed or had a gain – either in her private or professional life or in analysis – this was followed by a destructive attack. In the transference, her mind would do the same movements that her soma did. She would attack to abort or to avoid any mental conception. This drove me to conclude that both her soma and her mind repeated a pattern imprinted on her unconscious.

In the course of the many years through which this analysis spanned, we came to understand that she was the survivor of a twin conception, that she had struggled with her twin for space and nutrients and that the death of the twin had left her with a strong persecutory guilt. We also came to understand that her disruptive and destructive pattern of behavior was the acting out of the abortive imprints she carried at the core of her own self. What prevented her from being able to benefit from her gains in life and analysis were both the expression of persecutory guilt feelings as well as abortive imprints. This also prevented her from keeping her concepts, making her repeat the abortive movements she had once witnessed and felt threatened by.

From this analytical experience came a first paper which I named "The Anatomy of a Murderous Mind" (1983). I shall briefly summarize some of its main theoretical conclusions:

- In the utmost depths of our minds lies a basic matrix which contains the imprints – recorded by means of a *cellular memory* – of the whole process of our biological experience, from preconception to birth: starting from the formation of each of our two basic germinative cells – spermatozoid and ovum – up to the moment of birth.
- From this basic matrix derives the raw material of the unconscious phantasies which will get triggered whenever a specific circumstance bumps against one of these basic registers. At that very moment, what is contained in this "corpuscle" of memory in the *evoked* basic matrix will surface and settle in the mental space with all the affective–emotional coloring which belongs to that first original experience.[2] This will be so for the basic emotions of anxiety, anguish, envy, jealousy and the feelings of rejection, exclusion, abandonment, helplessness, distress and deprivation; as well as for adoption and acceptance – just to mention a few. We can therefore consider that all these emotions are phantasies – emotional memories, evocations, transferences.
- Thus phantasies are memories. They correspond to psychic representations of the imprints of early sense impressions (beta elements) which

> are recorded, tainted by the feeling of what – at that given moment – was sensed to be happening. The fact registered by the cellular memory occurred at a moment when the mind still had no conditions to "know" about it; its storage may have undergone distortions, superpositions or deformations. But the basic coloring is maintained.

Going further down to some more details on the constitution of the basic matrix, I wish to stress that its earliest imprints refer to the experience of the two germinative cells in the following sense: (a) what each of them underwent since its respective origin up to the moment of its mating; (b) the "relationship" established between the two cells before, during and after the heterosexual encounter; and (c) the vicissitudes and torments underwent by what now stands for the integrated couple – the concept – submitted to a violent struggle for life just after its first "birth," due to the destructive attacks from its first environment, giving rise to "feelings" of panic, and threat of being destroyed, aborted.

In fact, physiological destructive substances produced by the mother's body are activated in order to destroy and eliminate this new life that has just been created and represents a foreign body. The mother's immune system seeks to reject, destroy and expel it: 75 per cent of the fertilized eggs are destroyed in the fallopian tube.

Thus the moment of mating, fusion and fulfillment may be experienced as joy for life being created but it may also be felt – mostly on the spermatozoid's cellular memory side – as a moment of torture and destruction, in which it loses its previous original identity: it loses its tail, its head swells to four times its original size and opens up to deliver its genetic load to the ovum. The spermatozoid is forever undone: it disappears as such, undergoes a transformation, but loses its former identity.

Depending on what sort of imprints prevail, this moment may stand for a very basic human trauma: the trauma of conception. If this is the case, the prevailing imprint will contain the message that the coming together of the two cells has the meaning of something that should never have been, a dangerous experience to be forever avoided; heterosexual mating becomes something dangerous, castrating, annihilating, deadly.

In order to help understand how I was led to the visualization of what I just presented, I shall briefly introduce the path I followed. In the early Seventies Bion's ideas were starting to be known in Brazil. From 1973 onward, he visited Brazil once a year, for lectures and seminars, until 1978. I had the opportunity to get acquainted with Bion's ideas through supervisions, clinical seminars and lectures. These contacts with Bion changed my whole approach to the understanding of the psychoanalytical experience. I started considering the session as an encounter of two minds, following the biological model of conception, whose outcome was meant to be the discovery of the unknown.

Certain vicissitudes in the establishment of the analytic link started calling for my attention. I would observe situations which both roused my curiosity and astonished me. As I would make my mind available to the analysand's mind in order to contain it and help him process whatever required to be processed, I noticed that he would often act destructively in relation to this space and function placed at his disposal: he would either turn against any positive gains resulting from our analytic work and attack them destructively; or he would act treacherously, producing false material, leading me to interpret contents that were uninterpretable; or he would withdraw behind an impenetrable "protective shield."

The available psychoanalytical theories were of little help to really understand and handle such situations in order to be able to achieve psychic change. My supervisors offered me worn out Kleinian or Bionian theoretical notions referring to greed, envy or an urge to destroy. Such interpretations would not produce any real effect or mental change. I realized their ineffectiveness to undo the psychopathological patterns. They were merely descriptive. I felt an urge to reach beyond the surface. I wanted to understand what produced such destructive mental movements. I wanted to understand the origin of envy, the psychotic part of the mind, the attacks on linking, the perverse part of the personality. I wondered why a mind would avoid mating with another mind. What sort of pain was feared and avoided? Why would a mind suddenly retreat and hide beneath a sort of protective shield?

I had at my disposal years of listening to Bion's contributions communicated through metaphors. It was a matter of deciphering them. And I tried to do so.

One particular metaphor – maybe more than any other – became an especially powerful seed to be developed. In a Clinical Seminar (1978) in São Paulo, Bion stated:

> According to our theory . . . it would be useful on the way to finding her-self, to find this self which is fulfilled. And when I say the full-filled person I'm really meaning that a man or a woman can't be fulfilled until they have found their mate. Then potentially one can become fulfilled. If these two personalities could come together in the kind of way that their bodies can come together . . . you can bring together a penis and a vagina, a mouth and a breast . . . if only the same could be done mentally, then the person could become fulfilled. Now, on the way to that position it is possible that analysis might help. But the relationship in analysis is different, because it is not the fulfilled position. Therefore, the relationship between the analyst and the analysand is not permanent, not satisfactory, nor adequate. The relationship between them could be called a "transference", "transient" is not permanent . . . it's like a lodging house that you find on your way to

> somewhere or other. On the way! . . . So analysis could in a sense be on the way to the real thing . . . And yet, you know, it is curious, there is a sort of awareness that there is such a thing as a real thing which would correspond to what we call "fatherhood", or "motherhood", or "parenthood". We may not know what it is, we may not have found it, and it is quite possible that we never shall, nevertheless we can know that it is somehow there. And we can have this kind of aspiration towards it . . . All these discussions are really simply transient affairs. They are talks, which can be a stage in the journey towards a real communion between two people.

Among the many memorable things Bion used to say was that *the biological unit is a couple. It takes two human beings to make one* (1978). And he proposed that the meaning contained in the word "at-one-ment" which among other things means "to become one with one's own self," designates a form of "*bringing together not only body and mind, the prenatal and the postnatal personalities, but proceed also to the marriage of the spermatozoid and ovum which gave origin to that particular individual*" (quoted in Mello, 1980, pp. 77–82).

Long years of reflection, pondering on the analytic experience and the vicissitudes referred to, led me to conjecture about the existence in the mind of mnemic traces of traumatic prenatal experiences, from preconception to birth, which would have been imprinted on the soma – by means of a cellular memory – and remained stored there. The difficulties observed, particularly regarding the fertile mating of the two minds, made me consider the possible occurrence of a trauma experienced at the moment of the biological conception – first heterosexual mating – imprinted on the basic unconscious matrix and reactivated by the experience of the now mental mating of the analytic encounter. The visualization of this pattern – the traumatic imprint of conception's experience – a realization made possible by observing what happened to the analysand's mind when brought into contact with the analyst's mind, or when he conceived something mentally, allowed me to consider the existence in the mind of an inscription of a destructive physiological discharge fallen onto the product of conception – the recently conceived concept – which had been recognized as a foreign body, and attacked in order to be destroyed by the mother's immune system.

Such an experience would result in the presence of a catastrophic feeling that would follow any new situation whose content was linked with the meaning of conception, birth, growth or development. The presence of such catastrophic feeling, which may be experienced when biological conception occurs, would lead the mind to try to prevent – defensively – the establishment of mental links, thus attempting to avoid the repetition of the pain felt during the original traumatic experience. I understood that in some of the "here-and-now" moments of the analytic encounter, to me would be assigned the role of the patient's once endangered, suffering or victimized self: either as spermatozoid, concept, embryo or fetus; at other times, I represented the threatening agent – a foe.

The vicissitudes observed in the establishment and the maintenance of the analytic link – usually referred to as "attacks on linking," "negative therapeutic reactions," "patients difficult to reach" – were being visualized as proceeding from these earliest, cellular levels. The impediments that arise to the realization of the analytic encounter could be understood as difficulties reproducing a traumatic occurrence experienced at the time of conception.

I realized that the psychoanalytical setting and encounter favor the emergence of certain behavior patterns – that once were only biological and now are mental – since they were recorded in deep protomental furrows. They emerge in the "here and now" of the transferential scene, because they refer to imprints of traumatic (therefore not worked through) experiences, and also because they were recorded in a preverbal period. Such "points of trauma" originated long before the time and place to which the current theories would attribute their origin, hinderering mental development and growth.

I then put forward the hypothesis that the destructive performance in which my patient's mind would occasionally engage during the analytic experience was a communication by means of an acted-out language, employed to convey some traumatic experience to which he had been submitted at a very early stage of his existence, imprinted merely on his sensorial level (beta element). This results in the patient being unable to communicate such situations through verbal free association, as classical psychoanalysis would consider proper – because *his* mind does not "know" about them. Because it represents a knowledge "*unknown*" to the mind, the self feels an urge to have it revealed in order to be able to transform in into thoughts and thus deal with it mentally, working it through. Otherwise it will go on reappearing, repeating compulsively its auto or hetero destructiveness. The only language he can employ to convey such early experiences is acting them out in the transference.

Thus the "acting out" could be understood as a sort of "Rosetta Stone" of the very early imprints, and represent – once deciphered – a precious source of information, thereby becoming an important tool for grasping the meaning of communications about very early life-threatening experiences which happened somewhere on the way from preconception to birth.

Thus, through this new way of looking at the analysand–analyst interaction in the analytical process, a new light could be shed on the meaning of negative therapeutic reactions in psychoanalysis. The disruptive mental movements and attacks on analysis, on the analytical link, on its products or achievements, could be looked upon as re-editions of very early prenatal traumatic experiences sensorially imprinted on the concept, embryo or fetus when it felt the threat of being annihilated, aborted or destroyed.

Quoting Bion (1978): "You can't forget something which you don't remember. So, first of all, you have to remember it and then you can forget it. Un-forget what is forgotten."

Clinical illustration

I shall now present some clinical material from the analysis of P., with which I wish to illustrate how these theoretical concepts take shape in the process of an analysis. I will focus on four main mental features of P. and link them to a hypothetical prenatal source based on cellular memory imprints: (a) his difficulty to establish mental links in the "here and now" of the analytic encounter – which I associate to the trauma of conception; (b) his constant negative therapeutic reactions – which I link with the attacks of mother's physiology as soon as he was conceived, causing him a dread of being aborted; (c) his constitutional envy – based on the negative and hostile relationship of his first heterosexual cellular couple, also responsible for (d) his incapacity to bear situations which stir in him feelings of being taken advantage of or exploited while somebody else benefits at his expense.

When he first came to see me, P., a 42-year-old specialized engineer, had been fired from his job a few months before. He was looking for analysis because he realized he was sabotaging himself in life in general and, particularly, in his work. His performance was inefficient; he would putter about and waste time with trifling matters, putting off any important task until there was no time left to get it done.

At first, his reports were very boring, told in a metallic and very dull tone. He never called either his work colleagues or the companies he had worked for by name; he always used the term "company" when referring to his work – a word he pronounced in a manner that irked me profoundly. I could not follow his "nameless" accounts; it was always "the guy" or "the company where I worked." Nothing was named or had any particular feature.

Right from the first sessions, I noticed that P. did not establish an analytic link, nor did he achieve an analytic mating with me. He neither associated nor "dreamt," and did not offer the conditions to establish an oneiric atmosphere in the session. He turned to me to provide him with solutions to "psychological" problems or questions – ready-made packages he would bring from home, situations he claimed were beyond his understanding, for which he wanted me to give him explanations or solutions. He would ask standard questions and narrate dreams without producing any associations, giving me no clues which would enable me to interpret. At other times, he would behave as though he was not very smart – a kind of "dimwit" – and incompetent. I found myself concerned about how to pierce the layer of impermeability in which he wrapped himself and which prevented him from making any mind-to-mind contact with me or any kind of contact with his own self.

I shall start by focusing on the particular session in which I was first drawn to intervene with the frame related to cellular memory (spermatozoid/egg and concept) to deal with P.'s difficulties in establishing inter and intrapsychic links as well as to address his attacks on linking. After a couple of months' work, there had been a sudden positive and fugacious change – something in the previous day's session had made him break his inertia. He told a dream much more full of life. However, the following day, the old still atmosphere was back again.

On facing this negative therapeutic reaction, it occured to me that it was the re-edition of a "pattern": I fell back on the pattern of the attacks of mother's physiology on the newly conceived concept. I roughly described the process of human fertilization and what happens at the very beginning of its existence: the egg with the same DNA as the mother's; the spermatozoid with the same DNA as the father's, but different from the mother's; the one that enters has its tail cut off; it is undone and will never again be what it had once been. The self is born. Its DNA is different from the rest of the mother's body, which at once stirs an attack meant to destroy it. All this remains imprinted. I proceeded,

> Therefore, when a new birth happens inside of you, when a movement of life is stirred, immediately an anti-life mechanism is activated. So, there are two different moments: a first one which involves life-creation, and a second one in which is stirred a movement of destruction of this very life which has just been created.

This was followed by a sequence of sterile sessions, revealing a state of mind which refuses to mate, doesn't want to let itself be fertilized and which is not "married" to its own self. It is not an "integrated (internal) couple" who speaks; he doesn't produce a "pregnant," wise and competent speech. It is merely repetitive, empty, recitative; it is not the product of the place of creation.

I felt caught in a trap: I saw he was depressed because he was unable to act. I remembered he had been referred to a psychiatrist who prescribed an anti-depressant which he never took because he wanted to paint the living room wall first and was afraid the medication would make him feel dizzy. But he never got to paint the wall and continued to be depressed because he didn't do what he thought he ought to. He had created a full vicious circle, a "no-way-out" situation. Total immobilism.

After one particular session, I realized that I had felt a very strong impulse to send him away, to get rid of him, due to the vicious circle leading to a deadlock and the no-way-out situation. At the next day's session I decided to transform this counter-transferential feeling into an interpretation, when something similar happened again:

> There must be a very strong inscription inside of you referring to having been submitted to a great threat of being aborted. So here, with me, you act as to make me send you away, abort you. Perhaps this is the reason why, in your work, you act in a way to provoke situations to be sent away. This would be a way of acting out something that once almost happened to you . . .

After I finished my intervention, with him listening very carefully, he said: "What you just said makes a lot of sense. . . . All my mother's pregnancies were high-risk pregnancies."

I will now focus on the circumstances that led me to the instant in which I visualized a second pattern. I will describe how – during a session – I suddenly came up against something that led me to conjecture about the existence of a configuration to which I shall refer as "the trauma of conception." The introduction of this variable produced a significant change in the functioning of P.'s mind, and impacted his performance during that particular session.

Today again he had nothing to say, nothing would be of help, he was depressed, he didn't know why. I interpret: "You're telling me you're sterile." He denies this – because he cannot let the seed fructify. I intervene . . .

I follow closely each of his movements, showing him how he sterilizes everything: whichever path he takes leads to a "no place"; all of his different movements lead to a void; all of the different paths attempted by him end up against a blank wall.

I describe this and point it out to him. I use the model of a sterile couple who because of their sterility will bring to the end of the line their hereditary genetic transmission. He produces some associations which contain this end-of-the-line notion. Then suddenly something comes to my mind and I tell him: "Your biological conception must have been registered as such a painful and traumatic experience that now you avoid any situation that might take you back to it."

Once again I describe what happens to the spermatozoid. It is a transformation which results in a new being, but it ceases to exist in its original identity. He responds to this, recalling that as a boy he wanted things to remain as they were, unchanged. He was once given a soccer ball for his birthday, but instead of going out with it to play with his friends, he left it wrapped up in plastic under his bed. He had a 500 cruzeiros bill that he had put away carefully so that it would never be used, and when his father took it to buy some Coke, P. ran desperately after him begging him to leave the bill untouched.

With this association, P. was correcting my understanding: he clarified that not only the spermatozoid – as suggested by me – but also the ovum, had suffered a trauma. It was an ovum which did not want to be penetrated so that its DNA would not be changed and become subject to attacks from the mother's physiology. The 500 cruzeiros bill he didn't want to be changed had bearing with the spermatozoid's transformation process: it "invests" its identity – its genes – and from this investment results a completely different product. It occurred to me that perhaps this was why he could never accept any interpretation of mine, nor any evidence of progress, because that would promptly trigger the experience of terror.

When I mentioned the ball wrapped up in plastic as standing for the ovum *that wants to remain protected so as not to be penetrated* – he added: "*Just like a condom that prevents fertilization*" – thus preventing any change, any transformation, in the *status quo*.

When P. sterilizes the meaning of my interpretations (the fertile seeds) before they reach him – when he denies my interventions or when he "fires a missile" that blows away anything I am about to say – it is in order to stop stirring up and reliving the experience of the spermatozoid being annihilated. He puts on one side the ovum wrapped up in plastic so that it might not be fertilized, separated and far away from the spermatozoid, in order to prevent the encounter, the mating and the undoing.

Some sessions later . . .

P: After yesterday's session, I went swimming . . . and thought of several things there'd been no time to mention . . . (he says something that confirms the things I had shown him about not wanting to mate) when I was 17, I talked to my father about undergoing a vasectomy. Later when I would get married, I could reverse it so as to be able to have children . . .

A: You're saying that you remembered something which confirmed what I have told you . . .
He immediately retracts:

P: No, it doesn't confirm it, but . . .

A: I point out to him the movement he made to promptly take back what he had just said: I tell him that *when he realized that he was mating here with me, he felt anguish stirred by his feeling imprisoned inside of me.*
In response to this, he produces another association in which he again corrects my understanding, calling attention to the other part of the couple:

P: When he and F (his current partner) were young, they went to a friend's wedding. Somebody asked whether they were also going to get married, and he replied: "Good Lord, no! . . . the very idea of having to walk down this aisle . . . attacked by 80 serpents . . ."

A: His terror of mating with me comes both from the spermatozoid, whose register was one of annihilation, and from the ovum, which on entering the tube – aisle – saw itself surrounded by spermatozoa – the serpents – that promptly attacked it, *stirring up its terror*.[3]

A few weeks later, in a session during which I perceive his maneuvers to carefully promote disencounter and disconversation, I introduce a hypothesis for his need to promote them:

> I go into detail about what I understand as being the source of what was happening: I speak about the first heterosexual couple, the first mating that must have been registered by him as something very traumatic, very anguishing, which he now wants to avoid at all costs. I again mention the trauma felt by the spermatozoid, which I describe in small details, ending with: it contributes to the "fattening" of the ovum, which benefits from and develops at the spermatozoid's expense. And also the ovum will be attacked by the mother's physiology as it has never been attacked before. This is why it is "conservative" and does not want to be penetrated, so as not to be "changed." It does not want to be transformed because this causes it a lot of pain. His ovum resists, it remains wrapped in plastic "like a condom that prevents fertilization." Because from the moment the DNAs merged, he – the concept – was no longer a cell of the mother's body and became a target of the attacks. This is the trauma on the ovum's side. The spermatozoid's trauma consists in the loss of its original identity. I point out how he behaves in order to prevent our encounter, the maneuvers he employs smartly to prevent it. Also how he swiftly and competently aborts the seeds or what has just been conceived. He undoes it, turns it into something useless. It is an attempt to try to prevent something that happened in the past, which he wants to stop from happening again. I point out how he tries to separate the ovum from the spermatozoid, keeping them far apart, one from the other.

He is to be interviewed for a possible job. He "dilly dallies" so as to arrive late for the interview, but it works out anyway. During his account, I feel very sleepy. I use this to say:

A: You feel ambivalent towards me today. You are reluctant to penetrate me and give me your fertile seeds . . . the spermatozoid delivers its cargo, and immediately afterwards is undone, destroyed, while the ovum benefits from it, grows and fattens.

P: When you mentioned the spermatozoid, it occurred to me that I make an effort, run ahead, I am triumphant and it is you who gain! It's like at my job, I felt I was really putting a lot of effort into my work, working very hard to get a miserable salary at the end of the month, while all the profit went to the company . . .

He starts next day's session saying that on his way he felt like not coming, he had nothing to say.

A: It occurs to me that you cannot stand that I would benefit at your expense . . .
He interrupts me:
P: You shine!
Silence. I intervene. The silence continues. I return to the first couple:
A: The imprint of your first original experience is very deep: when the spermatozoid handed over its entire genetic load to the ovum and was undone, it disappeared, while the ovum benefitted, took advantage, grew and enriched.

I show him how something imprinted at the very beginning of his cellular existence was governing his life, determining his behavior; his performances were ruled by this inscription. I remind him how he reported to me his behavior at work: he wasted time with unimportant matters, until there was no time to do the principal task; and this was how he sabotaged the company.

P: You mentioned something that I had never considered quite this way. I always thought I was sabotaging *myself*, and now you are pointing out that I was sabotaging the company. I had never seen it from this angle.
A: Here also you thought you were sabotaging yourself when you were not working with me. Today you realized that you do not work in order to sabotage *me*. To prevent *me from shining*.

P. starts to work at a new job, after having remained a whole year unemployed. He starts boycotting himself right from Day One. I interpret that his collaboration to the company would result in an increase of its annual profit – that was why he had been engaged. But this was a situation he couldn't bear: his was a low salary, and with his work he would be contributing to increase his boss' profits fourfold (this had been the figure he had mentioned the day before). I describe to him the spermatozoid–ovum/exploited–exploiter relationship.

He is warned at work that if he doesn't improve, he will be fired. And this is what happened.

A year later

After having remained another whole year unemployed, an extraordinary chance is presented to P. Through an old friend he is appointed for a job in a big multinational company with very favorable financial conditions and many fringe benefits. The process of his being contracted extends over several months. The friend who was the go-between wishes to be included as P.'s partner if the contract works out.

After a while, I notice the appearance of P.'s sabotaging movements with which he once again threatens the possibility of getting the job. What emerges is that he cannot stand the idea that the friend – who brought him this opportunity – might also benefit once he benefits. He overtly expresses that he will not favor his friend. Envy and ingratitude are the theme of several sessions.

It becomes evident that P. would rather destroy this unique opportunity than favor someone else. I remind him of his destructive movements at his last job, where his task was to increase by fourfold the company's benefits while he earned a low salary. I also focus on his sabotaging analysis in order to prevent me from having success in my work with him. Once again he is confronted with the reality that he is capable of causing harm to himself – even of destroying himself – just to prevent anybody else from deriving a benefit.

I came to understand that there was a twofold source of the carving of his auto-destructive pattern: Firstly, his mother's immunological and physiological attacks on him as a concept, embryo and fetus, were repeated as a pattern imprinted by his first original experience. His attacks against himself represented movements of obedience to this Goddess of Destruction who was thus being worshipped and whose desire was being accomplished: "*If I destroy myself I shall perform my mother's wish.*" So when facing a new chance of being successful, his boycotting movements were auto-destructive movements repeating the physiological movements of his biological mother. Secondly, there was the hostile and antagonistic spermatozoid and ovum original couple: the anger of the spermatozoid for having been used to favor the ovum, leading to the carving of the pattern of envy.

This was worked through thoroughly and the effect was amazing. P. understood he could not change the original threads that had woven his very first fabric. But he could modify this pattern now; he was free to weave a new and different one using new threads of a different quality. This approach produced a very positive effect. He realized he did not have to destroy himself. What could now be done was a new programming – a re-patterning. The old pattern – the auto-destructive device – could be deactivated.

This insight promoted an evident change in his attitude during the sessions and life in general. He felt amazed by the power brought on by cellular memory insights. A dream pointed to this. It brought evidence of the installation of a new internal equipment and the acquisition of a new identity. Introducing the dream, P. explained that when he was a teenager living with his family elsewhere, they came to São Paulo and stayed at an aunt's house. The dream: P. had asked for a new telephone line to be installed in the aunt's apartment. But as there already existed one, this could only be done at the building's entrance desk. In the next scene, he sees himself moving into the analyst's house. He knows it might be inconvenient for me because I have my private life and a family of my own. Still that is where he wants to move in. He then sees himself having to travel abroad (this is a potential fact, as he might have to travel in order to sign the contract for his new job). He realizes that he has forgotten – at his parent's house in a far away city – his old passport, which contains the visa to the country where he is meant to go. So he hurries to fetch it. He will travel abroad with two passports: the expired one containing the visa, and the new one.

Final comments

I hope that by presenting this clinical material I have been able to achieve the purpose I had set out to achieve: to evidence the way in which certain traumatic situations belonging to the primordial prenatal period and related to cellular memory become manifest in the course of an analysis, and how they can be grasped and understood, especially when impasses are reached. Because I conceive the analytic encounter as the mating of two minds – the analytic couple forming a heterosexual fertile couple – I considered the difficulties manifested by the patient, which prevented the fruition of the encounter, as evocations and reproductions of the difficulties experienced upon the encounter of the first pair, namely at the moment of conception. I hope I was also able to convey how it is possible to grasp such situations, how they can be verbalized and the effect produced by such interventions. I also attempted to make evident how the very early sensorial impressions related to cellular memory (beta elements) may become alpha elements through the analyst's alpha function.

I propose that the recognition and inclusion of the prenatal psychic experience in the constitution of the mind (a) alters the concept of the internal world; (b) reports the roots of psychogenesis to an earlier period than the one usually considered; (c) modifies and broadens the understanding of certain psychopathological patterns; (d) enriches the understanding of the clinical facts which emerge within the analytic space; and (e) brings, as a result, changes in the clinical approach.

Notes

1 My special acknowledgments to Daniela Sitzer for her helpful text suggestions.

2 Michael Paul (1992) says something similar when he states: "These stages of mental development can dominate the mind of an adult and these memories and possible 'interpretations' arrived at by the foetal mind, can find expression."

3 See in Wilheim (1988, p. 165) the testimony of a patient of Farrant: "I experienced the terror felt by the ovum when besieged by thousands of sperms getting closer and closer . . ." See also Hitchcock's *The Birds*.

References

Bion, W. R. (1978). Clinical Seminar in São Paulo. In Wilheim, J. (1988) *A Caminho do Nascimento Uma Ponte entre o Biológico e o Psíquic*. Rio de Janeiro: Imago Editoria, pp. 17–330.

Jaret, P. (1986). Our Immune System: The Wars Within. *National Geographic*, 169: 6, pp. 702–735.

Mello, J. B. S. (1980). Dois Triângulos. In *Alter*, vol. 10 no. 2.

Paul, M. I. (1992). Implications of the Recognition of Foetal States of Mind: A Discussion with Dr. Alessandra Piontelli. Unpublished paper presented at UCLA Neuropsychiatric Institute, Los Angeles.

Wilheim, J. (1983). Anatomy of a Murderous Mind (Anatomia de uma Mente Assassina). Paper presented at a meeting of the Brazilian Psychoanalytic Society of São Paulo.

Wilheim, J. (1988). *A Caminho do Nascimento: Uma Ponte entre o Biológico e o Psíquic*. Rio de Janeiro: Imago Editoria, pp. 65–92.

Chapter 7

Thoughts without a thinker

Jane Van Buren

Bion's notion of wild thoughts, or thoughts without a thinker, presented western culture with a profound reversal in the understanding of how thoughts came to be. The concept "thoughts without a thinker" describes the mind at work at levels beyond the familiar signs and symbols. The recognition of mindfulness and significance existing beyond our ordinary reach of realizations and communications directed Bion further and intensely into a serious questioning of the meaning of words and beliefs and practices. He makes this point clear in his essay "Taming Wild Thoughts" (1997), in which he suggests that it is very difficult to find the origins of meaning in the individual and in the culture. He says,

> If we are concerned with physical diseases we have to learn the language the body talks. The human animal, unlike other species, can lie and has probably had a good deal of practice at lying and misinforming from a very early stage because feelings of guilt precipitate a proliferation of a capacity to lie and deceive.
>
> (Bion, 1997, p. 35)

He goes on to suggest that we probably do not know where to look for the origins of these wild thoughts, which are not yet tainted with rationalizations against the truth. He points out that there are a lot of tempting places to look:

> We are so familiar with psychoanalytic theories that we tend to forget the basic points so much so that it is difficult to say what they are. Sometimes we hear of analysis in a way that we think what a wonderful time we are having wandering amongst the weeds plucking the wild and beautiful flowers, but not getting anywhere near to disturbing the sleep of the sleeping beauty – the wisdom that lies fast asleep somewhere in the thickets, somewhere buried, not only literally under the mounds of the Ziggurat or the site of Ur of the Chaldees or Knossos, but what about the Oracle of Delphi? Is that voice in any way audible?
>
> (p. 37)

Bion had already realized another radical departure as he began to see that the troubled infant or patient was not dominated by his or her destructiveness, but by terror, overwhelm and catastrophic lack. As we know in the writing in *Second Thoughts* (1967b), Bion began to emphasize broken links as coming from the environment as well as the infant's distress. Crucially in the essay "A Theory of Thinking" (1967a), the lack of what he would later call a container was described as leading to a holocaust of missile-like bits of experience, pushed and pulled back and forth between the two participants; patient–analyst, mother–infant. Without the receiving mind, generations of unsolved hopelessness and helplessness rise up to plague both minds with a fear of living and of dying. Hatred, envy, and fragmentation accompany the failure of containment. These thoughts and the thinking that would accompany them are stillborn or distorted beyond recognition. Thus Bion suggests that thoughts without a thinker are in danger of being damaged at their roots, a situation in which their fruition and growth of mental capacities are aborted. The catastrophic abortion of unborn thoughts comes from trauma without reverie.

Bion felt that the great danger of growth and development was the burial of truth. Keen awareness brings intense feelings. Thinking about the danger and horrors of our existence on Earth, coupled with the growth of the capacity to signify and communicate, requires mental courage and new ways of making meaning. Bion realized how difficult achieving truthful realizations would be under these new conditions without succumbing to distortions and violent attacks. He thought that the infant's mind, or the patient's, needed assistance in maintaining realizations of the truth. He went on to talk about the language of achievement as the language of emotions before they become represented as concepts or ideas. He thought that it would be difficult to maintain the search for the truth. He says:

> I suggest that thinking is something forced on an apparatus, not suited for the purpose by the demands of reality, and is contemporary with, as Freud said, the dominance of the reality principle. A modern analogy is provided by the fact that the demands of reality not only forced the discovery of psychoanalysis but have led to the deflection of verbal thought from its original function of providing restraint from motor discharge to the tasks of self knowledge for which it is ill-suited and for the purpose of which it has to undergo drastic changes.
>
> (Bion, 1962, p. 111 as quoted in Grotstein, 2007)

The idea of the language of achievement is in contrast to the language of substitution and the theories of symbol formation, which have been valorized in psychoanalysis. Freud and Klein each in their own way believed that the symbol, or the use of substitution, is a crucial necessity for expansive mental life. In Freud's understanding, sublimation and substitution make creativity possible. For Klein, the extreme impediment to imaginative play comes from intense persecutory anxiety stemming from imagined damage to crucial internal objects. She also believed growth comes in the form of reparation, owning the injury to the internal parents and the release of the child's mental life from the harsh control of the superego.

Bion's notion of turbulence and inhibition of mental functioning reveals another of his reversals. He believed that the non-repressed unconscious is not the culprit that tears down the apparatus for thinking, speaking, and symbol formation. Bion, employing his concept of "O," understood the unconscious as a container of great truths that often became stranded inside the deepest layers of mental life. Instead of evolution from their forms as latent emotional signifiers, they were closed off, disavowed and distorted, arriving as distorted or diluted meanings. To grasp the implications of the innate richness of thoughts without a thinker at the deepest levels of mental life challenges and rocks established beliefs, expressed in the sensual realm, seeing, hearing, and conscious cognitive symbols. The journey of thoughts without a thinker seems increasingly difficult as the complexity of the mind has unfolded and the distance between originary "O" and the newer ways of surviving has increased. We might think that modern life has increased our chances of survival but we also know of the experience of alienation from our emotional life.

The contact barrier, formed of alpha elements, allows for production, exchange, and mixture of unconscious and conscious feelings and thoughts. Without the containing assistance of the mothering one(s) contact is forfeited and transformations from infinite to finite realizations and thinking is blocked. Symbols are thoughts to be spurred into significance, carrying the current emotional experience, or we might say "O" the most powerful, undiluted impersonal reality (Grotstein, 2007).

As myths and dreams are formed the possibilities of infinite powerful emotional truths can break through in a way that is tolerable to the mind of the subject. The balance is indeed delicate to achieve, to arrive, for example, at realizations that bring growth and knowledge without default into a breakdown and, paradoxically, a flexible boundary state between the experiences of different mental states – prenatal, postnatal, conscious and unconscious. The caesura is both separating and clarifying, but it can carry the unknown in such forms as to be horrifying or even pulling towards the void.

Growth demands change. New roads must be taken and bridges must be trusted for journeys into new circumstances and perspectives. Bion's departure from the traditional conscious/unconscious interface is based on the idea of growth. For him the evolution of emotional experience is the force that fuels mental life. Bion's new hypothesis of the understanding of the mind at work is a huge catastrophic change for western psychoanalysis, which is still very much taken by Freud's idea that the unconscious is problematic. Freud thought the desires that pulled for gratification were seriously opposed to the reality principle. Though dreams and even the complex patterning of neuroses involve remarkable ingenuity, the belief continues that the instincts must be tamed. Freud's insight that the transformation from id to ego was very limited nevertheless led the way for some understanding of the ability of the unconscious to present creative ideas and transformations.

Bion gradually moved beyond instinct theory, from the position of an unruly powerfulness to a concentration on the idea of immaturity, that the infant (patient) needs assistance with strange, disruptive emotional experience, particularly that of catastrophic change and the experience of the caesura. In "A Theory of Thinking" (1967a), Bion revolutionizes western thought about thinking by hypothesizing that thoughts precede thinking; that thinking comes about because of the need of the thoughts to be thought. Thus he elaborated the idea of thoughts without a thinker. From this vertex Bion proposes that original thoughts without a thinker were innate and difficult to communicate with; he also thought they were in a very dangerous position. They brought fresh original messages, but the messages they brought were disturbing truths to other parts of the personality, thus were hated, distorted, and even discarded. Bion also pointed out that the mind needs truth as the body needs nourishment. He linked this aversion to the truth to generational terrors and truths which, when unable to be contained, were projected into the children of the most recent generation and remained caught in a false system of explanation.

The fragility of the birth of new thoughts (freedom from lies) has everything to do with the caesura and catastrophic anxiety. One can see clear examples of this operating in political and international affairs. In *Taming Wild Thoughts* (1997), Bion directed his concerns to false beliefs and false gods. He held firmly to the position that truth is difficult to find and it can only reside in an unbound space where it can achieve its many forms and patterns. Bion also began to move towards understanding the ephemeral and transcendent; which break through the concepts of material or concrete pseudo-symbols. As he was doing so, the idea that feelings and emotions were the first cause of mental life was emerging. Bion believed that this trend brought forward the understanding of meaning. Connected to this is the development of thoughtfulness and also the capacities of the mind, which allows for recognition that part of itself is thinking or feeling differently than the observing aspect. The awareness of danger, feeling exiled from human contact and precariously attached makes the caesura more terrifying. Dramatic circumstances and small disruptions may be felt to be forces that shatter one's going on being, as "O" surfaces an enormous upheaval is potentiated.

The infant begins to fall apart. Repeated experiences with "O" and the lack of holding or containing, leads to a tragic mutilation of the subject's mind. The damaged aspect of a personality not only loses a sense of cohesion, but also cannot digest thoughts and feelings coming from without and within. The build-up of a projective identification, rejecting object, or obstructive object defeats the growth of meaning and budding thoughtfulness. The damaged aspect of the personality goes its own way, but with great limitations. Expelled by violent, hostile projective identification or transformation in hallucinosis, the chance of learning from experience is cut off. Finally the divide between the more troubled side of the personality and the more healthy one becomes ever more vast and deep, until it can hardly be reversed, or yield any solution to these differences.

The communication between the two takes place largely in the unconscious, or split-off realm. On the surface level, anxiety and dark thoughts dominate. Persecutory anxiety takes on a new dimension, seeming to be linked with the obstructive object that grows out of the failure of the container–contained and holding experience (primary maternal preoccupation is part of this), and fights the goodness and beauty of exchanges that promote the faith in and an appetite for life (Bion, 1967a, 1967b, 1997; Grotstein, 2007; Meltzer, 1986; Steiner, 1993; Winnicott, 1971). The obstructive object, or group, fights and undermines linking, and any open-mindedness leading to change. The obstructive group is cut off from experience and thus lives in a tomb of cruelty, harshness, and hopelessness. This aspect of the mind plagues the rest of the personality when there is any move towards growth and development.

Let us look at some of these processes in the context of an ongoing analysis. I wish to talk about a man who came into analysis with me experiencing very confused states alternating with a sense of deadness. The case that I want to share with you has undergone enormous and tumultuous change, passing through many caesuras. Mr. H came into treatment after a traumatic attempt at analysis. After suffering considerable abuse Mr. H finally broke off the analysis. He was very frightened and anxious, and as he later explained, felt uprooted and as if he had stopped existing.

Mr. H told me he had recently stopped stuttering. He still stammered, but only on certain words. One of these, interestingly enough, was any word that began with the first letter of his name. He explained that he had read a paper that argued that a schizophrenic mother causes stuttering. I felt both annoyed and impressed. The generalization seemed far-fetched and oversimplified, yet I was admiring of Mr. H's capacity to find ways to overcome his terrible problem. Such complicated feelings have continued throughout the analysis. Feelings of arrogance, stupidity and curiosity dominated his first year of analysis. Of course I am referring to Bion's paper "On Arrogance" (Bion, 1967b) in which he points out that the triad of arrogance, stupidity and curiosity indicates a primitive mental catastrophe. I felt terribly intruded on by Mr. H's pushing into me and watching me, and though this was unbearable, I was also disturbed by images of a small skinless creature that either arrived prematurely, or had not gained its postnatal orientation. My irritation in our sessions continued and intensified. After a long time I began to realize that Mr. H was driving me crazy. If I tried to follow his labored free associations, I became terribly depressed that I was failing. If I gave up becoming involved, I felt a terrible guilt. What I finally put together about this was that he was giving me an old experience of trying to be close with mother by inventing a way of communicating with her that mirrored her speech, while at the same time not being able to resonate with her projections into him. His confusion was profound; with the absence of a container and alpha function he succumbed and was overwhelmed by chaotic bits, which might have been thoughts or feelings, now shattered. As for me, I was overcome with confusion, chaos, and strong feelings of being trapped in an eternal void. The only hope I had under these conditions was that Mr. H and I were establishing a strong container–contained relationship. I believe this because I was so affected by his "senseless" goings-on. The words themselves were almost useless, although tantalizing. I was going through powerful, terrible, and terrifying emotional experiences. I felt morbidly depressed and so hopeless that I would welcome death. I was suffering from what I assume were the contents of his mind, that he had not been able to express. I saw babies lying dead, I felt problems of all sorts were not only unsolvable, but also lead to darkness.

This proved to be the case, because despite his continual failure to communicate his experiences, Mr. H was gaining some ground in being able to differentiate between internal and external events. However, throughout this stage Mr. H continued to be paranoid. His paranoia was founded early on when he remained in the hospital for ten days after his birth. He was born with a temperature, and the story goes that the doctors kept him in to treat and evaluate his health. I imagine from what he expressed to me, that he lost his mother, certainly her body, as well as her presence. He suffered acute abandonment anxiety and lost the opportunity for bonding. Furthermore, as I discussed earlier, mother was often in a strange state of mind, detached and confused. Mr. H attempted to bond with her eccentric presence. We went through months of echolalia, adhesive identification and violent projective identification. Again I felt overwhelmed, dejected and angry. I hypothesized he was living out, or attempting to bond with me the only way he knew how.

As these heroic efforts continued his internal objects seemed to take shape. Mr. H began to battle with these internal characters; the main ones in this period of analysis were his brothers. They were described as crazy, psychopathic and heinous characters. His hatred and bitterness were continued around the belief that his brothers had stolen money from his trust, set up by his mother to protect some of the money left to Mr. H. As the tale spun out, his brothers forged signatures of Mr. H and their mother, in order to take more control over the trust money.

This belief system was probably based on some facts, but since Mr. H's thinking was still corrupted by confusion and transformation in hallucinosis, I was severely frustrated to find any vestige of truth. I was severely frustrated by accounts of long meetings with lawyers stimulated by Mr. H's attempt to regain his property. In the telling, many mishaps befell Mr. H. The first lawyer complained that he couldn't understand what Mr. H was talking about. He also fell ill from "exhaustion and alcoholism." Other versions included lawyers who were stupid, incompetent, corrupt, and capable of bribery, so he escalated to even more lawsuits, not only against his brothers, but also against the lawyers who were helping him with his lawsuit. At the same time, Mr. H also became somewhat coherent. I believe he was making some small progress toward reflection and thinking, however, he had difficulty identifying what he perceived and what were his internal problems. He reported that some people could understand him and were thoughtful in their response to him. He said that they were very impressed with how much he had changed. Although he also described meetings that took place with the latest lawyers, as very tumultuous. It sounded to me as though no communication had taken place.

I felt very confused, but then I began to feel clear that I was witnessing a failure of communication between Mr. H and "mother." This realization was very hard won for me. It seems so clear to me now that up until this point I did not have the clarity of mind to organize my experience in words. It felt to me that I had been drawn into a regressive state of mind, alpha function in reverse, with boundarylessness, and lack of any sign of organization. And loss of time and space also dominated my mind. There was no room for thinking and taking in valuable experience. I felt disoriented and self-attacking due to my inability to know what we were going through. I stood up at the end of the session feeling dizzy and unbalanced. Mr. H prepared to leave the session, but he could not stand up either. He had lost his balance, his sense of gravity and was very disoriented, clinging to the walls and furniture as he made his way to the door. I was very concerned. These spells lasted for several weeks, physicians were consulted, but not much could be found as to what the sense of imbalance was about. Gradually these symptoms subsided. I maintained my analytic stance as best as I could, and it gradually became clear that Mr. H was suffering from catastrophic change. I felt intrigued and hopeful, but also worried. It had crossed my mind that Mr. H had broken through something very important. He trembled and became anxious. I searched my inner life to inquire what his fears were and how he had become so lost and unbalanced.

A powerful realization began to break through. A great many questions went through my mind. I was wondering why he had lost his balance. Why had he lost his sense of gravity? What was developing? Were there links forming that seemed shocking and unfamiliar? Had this happened to him before and why was it breaking through now? The old familiar signposts he had created were dropping away. In their place came flux, change, uncertainty, and fear of emptiness and disintegration. His dreams would qualify as what Bion would conceptualize as efforts towards dreaming – not quite successful, but I think helpful. Eventually he began to cast his dreams with people whom he knew, but were not necessarily close to him. It was often painful to try to understand what were the reasons for their presence. Often it seemed contradictory to what he was trying to say. So we might conjecture that these dreams carried wisps of thoughts and as he searched for his connection to them, he would lose his thread of connections and wander all over. His associations were very loose, and we both felt lost and bewildered.

During the period of Mr. H's dissociation his dreams did become more coherent. One dream of this sort was of two men on a bed naked. They were performing fellatio on each other. Despite the seeming perverseness of this dream, Mr. H was able to identify the men as his father and himself. The narrative was somewhat scattered as usual, but it was possible for both of us to have some associations. One could have an idea that Mr. H's dream was presenting an infant's use or need of a father; something that had been non-existent in his mind in the past, or considered useless. Father called Mr. H "miserable." It also came to my mind that Mr. H's father stammered for part of his life. I also remembered a much-repeated anecdote. Mr. H recalled that his father, upon hearing the news of his brother's sudden death, sat down for a moment looking visibly shaken and overwhelmed, then got up as if nothing had happened and went to work. Mr. H is somewhat more clear about his father's lack of emotionality than he is about mother's unreliable relatedness and thinking.

These associations or thoughts were very important. I believe they signified the emergence of his ability to dream, which depends on alpha function, a functioning contact barrier and the use of conscious and unconscious memories and feelings to communicate his concerns. Also, he developed a transference that seemed to be built out of the desire for infantile needs to be met by a "father me." This advance in the use of dreams certainly was not permanent. Mr. H relapsed into his fragmented attempts at making contact with his deeper feelings. Slowly and with great effort the caesura of meaning opened and Mr. H increasingly tolerated the upheaval of change, brought about by the fruit of alpha function. From these new capacities, two thoughts were able to make their way into his awareness with less debris in their pathways. Mr. H began to sort out the hallucinated from the real; the real being that which he had no influence over and no capacity to create. In this context he suffered intensely at the realization at how complex people and situations might be. He couldn't tolerate or digest the many contradictions he now recognized in his family, in me, and in himself. With the help of developing alpha function Mr. H became more flexible in his perceptions, however, it was still difficult for him to feel the emotions attached to them. Though I was relieved to be able to follow his spoken and thoughtful messages, the two main aspects of his communications remained unavailable. He felt no love or affection, no sadness, no hopelessness, except for the displaced anxiety associated with his extreme paranoid-schizoid phantasies and beliefs. He remained trapped in a narrow "whodunit?" construction. No shred of "I love" or "I need" colored his communications or thoughts, and deep bewilderment as to the motives of the actors in his plots continued. Earlier Mr. H had hurled gross accusations, "He's an asshole," "He's mentally ill," "He's crazy." A significant change emerged with the question, "Why should someone be so cruel?" This seemed very jarring to both of us. Mr. H attempted to find answers where before there had been no questions. Extreme paranoia was being replaced by uncertainty and some dimensionality beyond the either/or mentality. As you can imagine these changes were felt to be catastrophic. He would arrive for his sessions looking battered and exhausted. I felt concerned but he began the sessions immediately. At the same time he gathered his thoughts to the extent that I could often follow what he was trying to articulate. Mr. H seemed to know that he wanted to explain something.

From this point Mr. H's demons subsided. His paranoia began to shrink. Larger chunks of his psychic reality were relayed in dreams. One dream told of his crucifixion. He expressed his bewilderment and even ignorance of the significance of the images of this dream. I suggested he felt crucified in his family and pointed to the faint drops of blood dripping from his body. He agreed. "Oh, I never thought of that. As I was able to de-idealize everyone, in my analysis with you, I realized that I was abused by hatred and condemnation." This insight was based on a huge reversal of some of his realizations. In the next day's session he proclaimed that it didn't matter what the person said, as much as how their mind was working. "I always thought that people meant what they said, that they knew everything and I was wrong or at fault."

Mr. H was slipping out of his concrete prison and was beginning to view people and events as integrated, to the extent that he perceived different aspects of the same person, and he could see their growth, or changes. The idea of a concrete inanimate world now seemed ridiculous. Mr. H questioned how he could have ever looked at people and interactions as if they were things.

Conclusion: Getting a mind

Mr. H's analysis is an illustration of a magnificent psychoanalytic journey from meaninglessness to meaning. Mr. H's analytic progress had been extremely painful and arduous for both of us. The amount of buried truths was quite overwhelming, as were the legacies of neglect, lies, distortions, cruel projective identifications, and a hatred of change and growth. The effort itself to think and accept his feelings, or "O" or the deep emotional truth, was agonizing and required enormous determination and strength to ward off the insistent part of his mind that lied and tried to kill off any vestiges of truth.

Nevertheless Mr. H dared to mount the emotional Everest. Despite its jagged surfaces and slippery slopes of ice and snow he continued to cross the caesuras with terror and dread. He lost his bearings many times. Often we both felt like we were losing our minds. Remarkably Mr. H has recently explained to me that he has been building a mind and that the other members of his family had never had minds, at least the internal ones, and could not think. The authority of omnipotence was diminishing inside his psychic world.

At this time Mr. H began to demonstrate and express feelings of possessiveness and worry about my absence. He was thinking about my summer vacation, which was still some distance away. I think he had begun to realize, emotionally, that I was not a thing. It mattered to him if I was by his side or not.

References

Bion. W.R. (ed.) (1967a). A Theory of Thinking. In *Second Thoughts: Selected Papers On Psychoanalysis*. New York: Jason Aronson.

Bion, W.R. (ed.) (1967b). On Arrogance. In *Second Thoughts: Selected Papers On Psychoanalysis*. New York: Jason Aronson.

Bion, W.R. (1997). *Taming Wild Thoughts*. London: Karnac.

Green, A. (1972). The Dead Mother. In Green, A. (1972) *On Private Madness*. Madison, CT: International University Press.

Grotstein, J. (2007). *A Beam Of Intense Darkness: Wilfred Bion's Legacy To Psychoanalysis*. London: Karnac.

Meltzer, D. (ed.) (1986). *Studies In Extended Metapsychology: Clinical Applications Of Bion's Ideas*. Perthshire: Clunie Press.

Steiner, J. (1993). *Psychic Retreats: Psychological Organizations In Psychotic, Neurotic And Borderline Patients*. New York: Routledge.

Winnicott, D.W. (1971). *Playing and Reality*. London/New York: Tavistock/ Routledge.

Chapter 8

Nothing comes from nothing

Failed births, dead babies

Francisco Gonzalez

> I do not suggest that the event is related to the dramatic episode of birth itself, but rather that that dramatic situation, if borne in mind, is easier to use as a model to understand far less dramatic occasions which occur over and over again when the patient is challenged to move from one state of mind to another.
>
> (W. R. Bion, 1989, p. 48)

> Some infants, more than others, may have an idea that they ought to die, if not now, soon, if not acutely, chronically.
>
> (H. N. Boris, 1987, p. 353)

I will examine here a particular kind of birth trauma, we might call it, in which a person's primary mode of psychic functioning – the very form or configuration that subjective existence takes for an individual – might best be described as a kind of negative identification, in the sense of an identification with the negative, with non-being, nothing, or the void. The trauma of birth for these patients is that it has never really happened, at least not in a way that inaugurates birth itself as a living process, one that can depict the metaphoric movement from one state into a fundamentally different, higher order of development. In fact, one could say that without birth there is no primal setting for metaphor, and therefore no way to elaborate a psychological story from the fact of brute existence. For the kind of patient I discuss here, there is a profound condensation of life with death, and the installation of an anti-birth that produces a dead baby, an abortion, or a stillbirth as the foundational fantasy that organizes the personality.

Cindy tells me repeatedly that she just cannot decide if she can "cross over to the side of the living." In middle age she is struggling courageously with a terrible hole at the center of her being. For most of her life she was caretaker to her high-strung mother, a controlling and loquacious woman who feared all things new. The father, laconic and reserved, truncated his career in finance, unable to overcome his wife's anxieties about moving across the country: no job, however promising, could offer her the security of staying put.

One by one, other siblings left home – graduating, eloping, running away. Cindy stayed. By her adolescence, the father had already caved in, an emotional implosion fed by alcohol and disappearing acts. His absences stoked the mother's anxiety and her relentless clinging to Cindy, whose days were spent being filled up with the restlessness, fear, and paralytic indecision of her mother. Evenings, she cried herself to sleep alone in the dark, trying to empty herself out. "I loved being with her, but it was just too much," Cindy tells me, "she was glued to me." Father returned from his mysterious escapades as inexplicably as he disappeared, and his return erased the absence – a scene neatly spliced out of a movie. The family would go back to "normal": father in one room, watching TV, alone, mother in another, Cindy caught in between.

I took these stories as a depiction of a static mental structure or calcified state: an over-ripe Oedipal triangle as *tableaux vivant*, or rather as *tableaux mort*, frozen as they were in time, paralyzed by inaction and sealed in by silence. Eventually home left Cindy: the parents died over the course of the years, the house was sold by sibling decree, and Cindy was finally forced to move. She grew increasingly depressed, lost her job as a programmer, spent days in the house without leaving her bed. The thoughts of suicide she had been harboring in secret for years, now blossomed. Forced hospitalizations, shopping lists of medications.

Five years into a three-times-a-week analysis, she is still relentlessly haunted by thoughts of suicide, possessed at times by a deep and terrifying longing to join her dead parents, convinced that this eternal fusion is the only way to resolve the impossible problem of living. She tells me she feels "thrown out" into an incomprehensibly difficult and cruel world, defenseless and raw. She is constantly seeking safe refuge. Often she does not want to leave the office at the end of the session – "I want to cling to you forever," she says. At home, in retreat from the painful world of the living, she plunges into startling self-loathing, a violent upwelling of hatred and self-excoriation. She is unflaggingly menaced by the "bad voice," a maternal interject[1] that nags her for her stupidity and pushes hard for the final solution: *end analysis, kill yourself.*

"[S]ome mothers know their babies," writes Harold Boris, "and other mothers can't see the baby for the preconception. Preconceived babies have a difficult time getting emotionally conceived, let alone born" (1987, p. 355). The preconceived baby is the dead container baby, conceived as a storage place for the intolerable nameless dread of the mother. If birth marks the primal site of the original separation and the beginning of the long road of differentiation, the spring from which all future distinctions will be elaborated, Cindy just cannot get born.

As an event, a concept, and a metaphor, birth instantiates the foundational experience of origin, of starting out from somewhere and to somewhere. Birth promises a future. Not having been born, these patients do not conceive the unfolding of chronological time. Like Cindy, they are entombed or frozen in the eternal, a static or inhuman dimension of time, a negative nirvana. There is no fantasy of *what might be*; they are locked instead into the atemporality of *what might have been*: a being born that never happened.

As the foundational setting for the personality, this fantasy of the dead or aborted baby is catastrophic and closed in the extreme, a literal dead end. The cradle and the grave become fused, collapsing the grand potential space we call a life. Because of the condensation of life and death, entrance on to the stage of living in the world paradoxically carries with it the threat of annihilation. To be born is to be killed off. The only viable place is thus the claustrophobic shelter of the womb and the only available existence something akin to being as a fetus, totally dependent, lacking agency or the capacity for autonomous thinking. The only hope, if hope is the word, is to wait, outside of life, to be born.

Indeed these patients are a version of those living in Meltzer's (1992) *claustrum*, where psychological existence is confined within the body of the internal mother. Meltzer postulates intrusive identification, whereby the infant psychically forces its way into the internal chambers of the mother's body, identifies with this intrusion, and gets stuck there. The kind of patients I am trying to describe here are indeed those whose most vital center is locked inside of the primary internal object, unborn, saprophytically fused, even when some of them may employ a false-self carapace that permits some appearance of functioning in the world. They are painfully lonely people, with little or no experience or memory of love. In contradistinction to Meltzer's description, however, intrusive identification is how we might best describe what was *done to* these patients by the primary object. The intrusive identification came from the outside. Someone forced a way inside, too soon, violently, fatally.

Inversion of containment

The psychic landscape of these aborted or unborn patients shares a great deal with the scenes so usefully described by Green (1983) in the dead mother complex. Here the child must find a way to enliven the melancholic primary object and maintains this depleted object entombed within. The initial presentation to treatment is deceptively unclouded by depressive symptoms and the dead mother emerges, like a ghostly image developing in photographic emulsion, "as a revelation of the transference." In contrast, the patients I am describing here often enter treatment on their psychic deathbeds, deeply and chronically depressed – one foot already planted in the grave. They are more like the "undead" Sekoff (1999) speaks of in his extension of Green's work, horrifically suspended in a zombie world, the maimed provenance of "the deadening mother."

For unlike the drama of the dead mother, in this situation – which also places us on the lip of an abyss, void, or hole in the psyche and therefore carries vestiges of psychosis, autism, and perversion – it is the child who is required to be psychologically dead as a way of ensuring the emotional viability of the mother. (That the infant depends on this viability for its very survival, will link questions of existence with psychological processes in perverse ways, as we will see later.) This mother is overly full, we might say, rather than empty; spilling over, rather than imploding; frantically and desperately invasive rather than melancholically abandoning.

What takes place is a massive inversion of holding, a kind of psychological cannibalization. In a colossal reversal, the asymmetries of containment are switched, and it is the mother who takes the child as her emotional depository and regulator. The child becomes the "dark container" for the mother's "dark matter," as one patient put it. Winnicott (1969) describes the fruitful progression from object relating to object use, in which the object repeatedly survives the child's attacks and thereby incrementally establishes the difference between subjective and objective realities. With these patients, we might term what happens *mis-use as an object*. The nascent subjectivity of the child is at best grossly under-recognized, and the mother, who lacks adequate metabolizing capacity, projects raw emotion overwhelmingly into the infant.

Resiliency being a primary innovator of human psychological development, the child might typically deal with such a catastrophic situation by elaborating a false self as a protective shell, until a sufficiently safe environment allows the more vulnerable and vital germinal center to unfold and develop – that is, until the true self can sense the adequacy of a sustained containing process (Winnicott, 1955). In the patients I am trying to represent here, there is a pernicious (and typically unconscious) use of this very protective structure by the primary object. This use is something much more ruthless than the more typical failures of recognition that might lead to wounded self-structures and the panoply of higher-order narcissistic difficulties. Instead, *the primary object has opportunistically exploited the child's capacity to form a false self*, a capacity, after all, that demonstrates some proto-ability to metabolize emotional experience. A false self is in fact predicated on the ability to intuit the other's emotional states, to register and recognize impingement as such, and subsequently to mount some sort of stabilizing interpersonal regulation. A false self calms potentially turbulent waters; its whole purpose is to maintain interpersonal equilibrium by providing a smooth interface that counters the intrusiveness of others with the balm of acquiescence. It is this calm interface, this going-along-with that in fact constitutes the protective emotional shell.

I would like to draw a distinction between this kind of fortified false self and the "empty fortress" (Bettelheim, 1967) or shell-like enclaves typical of autism, described especially by Tustin (1981), with which these patients share a great deal in common phenomenologically. They can indeed look a great deal like autistic patients at times, but they have (and have always had, from infancy) a capacity to metabolize emotional exchange. Without this capacity they would not serve the functions the mother requires of them.

In the scenario of the dead baby, the mother or primary object is something like a hermit crab, appropriating the shell of the false self as a protective shelter for her own psychic vulnerabilities. But such a misuse of the child constitutes a forced evacuation of the child's psyche – a psychological evisceration. This is the psychic abortion with which these patients fundamentally identify. What is internalized, then, is an inverted containing function: one of being taken over, hollowed out and colonized, no longer a living child, but nonetheless alive.[2] The child has no option but to take this inverted object relation as the first template for the mind – it is needed and loved precisely as far as it is able to house the mother. It is this reflexive relation to self (I am an empty container for the use of the other) that constitutes the foundation for the early ego, or the seat of agency, or the proto-mentalization that will lead to mind.

This foundational fantasy establishes deadly paradoxes. The child's primary identification with itself (what it finds reflected in its mother's eyes) is something dead, an abortion, an objectified container emptied of its subjective contents. To the child's reflection in the mirror, this mother says not "that is you" but "this is mine." And yet, it is this very psychic death that authenticates the child's psychological (and to some extent its physical) existence. In order to live you must be dead, reads the sign over the gateway into this shadow life. Profoundly dependent on the mother, the child is the vessel she requires. Indeed, rather than gestating the mind of the child in its post-uterine life, the mother becomes something like the seed of a monstrous pregnancy in the child, a being who is brought into the world to serve as receptacle.

For such a child, to be or not to be will remain the principal and haunting question. One is hard pressed to find a viable answer: if the very ground of psychological existence is to exist for someone else, if I am, at core, someone else's possession and object, how can it be possible to exist *for myself* in any meaningful way? And if I am *for myself* does this not obliterate all that I am, for my deepest *raison d'être* was to be for another? And if I shatter everything, how can I be at all? Perhaps it is better to suspend the question.

Refusal to drive

One solution, then, is to remain in limbo, waiting to be born, the vital center of the self protected in a uterine non-living. Suspension fundamentally disavows the catastrophe of having been mis-used as an object; it tries to forget the aborted entrance of "me." A secret contract is struck with (extracted by?) the primary object: I will give you my self to house your need, since now, being nothing myself, I am needless. Such a solution requires a vigilant tending to the fires of negation, some way to erase subjectivity, burn up desire, to leave nothing but a hole. This passionate negativity, as we will see, is both cloak and dagger: it serves to hide and protect, to kill and to clear away.

When the question does crack open – and the entry into analysis is often precipitated by the cracking – there is hell to pay. Self-abnegation is the seal on Pandora's box for those who lead aborted lives, and any stirring of authentic desire risks unleashing uncontainable and demonic forces.

It is impossible not to be reminded of another patient, Jake, a man whose life came apart in late middle age. He had been moderately successful in a career as a concert pianist, was sought after in certain circles, had cut a few albums. When his mother died when he was in his 30s, he abruptly stopped playing, to the bafflement of those close to him. He had never wanted to play piano, an instrument he in fact hated. As a child he longed for a guitar, to build radios, to be a soccer star, but found himself complicit with his mother's dream that he play the piano as her father had done. Feeling somewhat more freed up after his rebellion of silence against the forces of maternal tyranny, he established himself in a music-related business and did well financially. Other than money, the work offered little but an occasion to complain: "it leaves me cold." Some ten years after his mother's death, he met an ambitious woman at a business function who took a liking to him. He went along half-heartedly with her courtship, putting aside his deep ambivalence in order, finally, to marry her. He presented for treatment in his late 50s, two years into a series of clandestine homosexual affairs: was he a gay, he wanted to know.

The first year or two of treatment in a four-times-a-week intensive psychotherapy was spent in a reconstruction of his life. I was skeptical at first, but while there were ways that we could view his relatively recent forays into homosexuality as defensive, it became increasingly clear that his affectional and sexual preference for men was a deep and vibrant river flowing through his life from childhood. I felt it was essential to keep my distance from any pronouncement about his sexual orientation, but Jake grew increasingly convinced, and convincing, that he was and always had been homosexual. Split off experiences, unrequited loves, nostalgic boyhood crushes, lusty dreams and a secret love affair with a roommate in college, all rushed forward to fill in a picture of a gay man sealed in an iron closet. For a short while Jake seemed to gain confidence and strength from the recognition of this seemingly lost self, but soon thereafter he began to unravel spectacularly. With reflection, what he now increasingly recognized was a sham life, more like a series of false-fronted movie sets than anything resembling flesh-and-blood experience. Mourning was foreclosed. He brooded over his regular mantras: "what might have been, but wasn't"; "the giant doors of eternity are slammed shut"; "there is nothing to be done about it." He began to self-destruct brutally, clawing away at the social fabric of his life, dismantling his family, using drugs, losing his job, and putting himself at risk sexually until he became HIV-positive. Despite vigorous interpretation, I felt impotent. Psychotherapeutic treatment became untenable as Jake turned increasingly to drugs in order to obliterate his pain. I referred him to a rehabilitation center where he continued ambivalently for at least a few years until I lost sight of him.

No doubt there are a number of things I might have done differently. Mostly I wish that I had been better able to help Jake to find a more productive way to remake himself, or to come to peaceful terms with what was actually livable in his life. At the time I was pursuing what might be called a soft Kleinian line, and thinking a great deal about Winnicottian holding, while focusing on the aggressive destructiveness and malignant envy in the transference, perversity (there were vivid childhood scenes involving excrement and danger), "attacks on linking" (Bion, 1959) and so forth. Perhaps, like someone who cannot believe he has really lost his keys, I just kept looking over and over again in the same places for something I could not find: a doorway into Jake's mourning. I was pained by the damage being done, and frustrated that I could not put a stop to it. Looking back on it now, I think I underestimated the necessity of the carnage (while I rue its lack of containment). The eruption of the devastating and furious story of personal annihilation unfolded naturally, necessarily, from the dark seeds that lay at the heart of Jake's psyche.

Opening the sealed crypt of the undead requires necromancy if the living are to be liberated, as Jed Sekoff (1999) has so eloquently written. The rituals of mourning and funeral rites of passage at the threshold of the grave facilitate the loss of the object. Without such a loss there can be no salutary evolution of mind. But perhaps before being able to quietly sit shiva in commemoration of the passing of the dead, the analytic couple must be beset by the frightful appearance of Shiva, the violent god of creation and destruction. If these dead baby patients have refused the mother of all mourning – separation – they have good reason for it: it is their only chance for survival. Emergence from the dead womb requires living out the deadly breakdown that has already happened; getting beyond the event horizon of the black hole in the psyche requires a Big Bang.[3]

Uncannily, Cindy and Jake have the rough outlines of a story in common. The father of each patient bought them a car as a gift; each had refused to drive it. The cars remained parked in the yard, unused, useless. The stories were different in many important particulars, of course, and each could be understood on multiple levels (including those concerned with adolescent development and paternal Oedipal dynamics, to name but a couple). But something about the insistence of the refusal drew me to the more primitive layers. Initially, and especially with Jake whom I treated earlier, I understood the refusal to drive as a transferential renunciation of the treatment: after all, I was trying to provide an escape vehicle from the fusional chaos; spite and perversion and envy would not allow its good use. There was undoubtedly truth to this reading, but what began to resonate more strongly was the therapeutic value of the negation. It's necessity. The refusal was as much an attempt to create, as it was to destroy. Like a toddler saying "no," refusal, denial, renunciation, negation in all its variegated forms, was a necessary way station on the road to a meaningful "yes." But how to say no to something when everything is already not yours? How to get out of the existential Catch-22: any rustling of desire is already someone else's desire, preempted, colonized by the other. Not using the car was like suicide: a refusal of the drives. But *whose* drives, that was not as clear. The father's? The child's? The mother's, lived through the child? When the rules of the game are appropriation, maybe the only subterfuge left is misappropriation. There was spite in the refusal, surely, but also proud defiance, a last-ditch attempt to preserve vital possessions by destroying them, like burning down the city to keep the invaders from taking the spoils.

In the world of dead container babies and hermit crab mothers – a landscape of double negatives, reversals, and inversions – there is a desperate need to clear some room, to carve out of existence something else, something other, to make *not*-me space in a field dense with *non*-me. Some drive for life in these patients intuits the need for potential space, for a true container, a living womb or breast, a receptive other. The part of the personality fighting for this reception struggles dearly to make itself heard above the din of confusion and the insulating walls of the fortress. Sometimes this requires a radical act of protest: self-immolation.

Nothing borne to being born

The course of treatment with such a patient is laborious and existential, at crucial times marked significantly more by the toleration of abjection and nothingness, by a living-through-something-with, than by anything approximating interpretation. There are long stretches, often early in the treatment, where the goal for the therapist is principally survival. Cindy leaked violently (it cannot be called crying) for almost the entire session, session after session, for the better part of the first one and a half years of treatment. I remember very little from that early time other than the experience of two overwhelming sensations: first, a catastrophic desire to fall asleep and become completely unconscious which took me over like an intravenously administered soporific; and second, a highly uncomfortable sensation of hatred. Though I could not make sense of them at the time, both were essential communications about her internal state: drowning in a flood of hateful feeling, getting sucked down a drain towards nothingness. Interpretations were made more for my benefit than hers, a way to keep myself afloat. I think her most pressing unconscious question was the essential one: could anyone bear what had happened to her. Perhaps the only significant intervention I made during this long interval was to endure the sessions and to encourage Cindy to continue. Somehow she must have communicated to me a faith that continuance mattered, for, remarkably, at no point did I consider ending the treatment.

It took a great deal of time before these unbearable sensations began to coalesce into shapes and narrative elements via the more conventional workings of the analytic process, namely the interweaving of historical material and the transference–countertransference story. What then emerged was a foundational fantasy of profound negativism, a kind of anti-primal scene that might best be described as an almost physical need for Cindy to join her parents in the conjugal bed, except that the parents (and Cindy) were dead, and the bed was a grave. This ache for ultimate stasis, which Freud (1920) might have labeled a manifestation of the Nirvana principle and Green (1998, 2002) an example of negative narcissism, is the antipode of Bion's caesura (1989), that strange point of division and of crossing over. "Investigate the caesura," Bion the mystic writes, "the link, the synapse, the (counter-trans)-ference, the transitive-intransitive mood" (1989, p. 56). But for a person that harbors a dead baby inside, this link – the bridge that crosses over from one territory to the next and infuses the crossing with mobility and life – is precisely what is missing. Without a template for transition, there can be no faith in the transitive nature of living or, for that matter, in doing psychoanalytic work in its more conventional forms.

Freud is clearly thinking of the mother's tender mitigation of the trauma of birth when he notes that "there is much more continuity between intra-uterine life and earliest infancy than the impressive caesura of the act of birth would have us believe" (1926, p. 138). It is the mother with her constant care that provides the enabling continuity: the mother's *care* now standing in for the functions of her *body*. Now, a mother's care and a mother's body are two very different kinds of things, but they are elementally joined for the infant through the fact of its existence. Without either, it would die. It is the tension between this continuity and the cataclysm of birth that provides the first lived template for metaphor, long before the advent of language.

Cindy was beginning to traverse the caesura. By establishing a setting for fantasy, the ghastly cemetery scene provided a shape, a birth into metaphor that allowed a furtherance of the analytic work beyond bearing nothingness ("furtherance" because this bearing, too, is quintessentially analytic: who would do it, other than an analyst?). Her thoughts of suicide continued, but my somnolence dramatically abated; the work became more lively, with currents of rich feeling: flashes of anger and disappointment, rough patches of frustrated irritation. The leaking morphed into weeping, as the tears now began to convey sadness rather than empty dissolution. Or to put it another way: live objects began to appear on the horizon.

This move out of the suspended animation of a negative fetal state signifies a righting of the original inversion of containment. It starts to become imaginable to be received, and by a Someone. But to create a place that might allow such conception, space is required. One must first tolerate nothing (Boris, 1987).

The emergence of something from nothing brings to mind another patient. Like Cindy, Beverly arrived quite depleted and collapsed; she had already been out of work for the better part of a year. A mid-level administrator in her mid 30s, she had accumulated a little money, but her parents provided the ample supplementation needed to keep her alive in what we came to call her "cave." She spent most days in her bed, watching television, surfing the Internet, or engrossed in a secret fantasy world about which she could say nothing for fear of its collapse: "it's an addiction, but I don't think that I can live without it, and if I tell you about it, it just won't really be mine any more." Beverly could be affable, with a dark edge tending towards sarcastic. She was painfully isolated from all but her parents. Her depression was severe, immobilizing. It was not uncommon for her to disappear from treatment for a week or even two at a time, often after a small break in the routine. She was adroit in wielding the technologies of "zoning out," both those enhanced (surfing the web or the TV) and those machinated purely by the mind. Zeroing out had a deep magnetic pull on Beverly, and she knew how to let herself drift towards its emptiness, how to make herself disappear, to become nothing. This ability, I thought, was what kept her from being overtly suicidal; she could approximate nothingness without having to physically annihilate herself by her adept manipulation of the virtual.

A vast sense of devastation opened early in the therapeutic field with Beverly. Again I could recognize its depths only in retrospect, realizing only a couple of years later how deeply unbearable the nihilism had actually been. Denial and therapeutic splitting on my part were perhaps among the few available technical provisions that helped to ensure the survival of the work. In this early time, Beverly came to sessions, if irregularly, she took her medication; there was otherwise little evidence of a treatment.

These periods of endurance, which require bearing nothingness (vast expanses of waste, –K, asymbolia), may well be the prodrome of the treatment, a gestation *ex nihilo*. These stretches have an amorphous quality, can be monotonous to the point of stupor, and are stratified with a dead, objectless aggressivity. There is something inhuman about them. They are borne or endured, the way one might endure crossing a desert, bearing the physical and emotional effects of severe deprivation: in an agony of thirst.

They are nihilistic rather than depressive, characterized by what is absent rather than by missing what was present.

They are also vital to the work, in the most literal way. A great deal must be evacuated by the patient in order to clear some sort of space for the birth of the self. Ill-timed interpretation of evacuation as a pathological mechanism may be counterproductive, replicating the original lack of receptivity, redoubling paranoid intrusions, and compounding the problem. Nihilism radiates from the patient, and must be absorbed by the analyst.

But neither did this mean that the analysis was to be a repetition in reverse, with the analyst now in the position of the dead container and the analytic work a fetus to be aborted. The most significant aspect of the work during this period was the living sustenance of a viable container, of something that could hold us both. Consultation was indispensable. Often containment was rudimentary: simply protecting the regularity of meetings (at one point considering with Beverly if it made sense even to continue, given the frequency of missed sessions: this engaged her) and maintaining an active stance that continually attempted to reach this woman who lived so close to zero. I think just the mere *fact of trying* superseded the content of any communication; it was, perhaps, the invitation of humanity in the voice that beckoned to this person who was so deeply lost, perched as she was on the edge of an abyss.

After the first couple of years of treatment Beverly began to emerge from her vegetative shroud, stumbling and pained, like someone who had grown too accustomed to the dark and now was blinded by the glare of daylight. Slowly we assembled a language together. Did I remember that term from mathematics – she wanted to know – called *epsilon*? I did, I thought. Wasn't that the smallest possible number that represented something, some infinitesimally tiny something that was just this side of nothing? Yes! – she sang out – Yes, that's right! And her voice proclaimed that in that moment we had finally touched on something, a filament of a bridge across a dark divide.

The path to getting born, for these patients who were never conceived, crosses a vast field of nothing. Bearing what is absent inaugurates the possibility of loss, and the beginning of transformation. The trick, perhaps, is to let our eyes adjust to the dark, to allow the story of annihilation to form out of the shadows. It can be a lonely enterprise. Poets know the capabilities of nothingness, its empty annihilations, of course, but also its potential as a place of emergence. Lear foreshadows both when he asks his daughter, Cordelia, what she can say to demonstrate her love for him. Their exchange is well-known:

Cor. Nothing, my lord.
Lear. Nothing?

Cor. Nothing.
Lear. Nothing will come of nothing. Speak again.

(*King Lear*, Act 1: 87–90)

"Nothing" is not the response Lear wants to hear, but it is the true response, the only one that might open a genuine path to the heart. Lear will have to bear much nothingness; he will be progressively divested and ultimately devastated. This is the terrain we must enter if we are to hope that out of the nothing that is annihilation can emerge the nothing that is the capacity for something to be born, and for the chance to speak again.

Notes

1 Christopher Bollas (1999, p. 95) coined the term in reference to the dead mother complex. "An interject is an internal object that arrives in the internal world either due to a parental projective identification, interjected into the self, or to a trauma from the real that violates the self, or both."

2 My description of phenomena in this paper is meant as a fictional depiction of an unconscious foundational fantasy, that is, one that provides fundamental psychic organization for the mind. It is fictional in the sense that it exists merely as a model in the mind of the analyst. Nor is it a comprehensive model, mapping only one region of the patient's mind. Our minds are more like dilapidated buildings – repaired and remodeled over time by many owners, with the material at hand – than like the concentric, mythical onion.

3 The event horizon of a black hole is the threshold past which nothing, not even light, can escape the strength of the gravitational field at its core. The absorption of light renders the hole's interior invisible, and indistinguishable from the black space around it. (www.wikipedia.org/wiki/black_hole)

References

Bettelheim, B. (1967). *The Empty Fortress: Infantile Autism and the Birth of the Self.* New York: Free Press.

Bion, W. R. (1959). Attacks on Linking. *International Journal of Psychoanalysis*, 40: 308–315.

Bion, W. R. (1989). Caesura. In *Two Papers: The Grid and Caesura*. London: Karnac, pp. 35–56.

Bollas, C. (1999). Dead Mother, Dead Child. In G. Kohon (ed.) (1999) *The Dead Mother: The Work of Andre Green*. New York: Routledge, pp. 87–108.

Boris, H. N. (1987). Tolerating Nothing. *Contemporary Psychoanalysis*, 23: 351–366.

Freud, S. (1920). *Beyond the Pleasure Principle*. In *The Standard Edition of the Complete Psychological Works of Sigmund Freud, Volume XVIII (1920–1922)*. Trans. J. Strachey. London: Hogarth Press.

Freud, S. (1926). *Inhibitions, Symptoms, and Anxiety. The Standard Edition of the Complete Psychological Works of Sigmund Freud, Volume XX (1925–1926)*. Trans. J. Strachey. London: Hogarth Press.

Green, A. (1983). The Dead Mother. In A. Green (2005) *On Private Madness*. Madison, CT: International Universities Press, pp. 142–173.

Green, A. (1998). The Primordial Mind and the Work of the Negative. *International Journal of Psychoanalysis*, 79: 649–665.

Green, A. (2002). A Dual Conception of Narcissism: Positive and Negative Organizations. *Psychoanalytic Quarterly*, 71: 631–649.

Meltzer, D. (1992). *The Claustrum*. Gloucester: Clunie Press.

Sekoff, J. (1999). The Undead: Necromancy and the Inner World. In G. Kohon (ed.) (1999) *The Dead Mother: The Work of Andre Green*. New York: Routledge, pp. 109–127.

Shakespeare, W. (1997). Blakemore Evans, G. and Tobin, J. J. M. (eds.) *King Lear*. In *The Riverside Shakespeare* (Second Ed). New York: Houghton Mifflin Harcourt, p. 1,304.

Tustin, F. (1981). Psychological Birth and Psychological Catastrophe. In *Autistic States in Children*. Reprinted 1999. New York: Routledge, pp. 96–110.

Winnicott, D. W. (1955). Metapsychological and Clinical Aspects of Regression Within the Psycho-Analytical Set-up. *International Journal of Psychoanalysis*, 36: 16–26.

Winnicott, D. W. (1969). The Use of an Object. *International Journal of Psychoanalysis*, 50: 711–716.

Chapter 9

The origins of the unconscious[1]

Framework of the future mind

Arnaldo Chuster

> Even in the best interpreted dreams, we are very often obliged to leave a place in obscurity, for we note, during the interpretation, that they occasion a narration of thoughts of the dream that do not allow explanation and that do not make any other contribution to the content of the dream. This is the umbilicus of the dream, the place where it rests over the unknown.
>
> (Freud, 1900, p. 511)

> I don't suppose there will ever be a chance of knowing, so to speak, what a fetus thinks, but – to go on with my scientific fiction – I suggest that there is no reason why it shouldn't feel. I think it would be quite useful to consider that some stages of fear, of intense fear, are more easily visualized or imagined by us if we think of them as thalamic fear, or as some sort of glandular manifestation such as something to do with the adrenals, or what later turn out to be the genital structures. You can look at this as you like, say as memory traces, but these same memory traces can also be considered as a shadow which the future casts before.
>
> (Bion, 1979, pp. 236–7)

> Thought without a thinker, may assume the appearance of reality or of a hallucination.
>
> (Bion, 1980, p. 84)

Introduction

This work has as a starting point and point of arrival questions regarding the methodology of psychoanalytical investigation of the origin of the most primitive mental states. In other words, it deals with the origins of the human mind, more specifically, the origins of the unconscious.

A review of the literature on the subject, verifies that very little has been written about it. It can be said that since Freud, priority has always been given to investigating the origins of the contents that are *in* the unconscious, but very little attention has been paid to the origins of the unconscious *itself*, which we could consider as the most primitive mental state of all.

Laplanche and Pontalis (1967), referring to the origins of the unconscious, mention that the two original mechanisms described by Freud – original repression and protofantasies – are not related by him between themselves. They suggest that both perform the same role, but the suggestion does not advance and does not explain whether it is one or the other that occurs first, or if they are simultaneous. At any rate, there is no study about the origin of the primary repression or about the protofantasies that advance beyond the filogenetic theory. It can also be considered that *if* the protofantasies are by definition the nucleus of the unconscious, although not the unconscious deriving from repression, the effective existence of the unconscious is already dealt with.

Green (1967), when discussing the question, showed that in the Kleinian system if we have to indicate the relation between the original fantasy of Freud and the Kleinian conception of unconscious fantasy, it is clear that the two conceptions conform very badly with each other. In Klein the unconscious fantasy is understood as the psychic equivalent of pulsion, the unconscious is already accepted as a given fact, originated by the theoretic system of pulsion. But in Freud the original fantasy is the primary organizer of the unconscious. In fact, it is the "sensibilization" of the original fantasy, says Green (1967), that activates the repression and constitutes the unconscious. But Green does not explain what comes to be sensibilization. The first repressions organize the posterior by the attraction that the repression exercises. The original fantasy is, therefore, what the unconscious sustains of its origins and whose effects impel the individual to move their interests and activities as far as possible from the theme, although the appearance always arises in the field of these displacements to beyond the origin.

In addition to this, as an intrinsic part of the concept of modernity, in reality one of the pillars of modernity (Chuster, 1998, 1999), the unconscious is, in general, accepted as a given fact. Such a position may inhibit the doubts or the quest regarding its origins. Such inhibition from an epistemological viewpoint is no different to theology when approaching the question of the existence of God. But as we accept and/or suppose that psychoanalysis is a scientific area, the quest must not stop: when, where and why did the unconscious originate? And the unconscious being, for the psychoanalyst, above all, a notion that originates from the *experience* of analytical treatment, what are the practical implications of this questioning?

Finally, one must always emphasize that the unconscious, in the full sense of the term, is found in a relationship of essential distancing from the phenomenon of the conscious. A phenomenon of another order is dealt with, and this distancing is marked at the level of subjectivity. But subjectivity of that which proclaims knowledge is the conscious. Then it is difficult to see how the unconscious can, in its conditions of inaccessibility to the conscious, provide evidence of it. Therefore, in the first place, the unconscious is a hypothesis of the unconscious, which takes us to the field of ethics more than to knowledge. For if there is a need to try to establish the existence of the unconscious, such as in verifying a hypothesis and, considering how this hypothesis determines a *practice* that attends human suffering, it becomes fundamental to consider the ethic that conducts the project of understanding and construction of this hypothesis, as it can be constructed in a form that ignores suffering or, at least, forms in which suffering can appear.

In the light of Bion's ideas

Bion, following Freudian tradition, recognizes that one of the fundamental discoveries of psychoanalysis is the existence of primitive mental states, primitive thoughts and ideas, primitive patterns of behavior.[2] Nevertheless, in Bion, one will find a surprising *investigation* of those most primitive states and their remnants, an investigation that introduces effective new matters to be investigated.

A synthesis of this openness is found in the article Caesura (1977), inspired by a quotation of Freud, from *Inhibitions, Symptoms and Anxiety*: "There is much more continuity between intrauterine life and earliest infancy than the impressive caesura of the act of birth allows us to believe" (1926, p. 101).

In developing the article, Bion questions the veracity of this statement and asks: "are we to consider that the fetus thinks, or feels, or sees, or hears? If so, how primitive can these thoughts, or feelings, or ideas be?" (Bion, 1997, p. 44).

Furthermore he said: "I can imagine that there may be ideas which cannot be more powerfully expressed because they are buried in the future which has not happened, or buried in the remote past in such a way that it can hardly be said to belong to what we call thought" (ibid.).

In this way, Bion postulates that clinical situations exist that can pass totally unperceived because they do not form part either of what we call unconscious or of what we call conscious. They belong to a *third* realm; much more primitive than the two others and the closest to a definition he suggests is an *inaccessible mental state*.

Immediately, such a distinction, by undoing the classical dichotomy unconscious/conscious, may cause perplexity, and even confusion, unless we are able to understand that Bion, referring to the most primitive states of human life, implicitly proposes that the unconscious goes far beyond what has been described under the aegis of the term "Freudian unconscious." In other words, taking the hypothesis of unconscious to its limits, the so-called "Freudian unconscious," is only part of something wider, which Bion also called "O," when he investigated transformations (1965) within the analytical field. It is this *void of Being*, the infinitude behind all human existence, which causes the unconscious to be always in creation and in expansion, while, simultaneously, it has a conservative movement of repetition of forms.

The present work is intended to discuss some ideas regarding the utility of a theory combining these two movements – *repetition* and *expansion* – translated, respectively, by the relation between the origin of things that are *in* the unconscious and the origins of the unconscious *itself*. To do this I will resort to a mythical language, a species of science fiction, following the same methodology as Freud in *Totem and Taboo*[3] (1913). It is noted that, following Freud's model, I resort to various current theories to describe the spectral model, which is non-linear, descriptive and indeterminate, that proves the concept of the *psychoanalytical object*[4] of Bion (1962).

This type of resource is recommendable for it permits development of a language that is not directly psychoanalytical (as that of a myth or fiction[5]), so that the interpretations derived will not be saturated by observations that only precociously confirm the analytical theory utilized. Such confirmation is inevitable at some point, and as Bion says, it creates a *circular argument*[6] which we can compare to a kind of focus that establishes a field of investigation. After this everything depends on the diameter of the focus: the narrower or more saturated the focus is, the less psychoanalytical it is in the sense of *imaginative capacity*, the capacity which, as we will see, is the *link between analytic intuition and the Language of Achievement* (Bion, 1970) – the psychoanalytic language par excellence.[7]

The other vertex of this resource is to produce what Bion called *analytical preconception*, that is the vehicle of the *analytical function of the personality* – a function that decides the facts that promote the transition of the "*knowing about*" to "*becoming O*." On the part of the analyst, this function selects the facts that produce *psychoanalytical transformations*: the *emotional experience* that can lead to an interpretation able to promote a *transformation in "O"* or a process of "*how to become what you are*." These transformations are called *creative interpretations*.

In a general direction, the two vertices described above mean the more saturated by formal theory an observation is, the less is the *imaginative capacity* of the analyst, and the fewer possibilities he has to work with the idea of expansion of the unconscious, remaining more subject to the repetition of distinct forms of interpretation.

The analytical pre-conception can also be considered as an instrument which, in addition to increasing the possibilities of providing creative interpretations, diminishes the possibilities of providing interpretations saturated with memory/desire, although in the analytical process these will be inevitable at some stage, for they are part of the instability and irregularity of analytical development and of the vulnerability of the analyst faced with a series of external and internal factors.[8]

I am particularly alert here for the more saturated interpretations of memory/desire which place themselves significantly at an extreme opposed to so-called *creative interpretations*, which have, as has already been noted, the meaning of the Language of Achievement (Bion, 1970) and are related to the increase in possibilities to produce a *transformation in O*.

An auxiliary vertex on the imaginative capacity in analytical practice

In my paper "A brief survey on the differences between fantasy and imagination in the light of Bion's ideas" (2005), I tried to show that the analyst loses capacity for creative interpretations if not syntonized with the rhythms produced by what is called *radical imagination*. I reached this hypothesis investigating the problems deriving from not taking into account the differential between fantasy and imagination for, as has already been said, it is *imagination that established the link between intuition and the Language of Achievement*. If we remain only under the influence of fantasy, intuition will make links with common languages and even scientific and theoretic languages, but not with psychoanalytical language. Using the differential it is possible to perceive, and take into account, that there exists an area in the human mind that *creates* something that is not an image or a photograph of reality.[9] It is these creations that we constantly meet with in the clinic, both when we analyze dreams and when a patient brings an image of the world that is private, totally *singular*, and makes us come upon something that was not there before. Therefore, there is a moment, in the transient analytical relationship, in which you could say that the unconscious was created and what there was before it expanded. It is in this original transience that one can consider the most primitive of all *experience*, capturing the rhythms of radical imagination as well as its failures. It was in order to try to describe this that I created the title of this paper, a fiction that is called: The origins of the unconscious: Framework of the future mind.

The term *radical imagination* is borrowed from the philosophical work of Cornelius Castoriadis (1997), and with small modifications of a practical order, I tried to describe *the original element of intuition*, seeking to differentiate it from the Kleinian notion of projective identification (unconscious fantasy), which arises later (for I understand that the Kleinian concept already implies the existence of an unconscious). However, the radical imagination, as origin, represents a nucleus of the preconception, originating the *first realizations* in the world of the embryonic mind, before the distinction of any object. But how does this happen? And should we call the final products of these realizations "conceptions"? And how is the product of this "embryonic mind" formulated and maintained even after birth?

The radical imagination,[10] in its first habitat, is naturally activated by acoustical and kinesthetic *rhythms*,[11] such as the rhythm of the mother's heart, the rhythm of the baby's heart, the intestinal peristaltic rhythm, the rhythm of the bladder, the balance of amniotic fluid, all of them expressing the mother's day-to-day routine, and therefore, the society around – the imaginative possibilities are infinite. However, what stand out are the effects of those rhythms and oscillations in this "pre-subjective" world: they provoke a species of explosion which opens space and creates a kind of cylinder[12] or an " empty window" whose frames are made of *time*. Time that begins to organize a pre-view of the world that is to come. In this sense, the psychoanalytical model of Bion is prospective and temporal: the mind of the fetus develops, expands, in the "prevision" of having to cope with certain situations that will appear in the gaseous medium, but in a certain way have already arrived as a *memory of the future*. The window (preconception) is a preparation for future situations (and can develop adequately or can transform into pathologies). It is always original to the experience of expansion, and relates itself to the dominion of imagination. Repetition, which is in the ambit of fantasy, is still not dealt with.

It is worth noting that a theory about an *inaccessible mental state* must permit that all questions inherent in the creation of meanings during psychoanalytic work can be applied. It is *radical* (a root of all concepts) because it creates *ex nihilo*. It does not create images in the visual sense, but pure forms, not saturated, that can transform into all types of images (as, for example, an acoustic image, that activates the precedent productive imagination to a creative interpretation).

After describing my science fiction I shall raise a few questions, which might be related to the vicissitudes of the origins of the unconscious, through a few clinical situations. Although, as we all know, to place such experiences in reports is easier said than done.

The origins of the unconscious: The embryonic frames of the future mind

There was a moment in the evolution of the species (between 4 to 2.5 millions of years ago) when a kind of primate, 120cm tall, inhabitant of the African savannas (probably the Australopithecus), developed a refined capacity to observe his predators. This ability produced important developments in his central nervous system (or vice versa[13]). At the same time, he developed an ability to use his vocal chords, which had extended much more than the other species, for he was walking on two back feet (it was easier and faster to carry babies and things) and stretching his neck to look at the distance in order to keep a better vigilance against the predators (a kind of tiger which ate him and a kind of elephant which trampled him). His vocal chords became capable of producing varied and differing sounds (a species of preconception of the human language) which could cause fear and paralyze his predators. This language also served as a model for throwing things (stones and branches of trees, which were later transformed into lances and bone arrows) that could hurt and cause pain and, eventually, kill the predators. It was also not very long before he discovered the power of the shouts of a group, which added the potential capacity of attack and defense. However, these combined abilities caused catastrophic changes in the species.

At first, the newly developed abilities made him observe and feel the presence of a terrible, invisible and constant predator: a huge tension caused by the observation of signs coming from the intimacy between biosystems separated from each other by millions of years in the evolutionary scale, such as the distance between the origins of the peripheral nervous system and the appearance of a developed central nervous system (a difference of around 550 million years).

Owing to this enormous tension (which today may be called persecutory anxiety), the systems approached chaos, and as happens in this kind of event, the almost chaotic system *autopoietically* (Zeleny, 1981) produced a solution: the *space*, that was naturally linear, bidimensional and concrete, present in all living species since the beginning of evolution, *folded* in an attempt to reorganize a relationship between the systems. However, this resulted in the production of a new approach to chaos, with the appearance of experiences of *time*, plus experiences of outer and inner space, in addition to massive perceptions of loss of individuality with consequent fragility and helplessness. This complexity gradually became what today is called thinking and mental space.

With the increase of these persecutory and frightening experiences (protothoughts), the tension of the loss of individuality (perception of dependence and loneliness), which can be defined as *constitutive*, became so powerful that the folded space reached a point near *chaos* again and once more, autopoietically, produced another solution, this time *a force of disconnection*, which started working simultaneously with the force that kept the system working.

Because of the conflict between the two forces, fully described by Freud as life and death instincts, the biological erosion and procreation which had so far followed the natural cycles as in the rest of the animals, acquired an autonomy that abolished nearly all the animal instincts then occurring by virtue of time–space experiences (triangular). In addition to this, whenever the complexity reached a specific limit of tension, the species became capable of voluntarily and violently auto-disconnecting from the other members.

In order to maintain the equilibrium between the opposite forces, the folded space was forced to change objects between external and internal mediums. This produced a function equivalent to a digestive function, the basis of a rudimentary language that is still evolving today. However, due to a part that was still confusing the external with the internal, which means an extra source of the disruptive tension, the system approached chaos again, and the new solution was to close completely over itself, acquiring a defensive cylindrical form. Thus, the digestive function also acted in executing a function of closure, like a sewing function.

If successful, this first function (Bion called it *alpha function*) creates a kind of net, which Bion called a *contact barrier*, clearly separating the external world from the inside. But if it fails it creates a kind of a tissue composed of irregular holes (which Bion called the *beta screen)*, which could bring back the previous confusion between external and internal worlds (Bion, 1962).

Digested and non-digested objects compose the two basic elements for the language of the system, that is, according to Bion, *alpha and beta elements.*[14] From these two hypothetical elements the cylinder form can create other elements and grow towards a negative or a positive direction (if one considers the social tendency as positive, as this was the successful way to protect the species).

On the external part of the cylinder, the digestive function could be named an *alpha function of the Self* (Meltzer, 1997a), working to bring inside the system symbols of the group and of the culture (acquired symbols). Inside the cylinder is the *alpha function of the internal objects*, which transforms the acquired symbols into autonomous symbols (peculiar to each individual).

A brief discussion of the myth in search of a clinical application

Up to a certain point in human evolution the language of primates, whose representations are defined in a fixed and repetitive form by instincts, completely dominated communication. The Central Nervous System, up to then a servant of the other systems (and, therefore, of fixed representations), operated as in the rest of the mammals, in a *functional form*. That is, the pre-human sexual representation was linked to reproduction, through a sexual cycle, the estrus. Apart from that, pre-humans lived in hordes in a certain way ignoring one another, except when seeking food.

But there was a point when intense chaotic experiences in the complex association of the bio-systems, caused by a rapid and intense gain in autonomy of the Central Nervous System, meant that human representations were no longer fixed or predetermined by the reproductive function. The Central Nervous System ceased to be a servant and became the master of the systems and, more than this, created something that is, from the point of view of the animals, an aberration – the human mind. It produced another type of language (of dreams, idioms, deductive scientific systems, mathematical calculations, social institutions, laws and ethics). Hence, another way of functioning, which has nothing to do with the reproductive function, began to regulate the human species. One may call it *disfunctionalization*, a very disturbing and permanent source of emotional turbulence deriving from the existence of something Bion called *preconception*, whose theory[15] is fundamental for the understanding of the diverse questions raised in this work. It is postulated that it establishes a difference between the human psyche and that of the animal, and as the most ancient mental element, possesses manifestations that were already present in the intrauterine medium. After preconception, the human being became, irreversibly, a mental being in all its implications.

There is a range of clinical situations that can place us in contact with the latent or manifest existence of *chaotic experiences*, where it is useful not to start from the idea of what we call the unconscious, or even what is called the conscious, but to start from the idea of the *inaccessible*, for which a new window of understanding could occur. I am thinking here of those patients who suffer from diverse confusions, such as those mentioned by Bion (1962), who cannot dream; therefore they cannot sleep or be awake, that is, they suffer a confusion between being awake and sleeping.

I remember here the case supervised by Bion (1987), of a woman of 32 who never used the couch. She would enter and say: "Today, I will not be able to stay seated here." The analyst asked questions to clarify the position, but to each question the replies of the patient made the situation more confused. The more she was asked the less she explained. This was the mathematics of the situation. Bion called attention to the use the patient made of the questions of the analyst, which had the intention of not having to advance. He said that with a patient like this, he would begin to suspect that she did not really know the difference between dreaming and being awake, or that she didn't know the difference between a love affair and psychoanalysis. He said: "However, the most immediate matter is what to say to the patient?" (1987, pp. 6–7). We come to the moment when we give an interpretation. There are millions of them, but there is only one experience, and this is the experience that the analyst has with the patient. We can discuss the matter, but this is not psychoanalysis, it is about psychoanalysis. The feeling that the analyst has is that something is occurring and can only be known if the patient comes to it and gives opportunity to try it. In the end, this is the moment when things originate.

An equivalent of this condition is encountered in those patients for whom contact with reality presents great difficulty above all when the reality is their own mental state (Bion, 1970). These are patients who do not tolerate pain and frustration, and confuse them in a very specific way; they feel the pain but do not suffer it and because of this condition they cannot be helped to discover it. Consequently, they are also unable to "suffer" pleasure and this denies them the necessary encouragement to receive help from someone or from themselves. They behave as if an action should precede another action, in a mental movement that leaves aside almost all elements that produce thinking. They remain in a very painful mental state, living with the minimum amount of thinking and feelings.

Bion also mentions certain individuals who, after trying to do everything possible to free themselves of certain archaic and intolerable mental states, later in their lives feel the reappearance of these experiences in a very violent form: "There are certain premature and precocious developments that are too precocious and too premature to be tolerable. Therefore, the fetus, the id, does its best to cut that connection. In a later stage of life the individual can auto-disconnect" (1987, p. 224).

I also add here those patients who present a somato-psychotic (or psychosomatic) situation, that is, in whom a part of the body, or a system, or the functioning of the mind itself, is identified as a predator and, because of this, is attacked in various forms. We can include in these descriptions the exclusively human illnesses, such as autism, the autoimmune illnesses, diverse situations of immunological vulnerability, illnesses developed precociously, and even a situation such as eclampsia. The possibility that one may encounter such situations in the clinic, along with those that do not fit into these more evident areas, are much more frequent than we are used to admitting. To relate these states to an unconscious that has still not formed, to an inaccessible mental state, may bring a new understanding which will increase liberty of imaginative conjectures.

A quotation from Bion's *Memoir of the Future III, The Dawn of Oblivion* illustrates these states well:

> *24th "somite"*: You are prejudiced. If I knew that I would create a soul, I would have remained a fetus.
>
> *25 years*: If I knew that I had an ancestral somite so ugly, I would not have tried to cultivate a soul.
>
> (1977, p. 30)

Indications of the existence of these problems of basic mental development can appear in patients who confuse (sometimes grossly and at other times subtly) realizations and values such as: error with harm, failure with prejudice, criticism with denigration, loss of youth with aging, sincerity with sociability, intimacy with lack of privacy, friendship with social relationship, loving passion with passionate love, thoughts with thinking, envy with jealousy, voracity with efficiency, resolution of problems with control of situations, etc. These confusions very often have devastating consequences for the social system of the individual, leading to serious ethical distortions in human relationships. In a general way they are related to bad actions and bad decisions.

Very often these patients bring situations in which we suddenly experience something like being enveloped by a thick and strange mist that obscures our field of observation; our perception becomes restricted to some vague objects while others appear to have no connection with each other, producing a sensation of discomfort, or somnolence, or the uselessness of work realized. Very often perturbing images arise, along with emotions related to apparently strange facts at that moment, facts related to primitive emotions, disturbing scenes, and postural indisposition. John Milton, the writer and poet, called this "*oedipal gloom*"[16] (quoted in Cormican, 1982, p. 56). We are dealing here with a situation in which every question turns back on itself: What is happening with the patient? Is it the same as is happening to the analyst?

Case 1

A male patient, 47 years old, frequently complained of not sleeping well. His description of how he spent the night suggests those patients described by Bion who neither succeeded in sleeping nor being awake, for they didn't dream. However, with the evolution of the analytical process, after much work on his confusion between internal and external reality, this patient related that he dreamt at the weekend that he was in a session of analysis, but observed that both the analyst and the analysand were sleeping heavily. Then he wakes up, looks at the clock, sees that it is 5 o'clock in the morning, and says to the analyst, in a censoring manner, that he shouldn't have been there for such a long time. But, as the analyst is sleeping and doesn't hear the complaint, he only wakes him up to advise him that their time is up.

After relating the dream, the only thing that the patient said (with a certain irony) was that it was very curious that both were sleeping in the session. A silence followed and the analyst captured a sensation of tedium and repetition.

Here we have a patient who dreams that he is in a session of analysis and can be asleep and awake at the same time. He can also calculate and dream, or he can dream calculating and calculate dreaming, but when relating the dream he does not make associations, which appears calculated to explain to the analyst that this dream is not capable of being analyzed. However, the patient expressed himself through non-verbal language for I could observe him, while reporting the dream, design in the air with the index finger the number 5 in reverse with a circle around it and a final dot. This released in the analyst a series of rational and imaginative conjectures, starting with Freud, who showed that the numbers in dreams could be analyzed. It is also not prudent to assume that a dream is something that did not happen. On the contrary, it is more appropriate to consider that it is in fact that which is occurring at the moment.

Returning to the patient, it may appear that he was having a prolonged session that extended to the weekend: the rhythm was not broken. There is a delay that could attend what apparently could be a desire not to separate from the analyst.

An analyst sleeping could not interpret anything and could not end the session. But, on the other hand, in the session in progress the patient not associating anything could have gone back to "sleep" without having been woken up. In some way, distinct from the habitual, he had not separated from the analyst and he could remain in what we can call a state of sensory equality: both sleeping. There remains something linked to the language of the number 5, which dictated the condition of awakening (where the patient evidently did not act in accordance with initial intentions: one of his repetitive attitudes). The meeting of imaginative conjectures and rational conjectures of the analyst remembers the *private myth* of the analysand, an inquiry: could the number be linked to the fact of being the only son of a woman who aborted 5 times before being able to give birth to the patient, after many complications? (this mother was in coma for 35 days during the 6th and 7th month of pregnancy, due to the rupture of a cerebral aneurism). Transference of a failure of a maternal function? Did some failure by the analyst contribute to this? Or does the analyst always fails to separate? But in a certain way, the analysand knows all this, so to repeat interpretations with this content would be to give them a routine or, perhaps, doctrinaire character.

I have tried to emphasize in this work that, as in any other moment of analysis, the thoughts of the dream, to which we have access in the course of an interpretation, depend very much on the *creative imagination* of the analyst, which obligatorily makes the interpretations remain open without a defined conclusion following the ethic–esthetic principle of incompleteness[17] since they come from all sides of the intricate network of our world of thoughts – most of them we do not succeed in describing in clinical reports. Regarding this inaccessible entanglement, complementing his quotation regarding the umbilicus of the dream (p. 135), Freud (1900, p. 511) says: "From the densest place of this entanglement, arises then the desire of the dream, like a mushroom from its mycelium."

I think that this quotation refers to the most primitive mental state, which is almost chaotic, from where an interpretation emerges and can eventually reveal the content of the dream. Here also is where we see the crossroad between an interpretation that can be in some way saturated with memory and desires, interpreting a repetition of the analysand, or giving a *creative interpretation* that could reveal a mental *expansion* of an analytical link. It is in this last option that the understanding of the most primitive mental state, *the origins of the unconscious*, can perhaps help, permitting thinking that there is something "inaccessible" present, which could activate a *psychoanalytical preconception.*[18]

This patient, who came for analysis living serious conflictive situations due to the use of drugs, as far as it was possible for me to perceive, on many other occasions sought a sensory agreement with my interpretations. He appeared to listen to them, for he maked an affirmative gesture with the head. However, after some time, I perceived that he internally rejects the parts that disturb him and silently substitutes them for other false knowledge – this logic, privately impeccable, then becomes the vehicle of a false premise to arrive at a moralistic meaning (transformation in hallucinosis – Bion, 1965). As a result, he places the analyst with a moral function that he is obviously not authorized to exercise, silently disqualifying the analysis and any interpretation.

Such disagreements, being silent, and at other times conveyed through an agreement that is in fact not a communication of meanings, but a species of false propaganda, may be maintained indefinitely, and the "analysis" will "go along," with both participants "sleeping," always missing the moment to speak about what is happening right now in the session. This is the equivalent of remaining in an area saturated with memory and desire, which creates a link destined not to speak about what is happening in the session. At other moments it is, perhaps, equivalent to remaining in a state in which one is neither "awake" nor "sleeping."

This patient, in very primitive states of his life, that is, in "the inaccessible before birth" and, certainly, when he was a baby, felt, in various ways, the presence of a mother now completely absent, now exhausted and depressed, and developed a "window" of resentments which, later in life, made him incapable of pardoning failures in human beings, which also caused a lack of genuine interest in himself and in others. In the end, this incapacity to differentiate, in the human ambit, failure from an irreparable damage led to the construction of a world regulated by the moral annihilation of his concern with the truth and with ethics, which also meant he had sacrificed his ability to take part in life in favor of a state of torpor and, consequently, in the analysis, my interpretation of the dream.

In this material, I have tried to illustrate an aspect of clinical material in which a complementary interpretation could be thought of between repetitive aspects of the patient an aspect of the unconscious that can be called "inaccessible." This is to approach what Freud (1900) called the "*mycelium of the mushroom*," the entanglement close to chaos, before any meaning. There is a confrontation between repetitive aspects of the patient and an aspect of the unconscious that was never conscious of anything, because it remains inaccessible. In this situation could we observe what Freud metaphorically called "*the mycelium of the mushroom*," the network close to chaos, before any meaning? But what, more specifically, is this "mycelium" seen to be?

One can consider that "*the mushroom*" is a moment of integration of the elements of love, hatred and the thirst for knowledge (emotional experience) (Meltzer, 1997b), which up to that point had been dissociated and spread over a chaotic entanglement, in a state of profound uncertainty. It is the painful state of uncertainty that produces so many defenses, principally those that have anti-emotion links (–K, –L, –H). These experiences are situated in a "before" the word, therefore it is necessary to be able to imagine, and esthetically conceive, some form of interpretation of the development that adopts an ethic that places human respect for life in general on the first plain. What are called ethical–esthetical principals collaborate in this task.

Case 2

A 33-year-old woman patient started her session saying, with a mixture of sadness and anxiety, how happy the animals were because it was easy for them to become pregnant, then remained silent with nothing to say. She had been occupying the last week's sessions with her feelings of unhappiness for she was having serious difficulty becoming pregnant. The medical treatments that she had been trying had all failed. It could be observed that on this occasion any interpretation that she would receive in analysis would also fail. Why repeat what could be a difficulty to receive help? From the theoretical point of view, where there is what we call preconception, she was encountering an inadequate realization that only led to an infertile emptiness.

I could have proposed investigating her painful feelings of uncertainty in relation to analytical treatment (a routine interpretation), but instead I thought that it would be useful to open a window that could be called Oedipal preconception in a search for the realization as link K or "*thirst for knowledge*." Or better, that which is imagined, that which represents, whether on the conscious plain or the unconscious, is not determined by biological functionality. Even if this may occur from time to time, in human beings sexual life is entirely determined by unconscious fantasies. For this reason I asked the patient: "How many sexual acts whose objective is reproduction could someone perform in the course of a lifetime?" I also asked myself: "What is the profundity of the problem of reproduction? In what way do a couple involved with problems of fertility find themselves in the same position as religious fundamentalists who believe that they should only have sexual relations for the purpose of reproduction?"

I mentioned the analogy between a couple experiencing a problem of infertility (which I could represent by the couple Laius and Jocasta) and the religious fundamentalists, but I could also imagine that the problem of this couple concealed an analogy with primitive religions, polytheists and totemic, whose rituals were moved by the cult of gods of fertility. They are all motivated by a type of passion. What is the functionality of this passion or of any other experienced by the human being? To what extent does the sexual act, when it is only a submission to the totem, lose its beauty and is attacked and feared as if it was a predator? Can we call this envy – a species of need to inhibit the good objects that produce growth (Bion, 1970)? Or a necessity to interfere with the good object's capacity for the esthetic experience, and thus with the relationship with the truth (Meltzer, 1997b)? In what way does envy constitute the frame of certain windows by which the world is seen as a world of predators (Chuster and Trachtenberg, 2004)? Certain questions put to the patient in the analytical process necessarily do not have a reply and we cannot wait for an answer. Neither do they increase the knowledge about oneself. Thus, analysis is not a question of going to a kind of an Oracle, following the advertisement to "know thyself" indicated on the portal, and leaving there with the knowledge of destiny. Many things, and perhaps the greater part of the analytical process, unfold by the *emotional experience*, in addition to words, that certain questions, functioning as interpretations or constructions, awake in the analysand. Often it is the "rhythm" of the feelings behind the interpretations that permits the unfolding of the analytical relation (as in any human relationship). The maintenance of the rhythm is, therefore, essential to the analysis. The knowledge may not increase in the intellectual sense, but the mental space does increase, thanks to the movement of mental states and the filling of the "frames of the windows of the mind" with new realizations.

These windows, formed in the embryonic mind, still empty of landscape, when entering into contact with the mother who reappears soon after the birth, making the breasts available, gain the triadic landscape: the newly born, the breast, the mother. The breast remains at the crossroads, in the zone of the crossing of the relationship of the baby with the mother: it is the preconception of the breast being realized when realizing the Oedipal preconception. But we can always suppose that something preceded this crossroad; another crossroad formed, and it is not possible to imagine that this did not happen in some way with violence, for there is always a social reality, exterior, independent, transformable and separable, breaking the closure of any pre-object or any posterior object, allowing the above quotation of Freud in the inverse sense: *There is much more continuity between social reality and intra-uterine life than the impressive isolation of the fetus in the uterus permits us to believe.* Thus, many questions function as this species of "social invasion" in this world closed to meaning, offering a species of horizon of unknown events and unfilled landscapes: a spectrum of other possibilities to be experienced.

Case 3

A woman patient, 42 years old, starts the session, relating, terrorized, an uncontrolled attitude she adopted – but, contradictorily judged positive, for it obtained results in relation to her adolescent son, of whom she often complained in a mechanical way because of the disorderly way he cared for things. An interpretation that could be called "routine" tried in previous sessions to place her in contact with her adolescence and disorderly part, showing her that she was not being sincere in the session about her suffering. However, such interpretations did nothing to modify the depressive state she brought to analysis, for she said that she didn't suffer, for where she thought she should manifest irritation there was an "emptiness." This patient, who routinely confused looking after someone with sacrifice, and confused controlling problems with resolving them, lost her parents in an aerial accident when she was two months old. She was brought up by elderly grandparents.

Not only as analysts, but also as common people, we can have some knowledge that real mothers and fathers become irritated in certain situations with adolescent children and express an opinion – even if they don't like it at all. There is an important link between generations formed by feelings and opinions. The conflict between them is also essential for the acquisition of identity.

The patient said that the son became very shocked with the type of anger that she expressed. The husband, who was arriving home, also displayed shock. Both were livid and embarrassed. Although speaking of the presence of a terrified object, the patient proceeded in her habitual monotonous rhythm, associating her anger with a failed attempt to give up smoking (a few sessions ago when the subject of smoking came up I asked her if smoking could be considered as part of the indiscipline in her life or, perhaps, a species of symbol of a husband who treated her badly and smothered her – another of her complaints). At this session it appeared to me that she oscillated between being superficial and being euphoric and it seemed that her feeling was strengthened in her hatred, which she said she had never experienced (which can also be called mortal). I could, however, go further and imagine just how primitive this hatred could be. Four million years ago, pre-humans, or better, the pre-conceptions of humans, organized themselves into groups to defend themselves from predators. They had a circular disposition that remained practically stable during the nights on the savannas. On the periphery were located the defenders of the group, in a mental state ready to fight or give the signal to flee in mass; the appropriate sentiments for this external circle are hate, fear and alertness (initiative). In the innermost circle were the babies and the mothers who cared for them, those incapacitated by age or by wounds, the pregnant females, the small children. Their mental state was of total dependence on the rest, for their activities were focused on feeding and caring. Between the two circles were the mating couples. A male of the outer circle came seeking a female on the inside to mate, generally in a despotic form, threatening the children who protested and were deprived of the mother's care, or attacking some young male who wanted to emerge from the inner circle to the intermediary.

Through my imaginative conjectures I could place the masculine part of this patient in the external circle, emerging as a defender and protector of her family group. To do this she had to make contact with the ferocity of her hatred and with her stupidity (as she described the situation), with which to "educate" the dependent son to have "respect" for her husband. She, a sophisticated and cultured person, always very passive and apparently friendly, met unexpectedly the existence of a very primitive state, a world up to then inaccessible and violent, that was still to become conscious. As Bion says at the end of his article "Making the Best of a Bad Job": "That war has not ceased yet" (1979, p. 257).

Notes

1 Paper presented to the 10th Annual Primitive Mental States Conference, Los Angeles, California, 14–15 May 2005, with the title *The Origins of the Unconscious: "Wind-O-ws" of the Mind.*

An outline of this work was first presented to the meeting, Bion in Vashon, Seattle, Washington, 8–9 February 2005. I would like to express my deep gratitude to colleagues Jane Van Buren, Jim Gooch, John Stone, Katina Kostoulas, Kirby Ogden, Marianne Robinson, Maxine Anderson and Shirley Gooch for their generous listening and helpful suggestions.

2 "These primitive elements have consequences today, supposing, for example, that the remnants of the branquial pit develops as a tumor of the branquial pit. In this way, certain primitive elements may exist that are detectable in our personalities or minds that are, in fact, survivors and that are capable of proliferating in a beneficial form, but also in a cancerous form, a pathological form. This is the only reason that makes it interesting to attend a patient today, tomorrow and in the future in the event that he or she accepts being observed again" (Bion, 1997).

3 In this text, Freud uses a *methodology* that employs an *anthropologic* myth that describes the pre-historical mental state. It was not Freud's intention to practice anthropology, but to produce in anthropologic language a *theoretical* function about the *horde* as precursor of the family, describing the existence of a primitive mental state as the producer of unconscious objects (nothing more than his psychoanalytic model). At the same time, Freud gives filogenetic roots to the Oedipus complex, crossing them with the descriptions of the vicissitudes of the ontogenesis.

4 The concept arose in *Learning from Experience*, (1962, Chapter 22), through the formula: $\psi(\xi)$ $(\pm Y)$ (M), meaning: *preconception* $\psi(\xi)$ seeks a *realization* in the developmental spectrum *narcissism* $\Leftrightarrow$ *social-ism* $(\pm Y)$ to create a conception under the sponsorship of the inherent *complexity* (M) of a biological organism.

5 The oneiric qualities of this type of language, as will be emphasized throughout this work, best attend the *imagination* of the analyst, that can permit, as happens with a writer, who proceeds describing their characters, step by step, being surprised by their words and feelings, while the intrigue develops.

6 In reality a typically Freudian argument, for initially the focus assimilates an archeologist investigating origins. When it is supposed that they have been reached, the whole problem is relocated in a mythical way, reconstructing in the direction of the original question which, being remade, does not give answers.

7 Derived from what Bion (1970) called an "act of faith" that would be the scientific mental state of the analysis, that is, the mental state *without* desire, *without* memory and *without* necessity to understand.

8 In the work "Analytical interpretations and ethical-esthetical principles of observation" (44th International Psychoanalytical Association Congress, July 2005), I approached the question of the vulnerability of the analyst through the spectrum memory ⇔ desire, relating it with corresponding forms of interpretation to the transformations described by Bion (1965). These are: (1) "*explicative explanations*," which go from information regarding the factual reality of the analysis to an interpretation that is only knowledge about the mind of the analysand (corresponding to the transformations in K); (2) "*routine interpretations*" – a term used by Meltzer (1973), which understands as interpretations pathways in the memory of the analyst, basically aimed at explaining the present through the past. Examples are the classic Freudian interpretations: however necessary they may be, they always have an inevitable loss of significance for the analysand – and coincide with what Bion (1965) called transformation in rigid motion; (3) "*doctrinaire or seductive interpretations*," which correspond to the projective transformations described by Bion (1965), with accentuated loss of significance for the analysand. Examples are classic Kleinian interpretations saturated with meanings, which prevent the analysand from thinking and, also, the mutative interpretations of Strachey. According to Meltzer (1997a), mutative interpretations are grandiose notion with *furor curandi:* the analyst has a belief that he says the right thing and that his words will enter the head of the analysand, effecting a change of thinking. This intention would be equivalent to brainwashing and has the value of propaganda, therefore it is called doctrinaire; and finally (5), at the extreme of interpretative possibilities, I describe "*pompous interpretations*," which are totally paved with the desire of the analyst, with total loss of significance for the analysand, and can reach megalomaniac proportions, coinciding with what Bion (1965) called transformation in hallucinosis. *Creative interpretations* related to transformation in O emerge from tolerance of ethical–esthetical principles of observation: uncertainty of observation, incomplete interpretations, inability to decide points of relationship and complexity of the psychoanalytical object.

9 The belief that there can be such a thing is provided by ancient concepts of learning and the nature of the traces of memory. A trace of memory is not the impression of some type of external reality, as is the image of internal reality, but a modification of functional possibilities in the mental structure according to a process of *learning from experience* (Imbasciati, 2005).

10 The first difficulty in working with this concept is in the word "imagination" itself, which is commonly related to images. This is elaborated imagination. I am referring to phenomena that are not visual. They are essentially auditory and kinesthetic.

11 Objects (or experiences) exist that are olfactory, auditive kinetic. They are, in the intrauterine medium, very much more important than the visual object (or experience).

12 Such a framework also constitutes frames of the levels of the spectrum of realization of preconceptions, the spectrum narcissism ⇔ social-ism: believe ⇒ think ⇒ learning from experience ⇒ create.

13 The uncertainty about origins is always present. To observe these areas it is necessary to take into account the ethical–esthetical principle of undecidability (Chuster, 2002, 2004).

14 Communication between terrestrial mammals occurs through patterns related mainly to the rules and vicissitudes of the link. This is an iconic-analogical communication composed of kinesthetic mediums such as body movements, muscular tensions and changes in the face and in sounds of respiration. In human beings this language (beta elements) is still very strong and sensitive. We can place it in the external part of the fold, while in the internal part is placed the recently acquired digital language composed of alpha elements.
15 Some authors, among them myself, (1989, 1996), reached identification of innate preconception with what Freud called *proto-fantasies* (*Urphantasien*). I no longer share this theoretical comparison. I think that preconception has a new direction, as a nuclear element of the *psychoanalytical object* (Bion, 1962). With this concept, Bion introduces a *change of paradigm* to analytical understanding, whose corresponding scientific dimension is the theory of complexity (Waldrop, 1992). To the extent that I learned the concept better, my conception of the analytical process was modified. If before I was already distancing myself from the medical model and the concept of cure, it was clear that one could not furnish analysis to someone as if it was medicine, taken for a determined time, or prescribed for determined times until the symptoms disappeared. I consider that psychoanalysis is within persons, as a fundamental psychic function, in a potential state, varying from individual to individual – that is, some possess more than others – and these differences of *mobility* can be captured in practice. In other words, psychoanalysis is a specific sensibility to discover the meaning of life in general, which the so-called *analytical process* aims to bring to light and develop, in the event of finding the *Minimum Conditions Necessary* for realization.
16 A tragic confinement being predominant without outlet for the language where the fight for objects is evident and can be worked through.
17 The ethical–esthetic principles of observation (Chuster and colls., 1999, 2003, 2005).
18 The imaginative activity of the analyst, activated by preconception, and revealed to the analysand by the interpretation – or by a construction, or questioning – is a way to share feelings and anticipatory thoughts. It is connected with prudence in the action, which Bion (1979) describes as the *three principles of life*, substituting the two Freudian principles – pleasure versus reality – of mental functioning.

References

Bion, W. R. (1962). *Learning from Experience*. London: Heinemann.
—— (1965). *Transformations: Change from Learning to Growth*. London: Heinemann.
—— (1970). *Attention and Interpretation*. London: Tavistock.
—— (1977). *Two Papers: The Grid and Caesura*. Rio de Janeiro: Imago.
—— (1977). *A Memoir of the Future Vol. III: The Dawn of Oblivion*. Rio de Janeiro: Imago.
—— (1979). Making the Best of a Bad Job. In: *Clinical Seminars and Four Papers*. Abingdon, Fleetwood Press, 1987, pp. 247–257.
—— (1980). *A Key to a Memoir of the Future*. Perthshire: Clunie Press.
—— (1987). Evidence. In: *Clinical Seminars and Four Papers*. Abingdon: Fleetwood Press, p. 224.

—— (1997). *Taming Wild Thoughts*. London: Karnac Books.
Castoriadis, C. (1997). *As Encruzilhadas do Labirinto V*. Rio de Janeiro: Paz e Terra.
Chuster, A. (1989). *Um Resgate da Originalidade*. Rio de Janeiro: Degrau.
—— (1996). *Diálogos Psicanalíticos sobre W .R. Bion*. Rio de Janeiro: Tipo e Grafia.
—— (1998). Bion cria de fato uma nova psicanálise? *Revista da SPPA, Vol V: 3.*
—— (1999). *W .R. Bion: Novas Leituras, Vol I*. Rio de Janeiro: Companhia de Freud.
—— (2002). *An Oedipal Grid*. Paper presented at The International Conference on the Work of W. R. Bion, Los Angeles, California.
—— (2004). Uma Grade Edípica. In *W.R. Bion: Novas Leituras Vol II*. Rio de Janeiro: Companhia de Freud.
—— (2005). *Analytical interpretations and the ethical-estethical principles of observation*. Paper presented at the International Psychoanalytical Association Congress, Rio de Janeiro, July 2005.
Chuster, A. and Trachtenberg, R. (2004). Envy. Paper presented at The Bion Encounter, São Paulo.
Cormican, L. A. (1982). Milton's Religious Verses. In: Ford, B. (ed.) (1982) *The New Pelican Guide to English Literature*. Middlesex: Penguin.
Freud, S. (1900). *The Interpretation of Dreams*. New York: Macmillan.
—— (1913). Totem and Taboo. *Standard Edition 13: 1–161*. London: Hogarth Press, 1958.
—— (1926). Inhibitions, Symptoms and Anxiety. *Standard Edition 20*. London: Hogarth Press.
Green, A. (1967). *Les Discours Vivant*. Paris: Presses Universitaries de France.
Imbasciati, A. (2005). Psicoanalisi e Cognitivismo: Uma Nuova Teoria Sulle Origini e il Funcionamento della Mente. Roma: Armando Editore, pp. 103–111.
Laplanche, J. and Pontalis, J.-B. (1967). *Vocabulaire de la Psychanalyse*. Paris: Presses Universitaires de France, pp. 486–489.
Meltzer, D. (1973). *Sexual States of Mind*. Perthshire, Scotland: Clunie Press.
—— (1997a). *Meltzer in São Paulo*. São Paulo: Casa do Psicólogo.
—— (1997b). *Sincerity and Other Works: Collected Papers of Donald Meltzer*. London: Karnac.
Waldrop, M. (1992). *Complexity*. New York: Simon and Schuster, p. 67.
Zeleny, M. (1981). *Autopoiesis: A Theory of Living Organization*. New York: North Holland.

Chapter 10

Pre-verbal language in the treatment of a mother and infant

A clinical exploration

Annie Reiner

Increasing knowledge about early emotional life and the nature of primitive mental states has generated more interest in direct psychoanalytic work with infants and babies as a mode of clinical intervention. After a brief review of some of the literature on early emotional life and on the development of language, I will present detailed clinical material of a mother and baby – "Mrs. G" and "Ellie" – whom I saw together in treatment for ten months. I will examine the communication between them and the effects of verbal interpretations of emotional states on each of them. I will also present a few prenatal observations about Mrs. G's "interaction" with her fetus, observations which, despite their basis in psychoanalytic thought, must be seen to remain in the intuitive realm of what Bion called "rational conjectures" (Bion, 2000, p. 204).

Mrs. G was the identified patient, having been in psychoanalytic psychotherapy for a year before she became pregnant. She brought Ellie to her twice weekly sessions regularly for about five months, not wanting to leave her small infant. After that she brought her intermittently for approximately four months, ostensibly because of child care limitations, but her need for emotional support in understanding her infant was also evident from the start. For one thing, she feared a recurrence of postpartum depression, from which she had suffered after the birth of her first child, but she had also come to see that early trauma in her own life had contributed to a detachment from her emotional life which she did not want to visit upon her baby.

Theoretical background to work with infants

Johan Norman (2004) adapted concepts of repression and the unconscious to the infantile experience, speaking of repressed memories already stored in the young infant's mind. One little boy of three months, for instance, showed fluctuating interest in his mother which Norman related to his memories of having had his mother's anxiety projected into him. Having then split off his anxiety, along with his anger at her, the emotional link to his mother had been severed (Norman, 2004, p. 1118). This is in line with Fairbairn's (1952) theories, discussed below, regarding the effects of maternal projections into the child and the subsequent emotional detachment from the mother as well as from the child's own emotional reality.

Many of Piontelli's findings echo Freud's statement, "There is much more continuity between intra-uterine life and earliest infancy than the impressive caesura of the act of birth would have us believe" (1926, p. 138). Klein felt that a child was born with a character and that mental life existed at birth, and in "Caesura" (1975), Bion discussed the idea of vestiges of prenatal mental life, conjecturing about fetal, even embryonic, proto-mental memories analogous to physical vestiges of our phylogenetic heritage in fetal development. In her research, Piontelli (1987) saw evidence of a distinct individual character in the fetus observable through its behavior even in the early stages. The fetus is not isolated from the outside world, for it hears the mother's voice, heart beat and borborygmi, and feels her emotions through changes in arterial pressure. Through ultrasound, Piontelli showed the fetus' responsiveness to sound, touch and taste; at 14 weeks the fetus could swallow, suck and react to pain, with some form of primitive learning taking place as well. By 15 weeks, all movements seen in the fetus at term were already present. This already complex perceptual, motor and mental apparatus belied the image of intrauterine life as blissful nirvana.

Piontelli's (1989) observation of a case of twins revealed what appeared to be intra-uterine memories re-enacted in the child's play after birth. While still in the womb, Luke and his sister, Alicia, would gently stroke each other's faces through the membrane which separated them. At a year old they mimicked this activity in their play as one went behind a curtain and they reached their hands out affectionately, stroking each other's faces through the sheer fabric. They would then laugh, in what Piontelli felt was a reminiscence of their intrauterine experience.

Language

Since we use verbal language to communicate with pre-verbal children, the issue of language and the means by which the infant "understands" the interventions is a central question. It is not a question which can be definitively answered and we are often forced to rely on what Bion called "rational conjectures" (Bion, 2000, p. 204) or "science fictions." This is not so different really from our work with adults, for speaking to the reminiscences of an *internal* baby or fetus in an indeterminate universe of mental space, often separated from an adult patient's awareness by decades, may at times be more difficult than speaking to an actual baby.

Norman pointed out that infants read lips and facial expressions and "understand emotional meaning when there is a concordance between the lexical [verbal] and non-lexical [sounds, intonations, gestures] aspects of the spoken language (2004, p. 1106). Brazelton also investigated the infant's connection to the mother through tonal qualities of her voice (Paul, 1997, p. 148). Szejer (2006) raises the question of whether the child understands words, and while she thinks not, at least not in the way that we do, she speculates that he memorizes their salient characters, signifiers which can be modified as cognitive functions develop. My sense is that while babies cannot be said to *understand* the words, they nonetheless seem to *gain understanding* from the communication, a more passive, primitive form of mental processing. Those who have made interpretations to babies, or even just talked to them, may be familiar with the rapt attention, intense curiosity, and sense of presence in their eyes which makes them appear perfectly capable of understanding what we say. Of course, their understanding is far from perfect, and what understanding they do have seems related first of all to what we might call the "music" of meaning. Words which have deep meaning to the speaker have a different sound and resonance than nonsense or words spoken without conviction. Just as specific musical patterns evoke specific feelings – a minor chord will evoke a sad, somber or dark feeling – the musical patterns inherent in speech do as well. We can notice this when the lack of sincerity in politicians' speeches makes our skin crawl, for a conflict arises in the mind when language and intention do not match. Paul (1997) makes the distinction between authentic speech and imitative speech, which is a distortion of language and meaning. He also examines various non-verbal factors which contribute to our understanding of language. Prosody, for one, includes intonation and stress or emphasis, as well as the vocal signals of pitch, loudness, duration and silence. All of these contribute to the music of speech, which imbues it with meaning.

Babies do focus their attention when they hear meaningful language, a sign of interest which suggests it has some meaning to them. An interesting study by Condon and Sander (1974) tested early neonatal response to the syntactical elements of speech. Through microanalysis of films of babies exposed to speech they detected a relationship between the neonate's movements and adult speech patterns. They called this "interactional synchrony," where "the listener's body motions are synchronous with the speaker's speech" (1974, p. 99). "As early as the first day of life," they concluded, "the human neonate moves in precise and sustained segments of movement that are synchronous with the articulated structure of adult speech" (ibid.). They found, in other words, a primal organized response to the pattern of adult speech. The form and structure of language is thus laid down in the body long before one is able to speak, through countless rhythmic repetitions in the body. This capacity for interactional synchrony was found to be missing in pathological states, in subjects with aphasia, autism or schizophrenia.

If babies do not actually understand the words, what do they understand? How do we account for the fact, as we will see below with Ellie, that what they hear does seem to affect their behavior and states of mind? I raise the idea that on a primitive level the capacity to apprehend may be a function of projective identification, so that the child gains understanding through identification with the *understanding* of the Other, an *identification with the mental function of "understanding"*. This is an aspect of the mother's alpha function, in relation to which the infant develops the capacity to think (Bion, 1962), and it is based on the idea of thinking and a need for knowledge and truth as a primary need, an inherent *potential* which exists in the infant from birth and probably before. Grotstein (2004) saw it as a "truth drive," which he postulates to be a "hidden order that runs through the entirety of Bion's work" (2007, p. 52). It relates to Bion's notion of a pre-conception, a state of expectation for an inherent need which, when realized, can become a concept capable of being thought (1963, p. 23). We are familiar with Bion's example of the infant's pre-conception of the breast which becomes a mental concept through the experience of the link between nipple and mouth, but he also makes the point that the capacity to think does not develop automatically in the infant. Rather, it requires the presence of certain capacities and mental functions of the mother (Bion, 1962). From this perspective, the capacity for thought itself is also a pre-conception which must await its realization in the relationship with a conscious object. Since it is part of the as yet undeveloped psycho-physical potential to which each infant is attuned and toward which each is driven, I suggest that it is this which the infant recognizes in someone who speaks to his or her emotional experience in a mindful and meaningful way. This pre-conception of his own potential for thought and language allows him to sense in meaningful verbal communication a biological inheritance held for him in trust, as it were, in a kind of "memory of the future," as he is driven to develop that potential. We may see evidence of it when looking into the clear eyes of an infant and sensing depth, wisdom and a knowing soul. However, the child is neither wise nor knowing, at least not consciously, so what we are seeing is the *potential* for wisdom, a desire or instinct toward knowledge which can either be nurtured or obstructed, or even destroyed.

This idea is expressed metaphorically in the myth of Eden, where Adam and Eve are surrounded by the wealth of the Garden but have not tasted its fruits. Likewise, the child's mind contains the opulent wealth of his potential capacity for knowledge of good and evil, and for the transcendent knowledge of the mind which Bion calls O (1970). However, not yet having tasted them he does not know what they mean. They are seen to be forbidden for they engender the pain of consciousness – to taste them is to be cast out of the womb-like state of unconsciousness before the awareness of separate existence – of time, life and death – and be set upon the painful path of consciousness (Reiner, 2009). Essentially, one is speaking to the unconscious of the child, but more in the sense of Bion's unconscious, which he acknowledged was close to Jung's idea of the collective unconscious (Bion, 1978a). This represents the capacity for contact with a primal knowledge, the human inheritance of a mind which must be potentiated by conscious knowledge gained through the relationship with a conscious object.

Language presupposes awareness of separateness for it becomes necessary as a means of communicating between two people. Language itself is therefore felt as a disturbance to the infantile phantasy of fusion with the mother. In his discussion of his small grandson's "Fort/Da" game, Freud (1920) connects the child's first words to his separation from mother. Similarly, Bion's idea of the "no-thing" places the origin of thought, and so also of language, in the capacity for awareness of the mother's absence (Bion, 1970). The capacity to tolerate the attendant feelings makes a space available in the mind for the thought "no mother" to exist. Lacan also points out that the mother's act of naming represents a differentiation of mother and child. He calls language "the murder of the thing," meaning that the absence or lack of the object stimulates the desire to substitute a word (Muller and Richardson, 1982, pp. 400–2). But Green (1986) criticizes Lacan's exclusion of affects as a factor in language:

> While Lacan took his stand on the side of language and structural linguistics, banishing affects from his theory, Bion started with the most primitive emotional experiences and leads up to the most intellectual concepts. Today, I would say Lacan made the error of excessive abstraction.
>
> (1986, p. 11)

In Bion's theory, an emotional transformation is facilitated through a relationship between primitive affects and abstraction, giving rise to language and thought.

Self and other

Winnicott's (1949) idea is that the inseparable unit of mother/infant must be protected after birth until the infant is ready to bear separateness. The development of a true self depends upon the mother's mental containment of the infant's raw emotional experience through her capacities for reverie and alpha function (Bion, 1962). This provides a model for thinking in the infant's mind, and underlies the development of an authentic self. As we will see in the clinical examples, in the presence of trauma or the absence of this emotional containment the real self may be split off, walled off somewhere inaccessible even to the infant himself. In its place a false self develops, cut off from emotional life. These ideas of detachment from a true self capable of emotional contact, expressed in Winnicott's (1949) theory of the False

Self and True Self, also underlie Steiner's (1993) idea of "psychic retreat" and, on a more primitive level, Tustin's (1981) encapsulated states.

As analysts, it is easy for us to forget that familiar theories like projective identification, maternal reverie, and containment (Bion, 1962) also represent non-verbal transactions. The means by which these communications are transmitted from mother to child and child to mother remain a mystery, as do the means by which infants seem to process verbal language beyond their developmental capacities. The case material presented here is an attempt to provide more clinical evidence to illustrate these familiar ideas in the very earliest stage of life.

Clinical material

Mrs. G, a bright, capable 38-year-old mother of a three-year-old boy, was referred for treatment by her previous analyst who retired a year into their therapy. Early on, our treatment revolved largely around her feelings about this loss. It replayed an earlier loss at age four when Mrs. G's mother was temporarily incapacitated by a car accident and the patient was sent to stay with an aunt for an unknown period of time. No one attended to this little girl's feelings of terror, abandonment and confusion, feelings which were then split off and deeply buried beneath the false persona of a capable, all-giving idealized mother. As a result, Mrs. G's presenting complaint was amorphous at first. She was coming "to continue the work I started with my previous analyst," the nature of which was not exactly clear as Mrs. G seemed like someone who had never thought about her emotional life. She seemed satisfied with her life but was concerned with other people's needs to the exclusion of her own, and her hypomanic state reflected how frightened she actually was of any feelings at all.

Mrs. G's mother recovered from her accident, later starting a successful business after her husband's death when Mrs. G was 16. Though in some ways a loving person, Mrs. G's mother was narcissistic, and often cruelly critical. Though arrogantly self-sufficient, she looks to Mrs. G with child-like desperation to deal with emotional and practical matters in her life. This causes intense confusion in Mrs. G, who is similarly split, playing mother to her mother as well as to her successful but needy husband, Sam, and of course to her actual children.

Despite Mrs. G's emotional detachment she made sufficient use of interpretations to begin to feel a strong attachment to me and to our work. She began to experience this internal self-sufficient mother as a formidable structure in her mind which was violently opposed to any emotional need or real connection. She endured surprisingly deep feelings of loss before and after our first vacation break, fearing an irreparable change in our relationship. Her uncertainty as to whether I would return at all echoed her fear of her mother's "disappearance" after her accident.

Prenatal material

I had been seeing Mrs. G for a year when she became pregnant with Ellie, her second child. Before presenting more detailed material of the interactions between them, I will give some brief impressions of her relationship to her fetus during her sixth month of pregnancy.

In the previous session, her husband's childish demands had made Mrs. G angry and depressed. She had always excused his behavior but now, more in touch with her disappointment at his inability to consider her feelings, she felt sad and helpless, a frightening emotional challenge for her. On this day, however, she talked excitedly and non-stop. I became increasingly anxious at the effluvium of uncontained feeling and noticed that I'd begun to feel as if I didn't exist. I found myself wondering how the baby must be feeling, imagining, if my own experience was any indication, that she might feel frozen, petrified, in a sort of suspended animation, an attempt, perhaps, to still her mother's anxiety or steel herself against it. I asked how the baby was doing. "Oh, she's fine," Mrs. G said cheerfully, "she's sleeping." Her response, though certainly no confirmation of my feeling, made me wonder what kind of sleep the fetus was in, and if, like me, she had been pushed into an emotional retreat to escape from the anxiety to which she was being subjected. As I pondered this, Mrs. G also sat quietly. After a few moments she said cheerfully, "Oh, she just woke up . . . she's kicking like crazy." With nothing to go on but countertransference and "rational conjectures" (Bion, 2000, p. 204) I commented that I certainly could not know for sure what the baby felt, but thought it possible she had been feeling that no one was aware of her, a feeling I thought that she, Mrs. G, was still having about Sam as well. She became sad and said how ignored by her husband, as well as her mother, she'd been feeling. At some point she reiterated that Ellie was "really dancing around."

It was interesting to me that as Mrs. G turned her attention to her fetus in response to my question, Ellie became animated or woke up. I speculated that my recognition of my own feelings of being ignored and Mrs. G's subsequent ability to feel her feelings, may have provided enough emotional containment for Ellie to come to life. This is hardly a scientific conclusion; I offer these impressions as background to the environment in which this fetus found herself, and as a means to observe any continuity of behavior later on.

Working method

In the last month of her pregnancy Mrs. G's treatment centered largely on her fear and helplessness as she anticipated the birth. This caesura carried the feelings of the traumatic separation from her mother when she was a toddler, feelings which were now activated at any hint of change. Beginning to feel these feelings for the first time challenged a defensive structure which had long kept her emotionally anaesthetized. Starting the day after the birth, Mrs. G and I had a few weeks of phone sessions. For most of the next five months she brought Ellie regularly, clearly welcoming the support of another pair of eyes on this delicate creature for whom she was responsible. More attuned now to her own emotional life, Mrs. G had also begun to feel responsibility for her daughter's mind, and wanted to protect her from the kinds of projections she had suffered in relation to *her* mother.

Although Mrs. G was the designated patient, I chose to address my comments to whomever seemed most to need them at the moment and to whomever might make the best use of them, trying to be attentive to the complex interactions between them. It was at times a delicate balance as Ellie got some of the attention previously paid exclusively to Mrs. G and her internal, mental baby. Bion's important question about "how to get the interpretation to the right address" (Bion, 1978b) seemed relevant here, and not so unlike the challenge one faces with an individual patient, where one has to determine to which aspect of the personality to address one's remarks so that they might genuinely be received.

Session 1: 3 weeks old

This was one of the last post-natal phone sessions. Mrs. G was characteristically energetic, repeatedly saying how well things were going, how sweet the baby was, how good, etc. Ellie was fussing in the background and Mrs. G said, "She's cranky now, she just woke up." As Mrs. G continued on about how good things were, I found myself feeling anxious and exhausted. My suspicion that this was a manic reaction against an unconscious anxiety was confirmed when she said, "I asked my husband if he thought there was something wrong with Ellie because she's so calm. She'll just sit and look around, which Billy [her son] never did."

I mentioned how hard it was for her simply to sit and "be," how anxious it makes her, and she agreed, saying, "I schedule myself so I'm always doing something." I asked what it feels like if she's quiet. "I don't know," she said simply, implying that she never gets close enough to it even to imagine. I said, "I think you start feeling afraid a feeling may come up. Even now, you may be afraid that if you acknowledge any fear or helplessness in taking care of Ellie that it will somehow cancel out all the joy you're also feeling." She was silent, seemed surprised. "I don't want to get too negative, like I was with Billy," she said, "I mean *on some level you worry about everything*." She described her fear when walking Billy, afraid someone might attack her. "I'd go into this terrible scenario till finally I thought, either you walk the kid or you don't but you can't create this boogeyman out there."

We see something of her deep anxiety, feeling overwhelmed, worried "about everything," trying valiantly to contain it without being able to think about it. She seemed very interested when I interpreted that all these feelings then seem to loom outside her like a boogeyman, and she calmed down. She began talking lovingly about how much she enjoys playing with Ellie, but after a moment she said, "When Billy was born I couldn't really play with him . . . I feel bad I couldn't do it then, not that I completely screwed him up, I mean he's fine, but I guess I'm more in touch now." Her regrets and guilt became conscious here, but it is the guilt of a primitive superego – the "boogeyman" – and after another silence she reiterated how hard it is for her to sit. "I always feel I should be doing this or that." [Ellie was crying on and off at this point.]

I remarked that she seemed to be feeling a lot of judgements inside about what she felt she did wrong. "Constantly," she replied, "but in my defense, I'm better at it than I was with Billy." I acknowledged her appreciation of this positive change, then commented that she sounded as if she felt she was on trial. "I guess I do," she said, " I must put that on you, but maybe it's natural to feel judged since your job is to make me look at things I don't know . . . Still, our sessions have helped so much, in ways I didn't expect." I pointed out her complex feelings, both that I'm helpful and also someone to defend herself against. [Ellie cries] . . . "I'm changing her now, she doesn't like being naked, it's more of a helpless feeling without clothes . . . It's harder to be quiet on the phone, the silences feel so unnatural . . . if you're on the phone you're supposed to talk."

I pointed out that she seemed to feel she had to talk for *me*, to care for me, which may seem preferable to feeling so emotionally naked and exposed as we talk about her feelings. She replied, "My mother hates silence, she becomes helpless and asks me to solve her problems." I said that if something in the silence scares her mother, Mrs. G may not hear the *silence* but more the *noise* of her mother's fear and helplessness. "So maybe it isn't your silence that frightens you," I added, "but your mother's noise." There was a long silence. Finally, Mrs. G said, "Ellie just fell asleep." After another silence she said, "My mother has a lot of clutter in her house . . . I was just thinking, that it's like noise." "Like visual noise?" I asked, to which she replied, "Exactly, or spatial noise."

In this session, a primitive superego has emerged, warning her against feeling and judging her for being anything less than perfect. Although her real feelings remain split off, Ellie nonetheless feels them, just as Mrs. G felt her mother's "noise," a mental burden no infant can contain. Exposed to these projections over and over again, Ellie becomes agitated, but even in these first sessions Mrs. G began to be sufficiently gathered up emotionally for Ellie to relax. If unacknowledged, the immense anxieties beneath Mrs. G's idyllic picture of mother and baby begin to erode her genuine feelings of joy, as positive feelings turn manic. By the end of the session she was safe enough in the silence to have a creative thought about her mother's clutter as "spatial noise." We might say that Mrs. G is the space filled with that noise.

Session 2: 3½ weeks old

In this last of our phone sessions, Mrs. G reported a dream, a rare event for her: "I was looking out the window of my house. I saw a tornado coming toward me but it wasn't going to hit me. A lion then dropped out of it, but it was muzzled."

Mrs. G kept repeating that her dreams are usually more prosaic, and I sensed some fear and embarrassment over this production of her unconscious. Her association to the tornado was to reading *The Wizard of Oz* to her son. "He was such a colicky baby, Ellie is so calm." She then felt guilty comparing her children, as if it sounded critical of Billy. She said she wasn't scared in the dream, calmly watching the tornado and the lion with interest. "Lions are powerful but this one was muzzled so it couldn't have hurt me." She thought of the cowardly lion.

We see some scary images in this dream, and yet no fear, which I thought indicated something about Mrs. G's ambivalence concerning the nascent development of her capacity to feel. It was a complex dream, but I began by saying that I thought she was beginning to get a look at a powerful part of her mind which was unknown to her, which had somehow been tamed or muzzled. Certainly this was so after her mother's accident – she did not get angry or cry, for no one was listening to her. This dream indicated her sense that although the wild feelings were coming closer, they were still far enough away for her to feel safely removed from them, hidden inside, behind the window (in a numbed or encapsulated state). Based on her association to Billy's colic, however, I felt that the lion is also the baby Ellie, for while Billy was a roaring lion, she both fears and hopes that Ellie, like her, is a muzzled baby who will not cry. I recalled her discussion with her husband about how docile and sweet Ellie was, and the question, "Do you think there's something wrong with her?" She has an unconscious fear of having already muzzled this baby, as well as her internal baby, who cannot speak up or feel the passion of her inner life. Even having this dream is an embarrassment. She wants to feel and yet wants to remain safely cloistered from the turmoil of emotional life. Sensing her mother's fear, Ellie, too, has already muzzled her own wild emotions and put them to sleep.

Projective identification: Common dreams of analyst and analysand

Session 3: 8 weeks old

The analytic context is important in this next session, for I thought the patient was still reacting to a change in our session time four weeks before. For various reasons she had canceled the first three changed times, which was rare for her. When we finally met I raised the question of her having trouble adjusting to our new time. I interpreted her feeling that she had lost the 11am Thursday me and wasn't sure this new 2:15 Wednesday me could be trusted to listen to and understand her, if we would still have a relationship. She seemed surprisingly vulnerable to these feelings. The next week she called to cancel again (babysitting problems) but this time she asked for an additional session. I left a message offering her a Friday time. When I didn't hear back I was left wondering if she planned to come, if she had even gotten my message, and I started feeling I'd been cut off. I realized then that the 11am Thursday me whom she had slowly come to trust was like her mother *before* the accident, while the 2:15 Wednesday me was experienced as her incapacitated mother who must have seemed strange and unapproachable upon her return from the hospital. However, the little girl who had become the self-sufficient mommy was also different, traumatized at being left alone, and was now leaving me with all her split-off feelings of need and loss.

Mrs. G finally made it to a Wednesday session. She had Ellie in tow, now two months old, who was asleep in her stroller. She immediately made reference to our discussion in the last session – now two weeks prior to this one – about her difficulty adjusting to her new time. When I asked if she'd received my call she gasped, "Oh, I'm so sorry! I guess it slipped my mind." At this point I remembered my own dream of the previous night, which I will recount as I think it raises interesting issues about projective identification, as well as the correspondence between the unconscious of analyst and patient.

My own dream was about a close childhood friend – "Jane"– whose elderly mother had recently died. I dreamt *I was at Jane's mother's house – it was empty because Jane had sold it when her mother died. I felt bad for Jane . . . she was so sad.*

Although I had personal associations, including my concern and sadness about my own elderly mother's recent illness, my immediate association was between Jane and Mrs. G, who looked remarkably alike. Their features, even their expressions were uncannily similar, and they have the same color of curly hair. The resemblance is so striking that there were times I had to restrain myself from blurting out, "You look just like Jane!"

I thought that my concern about whether or not Mrs. G had gotten my message, and whether she was coming the next day, may have impelled me unconsciously to seek out Mrs. G through my dream in an attempt to intuit her state of mind. Perhaps, like a sort of long-distance maternal reverie (or as a baby does with its mother), I was somehow dreaming her dream for her, feeling her unthought thoughts. My thoughts about my dream informed my interpretation and I said that while she may be starting to feel that this was her time, I suspected she had another feeling about it as well. "I think forgetting to call me was a way of trying to let me know how it feels not to know where I am, as if the familiar me of the old time had disappeared." I related this to her anxiety of her mother's absence. Was she ever coming back? Had she, perhaps, even died? "You must have felt so frightened," I said, "about how *empty* the house felt without her."

"My house was literally empty," she replied, "my mother was gone, my father was gone, I was sent next door to stay with the neighbors before I went to live [out of state] with my aunt." She did not know for how long or what she felt, that time was a blank in her mind. I pointed out that the empty house was also how she felt inside in her mother's absence – empty of her thoughts and feelings, with no way to think about them. Referring to my interpretation about her efforts to think about my whereabouts by leaving me wondering where *she* was, she asked, "Do you think people communicate that way?" I said I did think she may have done so with me, having no other way, as with her mother, to let me know about these painful feelings.

Mrs. G sat quietly for quite a while, still fairly rare in our sessions. A moment later, at exactly 3:00, the time our session ends, Ellie woke up with a start, as if she knew the session was over, and began to cry bitterly. Her mother tried to comfort her and remarked, "She never cries this long." I thought that even in her sleep she may have sensed the depth of her mother's desire not to leave, relieved finally to have an ear for these old feelings. I said, "I think it's possible Ellie may be feeling what is so difficult for you to feel, that you feel sad to have to go and want more time with me." Mrs. G nodded. Ellie stopped crying, opened her eyes wide and alert and looked at me with a clear gaze. With the air cleared of those unconscious feelings of loss and need, Ellie no longer seemed to have to carry the full brunt of her mother's old sorrow.

It occurred to me that there was a connection here to that first session (above, p. 161), when Ellie, still in utero, woke up when her mother began to contain her anxiety and sadness. To say these are examples of projective identification still leaves a lot unanswered, for the means by which this familiar theory of non-verbal communication takes place remains a mystery. However, we had seen here two or three different instances of projective identification, with two of them at a remote distance. First was Mrs. G's communication of feelings of neglect, confusion and abandonment by "forgetting" to return my phone call, the second was my dream. The third, Ellie's distress at the end of the session, also seemed to represent a projection of Mrs. G's unconscious distress at having to leave. While there are no hard facts about these ephemeral, numinous aspects of mental existence, what does seem evident is that communication depends upon a transmitter and a receiver. One has to wonder how many billions of messages like these may be sent by babies and never *consciously* received, messages encoded in the minds and phantasies of our patients which may be discovered only in analysis decades later.

Although my dream surely had a level of personal meaning for me as well, I think it illustrates the kind of unconscious play, the emotional give-

and-take, which goes on all the time between mothers and infants, and in any intimate relationship, including an analytic one.

Session 4: 5½ months old

The previous weeks had been difficult for Mrs. G. She had become painfully aware of the importance of our sessions, a dawning awareness of her needs and our separateness. She began wanting her sessions for herself, so I was surprised that after about a month without bringing Ellie she had brought her again today. She was asleep in her stroller, which Mrs. G parked so that I could see her face. After just a few moments, Ellie opened her eyes and looked around, surprised and confused. She looked at me with curiosity for a long time. Finally I said, "I think you're wondering where you are now, and trying to remember who I am, especially since you haven't been here for a long time." She examined my face a moment longer, then relaxed and looked around the room, as if hearing my voice had oriented her within her experience. She now drank in all the familiar sights with big and hungry eyes, intermittently looking back at me. "She can't stop looking at you," Mrs. G noted, watching Ellie attentively. After a while she asked if Ellie wanted to come out of her stroller and her face lit up with a happy smile as her mother lifted her out. Ellie tried to engage me with smiles, eye contact and noises. "You want to say something?" her mother asked, to which Ellie "replied" with a distinct two syllable sound surprisingly like "Hello." She repeated this sound and I said, "Hello." Mrs. G and I both smiled with pleasure. Ellie then started "talking" to me more pointedly with deliberate sounds and a strong sense of intention. "You really want to talk to me, but you don't really have the words yet to say it," I said. She listened to me, then went on "talking."

Mrs. G continued to watch attentively, obviously enjoying this. Her capacity to observe and attend to feelings was notably more apparent, a factor, I thought, in what was clearly a "conversation" between the three of us. Her hypomanic quality had for the moment abated as she became more curious about her mind and who she was, and I had the impression that there was finally someone available in the room with whom I could have a conversation. I interpreted to Mrs. G that maybe she, too, had a lot to say to me but didn't know how to say it. "You may have wanted Ellie here again today to express your eagerness to talk to me." She replied, "I've been thinking a lot about what we were talking about."

She had spoken thoughtfully last time of a book she was reading about religion and the meaning of human existence. She thought the Bible had a lot of important ideas, but that religion seemed to give people easy answers. I had interpreted in that context that she felt our work to be a sort of spiritual quest in that it had to do with a search for meaning, answers to big questions about existence, including her mental existence. I thought she was drawing a distinction between established answers which religion offers about the meaning of life, and her growing sense that our work was about the two of us finding answers together, if we could, specific to *her*.

Today she spoke of her friend, Julie, whom her husband had said always goes along with other people's opinions. Mrs. G feared she was like that, but that since her treatment began she speaks up more with Sam. She said she liked Julie, "We can speak our minds to each other . . . She looks sort of conservative and sophisticated but underneath she can almost be wacky at times, unpredictable, she has an interesting mind that isn't just one thing." I interpreted her curiosity about relationships, and about ours, about how she can speak her mind to me even though, like Ellie, there are things she wants to say that she doesn't yet know how to express. Because I help her think about them, she notices my importance to her, and then also notices her curiosity, as well as her doubts and suspicions about me, a relative stranger to her.

She said, "I *was* thinking, I don't really know who you are. Even though you're supposed to be detached, you still seem to be who you are, so you can't be totally detached." I said that while we only meet in this room for a certain amount of time, she's still aware that I'm a real person, for whom she has real feelings of connection. "I think you can't quite figure me out," I added, "like Julie, I look conservative and yet I have these sort of wacky ideas about feelings and babies which I keep talking to you about." This discussion was quite a shift for her, as I often felt she was completely unaware of me. She had recently mentioned how disturbing it is that her mother always leaves without saying goodbye, "as if she just disappears." It makes Mrs. G feel she does not exist, similar to the feeling I often have, but did not have today.

Throughout our conversation, Ellie played contentedly on a blanket on the floor with her toys. As her mother began expressing more passionate feelings of connection to me, Ellie began to cry. When Mrs. G picked her up she stopped crying and nestled deep into her mommy's neck, then looked back at me with curiosity. I pointed out that just as Ellie seemed to have felt left out of our conversation, I thought that Mrs. G's curiosity about me also included some feelings about where I was, and with whom, when I wasn't there with her.

Further associations about triangular relationships seemed to confirm this idea, for Mrs. G then mentioned that she'd been thinking of Dr. Y (her previous analyst). She felt that in a way *our* relationship kept her close to Dr. Y, about whom she had fond feelings. I saw in this that Mrs. G's growing feelings of attachment toward me included her gratitude toward Dr. Y for sending her to me. But like Ellie having to check back with her mother, as if to make sure she still had a place with her if Mrs. G was engaged in a relationship with me, Mrs. G also had to check back to make sure that she was not betraying her feelings for Dr. Y. While on some level she probably represented Mrs. G's self-sufficient internal mother who would be opposed to any of these vulnerable feelings of need for me, this did not seem to be the relevant thing at that moment. The triangular relationship I was seeing did not seem to reflect pathological jealousy, but rather a need and appreciation for the objects, i.e. Mrs. G's appreciation of me and Dr. Y. We can see this in Ellie as well, for while she wanted to reassure herself of her relationship with her mother, her attitude toward me for talking to Mrs. G was not one of jealous hatred of me as a rival, but rather one of curiosity. The same thing seemed true of Mrs. G's feeling for me. Her curiosity about relationships in general, and me in particular, seemed motivated, at least at this point, by a genuine curiosity. As Bion (1978b) said, "The patient isn't interested in the analyst, nor is he interested in himself, but in the bit in between." The patient is interested in the connection between them, the *link*, and so in retrospect I felt that what I had first assumed to be jealousy in Ellie and in Mrs. G, was in fact this curiosity about connections – both dyadic and triadic. It reflected a kind of healthy Oedipal triangle, with gratitude toward Dr. Y as the "father" who has given the mother (me) a baby (Mrs. G). Deeper fears of real emotional attachment to me as a betrayal of her attachment to a detached internal mother would emerge at a later time.

The importance of this session lies in the opening of Mrs. G's curiosity about a relationship with an other, the beginning of a sense of separateness and genuine object relatedness. This tentative emergence of her real self had an apparent correspondence here to Ellie's developing separateness in her attempts at verbal communication.

Session 5: 6 months old

Mrs. G had just increased her sessions to three times a week. She brought Ellie today, as she did every Thursday, when she lacked childcare. Mrs. G said, "I've been wondering, what is the end result of this [treatment]?" I related her question to her anxiety about coming more often, not knowing what will happen. "I always like to know how things turn out," she replied. Ellie crawled over to her stroller and pulled herself up. "It's amazing," Mrs. G said, "she crawled once a few days ago and now she pulls herself up to stand. She's trying to walk." Ellie crawled toward me, and tried to pull herself up at a small table near my chair which holds a tissue box. She became frustrated and started to cry. This precocious behavior, for which she was neither physically, neurologically nor psychologically prepared, had started to feel overwhelming. She seemed to discover she was just a baby, and when Mrs. G picked her up, Ellie burrowed into her mother's neck, climbing and pressing into her body as if trying to get back inside a protective womb. She began looking to nurse and Mrs. G said, "She shouldn't be hungry," but nonetheless offered her the breast. Ellie nursed but was agitated and let out a desperate screech. "Oh-oh, it's the ugly sound," her mother said, shushing her anxiously. Ellie tried again to nurse but couldn't. I said to her, "I think you felt you had to be all grown and so you tried to stand up even though it feels too hard for you. You want to make sure you can still be Mommy's little baby." Ellie turned around and gave me a long hard look. She gave up the idea of feeding and sat facing me, watching as I spoke.

I thought that Ellie's precocious behavior was in part a response to her mother's anxiety about our work. I said to Mrs. G, "As you said earlier, it's very hard not to know the end result here, I think it makes you feel helpless, and scared, but it seems these feelings feel 'ugly' to you, as if only rational, grown-up feelings are allowed inside." She acknowledged that it scared her not to know. I added that like her own desire to know the end result Ellie also seemed to be showing her what it was like to feel pushed beyond her capacities. She pondered this a moment, then said, "I always push myself." I reminded her of how she tried to be all grown-up, pushing herself past the feelings of loss and terror after her mother's "disappearance." By denying the sad, scared little girl she was, however, she had lost her emotional moorings, and her self.

There was a delicate balance here between speaking to Mrs. G and to Ellie, for I was aware that Mrs. G may hear my interpretation as a persecutory attack on her mothering. Because of this, but mainly because Ellie was suffering such distress and confusion, I chose to address her feelings first. Their feelings were clearly linked in this session, though, and once Ellie's feelings were contained, I could speak more openly to Mrs. G, who then seemed able to begin to note the connection between them, and how Ellie mirrored her feelings.

Session 6: 9 months old

This session was two weeks before the Christmas break; Mrs. G had also missed the last session. Mrs. G was silent and Ellie was vocalizing a lot. "She's got a lot to say today," her mother noted; Ellie continued "talking." Finally Mrs. G said, "I can't remember what we were talking about last time." She frequently made statements like this, which I felt expressed both her connection to me and a sense that it is severed between sessions. I said I thought it had seemed to her like a long time since she'd been here because of our missed session, as if there were a big gap between us which could not be bridged. Ellie interjected, cooing and smiling at me, and Mrs. G said to her, "You need attention today." We were silent. Ellie came over to the ottoman near me and lifted herself up on shaky legs. She looked deeply into my eyes, then lowered herself to the floor, looking relieved. I said, "You look more comfortable there." She looked slightly confused and stood up again, as if to say, "Oh yeah? I can do this!" She immediately sat back down, looked back at her mother and started to cry bitterly. Her mother picked her up to nurse her. Ellie could hardly bear waiting for the breast, but when she started nursing she got distracted and began crying again. Mrs. G, frustrated, guilty and perplexed said to Ellie, "I didn't take it away." Ellie tried to nurse again but once more pulled herself sharply off the nipple and sobbed, clearly in great distress. Mrs. G explained to me that Ellie was hungry, but that lately she often distracted herself like this and fed fitfully, except during her morning and bedtime feeds. I observed as this continued, feeling their helplessness as well as my own lack of understanding. While it seemed to have to do with weaning, I didn't yet have a specific idea about the emotional meaning it had for Ellie. I said to Mrs. G, "I think it was more difficult for you than you know to have missed your session so, like Ellie, I don't think you're even sure what you need today. These feelings of need have been silenced in you, so you can't find the words for how bad it feels not to get what you want, and not even to *know* what you want." She replied, "My father and aunt always told me not to cry after my mother went away."

She had clearly learned her lesson well, and now told herself not to need me or miss me. She described this as a pattern, but then quickly devalued her feelings, saying, "Rationally it doesn't seem earth shattering." I acknowledged that this was surely so for the grown-up her, but the poignancy of her statement lay in the fact that missing her mother, or me (in the transference), did indeed feel earth shattering, and mind shattering as well.

She was quiet and I could see that she felt more vulnerable. Ellie, who had stopped crying, fed calmly. After a minute or so, Mrs. G mentioned that Billy was feeling terrified at the prospect of going to a new children's group over the Christmas break. She had empathized with him, telling him that she feels scared, too, if she has to do something new. She then said to me, "I don't like surprises." I replied, "At the moment I think the 'something new' for you is *our* Christmas break, which I think feels like your mother disappearing after her accident. So I think you're feeling, why re-connect with me today if I'm only going to spring that terrible surprise on you."

This hornet's nest of old feelings was coming more to the surface today and, like Ellie, Mrs. G also had a lot to say, the nature of which had been unsayable and unthinkable. Ellie, however, seemed to have felt them, and was acting out Mrs. G's inner drama, trying, like her mother, to be the precocious baby who didn't feel helpless, who could stand and walk and be all grown-up without needs or "irrational" fears. I thought that Ellie's agitation around nursing had to do with this emotional conflict, being fed the heavy burden of her mother's unconscious despair, anxiety and need along with the milk. Ellie's ambivalence about feeding and her rejection of her mother aroused even greater anxiety, however, as she then becomes aware of being in a "bad" world with a "bad" mother (Fairbairn, 1952, p. 66). As Mrs. G began to feel her needs, giving these unthought thoughts a home in her mind, Ellie was less burdened by her mother's feelings. With the mental space to experience her own emotional reality, she could feed calmly and do her own mental work.

Session 7: 9 months, two weeks old

Now feeling the strength of her needs, Mrs. G experienced acute anxiety which lasted for two weeks. However, as familiar schizoid defenses returned, numbing her feelings, the anxiety abated. Ellie's ambivalent nursing continued in this session and once again she started crying, burrowing into her mother's chest, trying for about two seconds to nurse again, crying, pulling away and repeating this again, till finally she pulled away with a loud shriek. While her behavior seemed directly related to weaning, it also seemed to point to the deeper issues in their relationship. It was painful to witness Ellie's violent confusion and helplessness and as she cried I said, "I don't think Ellie knows whether she should be inside you or outside of you. She's nine months now so she's been outside of you as long as she was inside and I think she's feeling scared as she begins to get a sense of being a separate person." Mrs. G agreed, then informed me that she had been slowly weaning. I said, "Since you've been feeling so vulnerable, especially now with our break coming up, I think you're also finding it very hard to feel separate and on your own."

As Mrs. G listened, Ellie stopped crying and Mrs. G remarked on this. I said, "It does seem that when you start to feel your feelings, even if they're unpleasant ones, Ellie doesn't have to feel them for you." Mrs. G replied with a sense of awe, "It's amazing really." Ellie crawled over to me and went under my chair, then began examining a bottle of water on the floor. She touched my shoe, clearly curious about me and wanting, I thought, to get inside me now, and to know what kind of milk or thoughts were in me. I reflected to her how interested she was in me, and in what I had said to her and her mother. She went on happily exploring and occupying herself around me, examining and touching my shoe, my leg, then looking up and smiling intermittently as she went about her business.

Mrs. G was silent, and apparently thoughtful, as she watched Ellie. "I'm thinking that I'll never be able to explore around here freely like she is," she said. I told her that I thought she was wanting her own time here, to see who *she* is as a separate person, and who I am, and that having to be the mommy here didn't leave enough room for her baby self to explore freely. She acknowledged that she had been thinking it was time to leave Ellie at home and have her own sessions. I felt it was important to explain to Ellie that Mommy had to come think about her feelings with me so that Ellie was free to have her own feelings, too.

That was the last session with Ellie. I felt it represented an important developmental step for Mrs. G, for it was the first time she indicated directly her desire for attention to *her* baby self, to feel her own needs without Ellie as an intermediary. In the course of these 9 months, and the 4–5 months during which she brought Ellie regularly to her sessions, Mrs. G became more attuned to her emotional life, which she was increasingly more able to experience in herself and her baby. She became fascinated by the connection between their emotional states, which in turn stimulated her curiosity about her own internal world. This included a lot of anxiety, the painful disappointment of her relationship with a mother who could not recognize her needs, as well as the difficult awareness of the impact her own unfelt feelings have on both her children.

This small glimpse into an intervention between a mother and infant at a primitive level of mental development obviously leaves many questions unanswered. Dealing with a child whose experience cannot be verbally confirmed presents a unique challenge. However, it provides a constant reminder that even with an adult patient one is exploring a world which is unknown and unknowable. While supported by our analytic knowledge we still have to rely primarily on our own intuition. Whether any child can understand the meaning of the words themselves or the meaning in the music we cannot say, but Ellie's responses to verbal language seemed to support the idea that she had listened to and been affected by what she heard. What also seemed evident to me was that interpreting the emotional reality of the interchanges between Ellie and her mother revealed what could only be described as a hunger for knowledge in this infant, and an ability to be nourished by it.

References

Bion, W. R. (1962). *Learning From Experience*. NY: Basic Books.

—— (1963). *Elements of Psychoanalysis*. NY: Basic Books.

—— (1970). *Attention and Interpretation*. London: Tavistock Publications.

—— (1975). Caesura. In Bion, W. R. (1989). *Two Papers: The Grid and Caesura*. London: Karnac Books.

—— (1978a). *Four Discussions with W. Bion*. Perthshire: Clunie Press.

—— (1978b). Lecture. Los Angeles, UCLA Neuropsychiatric Institute.

—— (2000). *Clinical Seminars and Other Works*. London: Karnac Books.

Condon, W. S. and Sander, L. W. (1974). Neonate movement is synchronized with adult speech: Interactional participation and language acquisition. *Science*, January, 1974.

Fairbairn, W. R. D. (1952). *Psychoanalytic Studies of the Personality*. London: Brunner Routledge.

Freud, S. (1920). Beyond the pleasure principle. *SE* 18. London: Hogarth Press.

—— (1926). Inhibitions, symptoms and anxiety. *SE* 20. London: Hogarth Press.

Green, A. (1986). *On Private Madness*. London: Karnac Books.

Grotstein, J. (2004). The Seventh servant: The implications of a truth drive in Bion's theory of 'O'. *International Journal of Psychoanalysis*, 85: 1081–1101.

—— (2007). *A Beam of Intense Darkness*. London: Karnac Books.

Muller, J. P. and Richardson, W. J. (1982). *Lacan and Language: A Reader's Guide to Écrits*. NY: International Universities Press.

Norman, J. (2004). Transformations of early infantile experiences: A 6-month-old in psychoanalysis. *International Journal of Psychoanalysis*, 85: 1103–1122.

Paul. M. I. (1997). *Before We Were Young*, NY: ESF Publishers.

Piontelli, A. (1987). Infant observation from before birth. *International Journal of Psychoanalysis*, 68: 453–463.

—— (1989). A study of twins before and after birth. *International Review of Psychoanalysis*, 16: 413–426.

Reiner, A. (2009). *The Quest for Conscience and the Birth of the Self*. London: Karnac Books.

Steiner, J. (1993). *Psychic Retreats*. London: Brunner Routledge.

Szejer, M. (2006). Talking To Babies. Lecture, Primitive Mental States Conference, Los Angeles.

Tustin, F. (1981). Psychological birth and psychological catastrophe. In Tustin, F. (1981). *Autistic States in Children*. London: Routledge, pp. 96–110.

Winnicott, D. W. (1949). Mind and its relation to the psyche-soma. In Winnicott, D. W. (1958). *Collected Papers: Through Paediatrics to Psycho-Analysis*. London: Hogarth Press.

Chapter 11

Transformations of early infantile experience

A six-month-old in psychoanalysis

Johan Norman

My argument in this paper is that there is a methodological dilemma connected with psychoanalytical knowledge of infants. In the field of psychoanalysis with somewhat older children and adults there is a continuous, mutual exchange going on between how we understand the course of events in the clinical setting and psychoanalytical theory; fruitful for both clinical work and theory. This fruitful intercourse is missing as a base for knowledge of infants, as the observations are not based on a psychoanalytical clinical setting. Psychoanalytical models of early infantile mental functioning are mainly constructions based on psychoanalysis with somewhat older children and adults according to 'the method of working backwards from a developmental end-point' (Harrison, 2003, p. 1382). We are left with uncertainty concerning the actual infant's infantile mental functioning, as the more adult mental functions – for example, verbal capacity and secondary repression – develop as early as at two or three years of age and then overshadow the infantile mental functioning.

Infant observation and observation in experimental research in different disciplines have provided valuable information about infants but do not offer specific knowledge about the interaction between infant, mother and analyst in a clinical psychoanalytical setting, with all the processes of mutual involvement, emotional links, transference/countertransference and interventions etc. that this involves. Parent–infant psychotherapy has in many forms applied psychoanalytical theory and method, and has gathered an extensive knowledge (for example, Fraiberg, 1987; Stern, 1995). However, although the infant or the parent–infant relationship is said to be in focus, there is a lack of development of technique to take advantage of the infant's capacity to contribute to the interaction and the process of the clinical situation as an active intentional agent. Furthermore, the clinical setting is usually based on one or two sessions a week, which means that affects and processes that evolve in the mother and infant often are left uncontained for many days and nights. This is not an optimal setting for a psychoanalytical understanding of the infant's mental functioning and interactional contributions. Attachment theory (Bowlby, 1988; Fonagy,

2001; Fonagy *et al.*, 2002) is a psychoanalytical developmental theory of the mind that has created its own language focused on the different qualities of attachment, while the ordinary clinical psychoanalytical high-frequency setting, with its technique and theory of the mental functioning and interaction of both the analysand and the analyst, has a wider aim. In this paper I have to delimit the aim and it is impossible in this context to bring into a critical discussion the attachment developmental theory.

I argue that it is possible to develop a method for infant psychoanalysis that is neither an application of 'adult or child psychoanalysis' nor a 'psychoanalytic psychotherapy,' but is simply psychoanalysis adapted to the requirements of the infant as analysand in the presence of the mother/father. The paper is based on Freud's assumptions, concepts and models, and the broad mainstream of psychoanalytical development since Freud, with special attention to Wilfred Bion's and some Kleinian and Winnicottian thoughts. I will focus on both the interactive and the intrapsychic point of view and, in particular, the concepts 'repression' and 'splitting,' studying whether they can be used and adapted as fruitful tools for understanding an infant in a clinical setting. The aims of this paper are: (1) to present my work with an infant together with the mother in a psychoanalytical setting; and (2) to explore some psychoanalytical theories and concepts, especially 'repression' and 'splitting,' as tools for the understanding of this case.

Ossian, six months old

A six-month-old infant and his mother were in a state of emotional turmoil when we started intensive psychoanalytical work. The setting was four sessions a week ad modum 'to talk with infants.' This means that the analyst talks with the infant from the start in order to open a mutual emotional link and receptivity with the infant, a technique I have described in earlier papers (Norman, 1997, 1999, 2001).

The beginning of the end of the analysis

Ossian, his mother and I had worked for five weeks, four times a week when Ossian – by then seven months old – invented a 'fort-da' (cf. Freud, 1920, pp. 14–15) game with his pacifier. Ossian had begun to play with his pacifier; he turned it in his mouth, turned it crosswise, turned it inside out, dropped it intentionally and then his mother gave it back to him or he took it back himself.

One day when Ossian was lying on the floor and his mother was sitting beside him, it was evident that he was playing when he threw away the pacifier. He could not reach it and he had not yet learned to crawl. He then found out that he could pull the blanket that covered the floor so that the pacifier was towed back to him. He repeated this several times. It was tempting for his mother to help him by giving him the pacifier but when she did so he became angry. When he had thrown away the pacifier so that it landed on the floor outside the blanket, his mother invented her part of the play – she held her hands so that Ossian could put his feet against them, stretch out his legs and in that way approach the pacifier. Ossian also created a special kind of tension when he threw away the pacifier and did not pull it back. None of us moved or talked. In the air hung an unspoken question of who would make the next move. This feeling of expectation implied that we all became attentive to an emotional field of links between ourselves. Finally, Ossian pulled the blanket so that the pacifier was towed back to him; he put it into his mouth and the tension was released.

Ossian's capacity to play as in the 'fort-da' indicated a change in his mental functioning that made termination possible. Two weeks later, after a total of six weeks of four sessions a week, my work with Ossian and his mother was finished.

Some theoretical assumptions and concepts

Setting and technique

In order to get a fruitful intercourse between psychoanalytical theory on infants and the clinical work, one demand is that the clinical observations are based on the listening process in a psychoanalytical setting. It is well known to practicing psychoanalysts that the analyst's state of mind in the analytical session has distinctly different qualities from the analyst's state of mind in everyday life. This is valid also when the analyst is meeting an infant analysand together with the mother but only on condition that the analyst is relating to the infant with 'the psychoanalytic state of the mind' (Green, 2000, pp. 45, 63) and 'the analyst's professional attitude, his technique, the work he does with his mind' (Winnicott, 1960, p. 161).

The external setting is simple: we meet in a small room with three low chairs, and a cotton cloth covers a part of the floor. I am sitting on a wheeled office chair so I am a bit mobile and usually at a distance of one to one and a half meters from the mother and infant. I never take up an infant in my arms. I try to offer four fifty-minute sessions a week. For an infant of Ossian's age I use no toys.

In psychoanalysis with somewhat older children and adults, language is central. But, although one of the aims of infant psychoanalysis is that it should be pursued according to general psychoanalytical principles, how can this be done when the infant cannot talk? The role of spoken language in work with infants is controversial and I regard the theory of the technique as an ongoing research project. My preliminary thoughts are as follows. In a spoken language, the lexical meaning and the non-lexical expressions are aspects of the verbal language. In order to achieve a correspondence between the lexical verbal expression and the non-lexical emotional expression of the prosody, gestures, body language and facial expressions, the analyst's verbal formulations have to be sincere expressions of what the analyst actually imagines (Norman, 2001). The infant is especially interested in the sound of words and the human voice when somebody is talking with him or her: 'Long before they can talk, babies are sensitive to the intonational contours that characterize a clause or sentence' (Mehler and Dupoux, 1994, p. 155). The infant reads the lips and the facial expressions, and can grasp emotional meaning when there is a concordance between the lexical and non-lexical aspects of the spoken language. Already from birth the human infant takes part in a world of language and is capable of discriminating phonemes, syllables and combinations of syllables (Mehler and Dupoux, 1994), and is soon able to differentiate the words in spoken language. The infant is attentive to the intonation and facial expression that is a part of the spoken language. The infant, through a recurrent primary identification, a pre-verbal intercorporality that proceeds faster than the visual reflex, immediately takes in these non-lexical aspects of the spoken words. By cross-modal perception the infant has, simultaneously, the sound of the syllables of the word and the emotional impact of the intonation, and the visual impact from the emotional facial expression. An infant of Ossian's age is building up experience based on the cross-modal perceptions of the sound of the words and the emotional non-lexical aspects. For the analyst, the lexical meaning is crucial as the analyst cannot create the non-lexical expressions in a sincere way isolated from the lexical meaning of the word.

The inflexibility of the infant's aversion and the concept of repression

By repression we usually mean 'secondary repression,' 'repression proper,' which consists of a pressure from ego and superego and simultaneously an attraction from the primally repressed (Freud, 1915a) to keep something away from the conscious. The concept of 'secondary repression' is not relevant for understanding the infant. My question is whether it may be possible and fruitful to adapt the essential meaning of the concept of 'repression' to the infant's requirements and to work out a concept of 'infantile repression.'

Contemporary experimental studies in psychology and neuroscience on the infant's memory (Hadley, 1989; Singer and Fagen, 1992; Schore, 1994; Solms and Turnbull, 2002) support the view that even very young infants have laid down memories of affective states and experiences. According to cognitive psychological and neuro-psychoanalytical terminology (Solms and Turnbull, 2002; Talvitie and Ihanus, 2002), the infant's memories are said to be implicit, meaning that they have an effect in mental functioning but cannot be consciously recalled, in contrast to so-called explicit memories. My references are to implicit memories. Memories of unsatisfied needs are connected with painful affects and the infant rejects the retrieval of the memories and the development of the affects. Freud formulates it thus: 'to suppress the development of affect is the true aim of repression' (1915b, p. 178). In his paper 'Repression,' Freud writes that 'the essence of repression lies simply in turning something away, and keeping it at a distance, from the conscious' (1915a, p. 147).

Some aspects of Freud's formulations on the functioning of primal repression may be relevant as a model for the mental functioning of 'infantile repression': 'We have reason to assume that there is a primal repression, a first phase of repression, which consists in the psychical (ideational) representative of the instinct being denied entrance into the conscious. With this a fixation is established' (ibid., p. 148); 'It is highly probable that the immediate precipitating causes of primal repression are quantitative factors such as an excessive degree of excitation and the breaking through of the protective shield against stimuli' (1926, p. 94). The infant's less-structured ego and weak, self-reflective consciousness offer no protection against external or internal excessive excitation, and it is primarily the mother's and father's containment and reverie that function for the infant as a protective shield. Both intrusive projective identifications from the containing object and inhibition of receptivity in the containing object imply that the infant's protective shield has been broken through and leaves the infant in a state of excessive excitation.

However, the term 'primal repression' in Freud's sense means that the fixation 'persists unaltered from then onwards and the instinct remains attached to it' (1915a, p. 148). My own studies on infants in a psychoanalytical setting (cf. Norman, 2001) point to the probability that this is not necessarily the case for the infant, and we thus have reason to make a distinction between the concepts of 'infantile repression' and 'primal repression.'

Connected with repression is 'return of the repressed,' giving rise to substitute formation. Substitute formation is a compromise-formation in which 'both the unconscious wish and the demands of defense may be satisfied by the same formation – in a single compromise' (Laplanche and Pontalis, 1973, p. 76). The concepts of 'infantile repression,' 'return of the repressed' and 'formation of substitutes' imply that we assume that the infant has an unconscious in the dynamic sense of the word (cf. Freud, 1915b, p. 166).

Splitting, projection and projective identification

The terms 'repression' and 'splitting' sometimes refer to similar phenomena and then it is a question of vocabulary. However, sometimes the terms refer to different phenomena (Hinshelwood, 1989, 1999). Melanie Klein refers to splitting and fragmentation of the object that also implies more or less a splitting of the ego (Hinshelwood, 1989). According to this line of thought, 'the young infant defends his ego from intolerable anxiety by splitting off and projecting unwanted impulses, feelings etc. into his object. This is an object relational perspective on the discharge of unpleasurable tensions and stimuli' (O'Shaughnessy, 1981, p. 178). The projection transforms the perception of the external object into a threat that has to be averted. 'Through the use of projection the distance between two parts of one person is converted into a distance between two people' (Hinshelwood, 1999, p. 8).

There is, thus, a difference between infantile repression and splitting: splitting functions with projection and projective identification, while repression functions with displacement, condensation and compromise-formation of substitutes. According to Hinshelwood, the 'use of the two processes [splitting and repression] seemed to be correlated with level of anxiety, not of development' (ibid., p. 8). This introduces the possibility that the return of the repressed, which implies formation of substitutes, may break down when anxiety increases and then, in order to defend itself, the infant resorts to splitting and to creating a concrete distance to the parent through projection.

Back to the start of the analysis with Ossian and his mother

A first phone call

When she called me, Ossian's mother had told me that he seemed to be unhappy; he did not cry but whimpered most of the day, and at night he slept only for a short while and then woke up with what seemed like a stomach ache, and he was then inconsolable. The parents had sought medical help for Ossian several times the previous month but the doctors had said that everything was all right. Ossian was eating poorly. He refused to take his mother's breast. Although his mother had kept on trying to breastfeed it was now interrupted. When Ossian was three months old his mother had asked a nurse at the child health station about some small spots on Ossian's skin and had been told that they might be a symptom of a severe illness. The parents were extremely concerned but after a couple of weeks received reassuring information.

I asked the mother to come with Ossian and I explained that my way of working is to turn to the infant and 'to talk with the infant' right from the start in order to try to establish a relationship with him in the presence of the mother. The sessions were recorded on audiotape and transcribed verbatim. When a dialogue is presented, it is quoted from the transcriptions. The parents have given their consent to publication.

The first session, a Wednesday, ten days after the call

Ossian's mother laid Ossian on the cloth, sat down on the floor and then took Ossian in her arms. Ossian looked attentively at me; he seemed worried, watchful and cautious, and also a little curious. I said to him, 'I see that you are looking at me. I know that your name is Ossian. My name is Johan. We don't know each other but your mother has asked us to get together to see if we can understand what it is that is troubling you and your mother.' Ossian, who looked at me attentively when I was talking with him, looked then at his mother, but rather soon he turned away from his mother and me and looked around the room. I followed what he was doing with my comments, quite simple descriptive comments, like '. . . and there is Mother, she is sitting there . . . you are looking around the room, you have never been here before . . .' He began to relax, and smiled at me and at his mother.

His mother began to talk with him, and Ossian gave her his attention and a few sounds in response. But Ossian began to whimper. With Ossian lying on the floor, his mother changed his nappy. Since Ossian's stomach was now bare, she showed me the brown spots on Ossian's skin, which they had been told might point to a serious illness. His mother told me that they printed out a lot of information from the Internet about this ailment and had become terribly alarmed. Ossian and his mother again seemed to be in a calm and friendly emotional interaction, and they resumed their conversation. Suddenly Ossian flung out his arms, coughed and cried as if something hurt. It looked as though Ossian had a stomach ache, as if something was grabbing hold of him, and he was frightened. I was struck by a sudden dread that he really might be physically ill. At the same moment I was reminded that Ossian had been examined by several doctors over the last few months and they had not found any illness. I realized that I was using this recollection for reassurance against my sudden feeling of dread, and I asked myself, 'A dread of what?' I realized that I was probably not the only one of us three in the room who was frightened at that moment. This train of visual/emotional thoughts from the moment I became fearful to the recovery of my reflection was almost instantaneous. Ossian's mother took him up in her arms, patted him and tried to divert him by pointing at something in the garden or looking at the lamp. Ossian sucked energetically at the blouse on his mother's shoulder; he whimpered and wailed, full of dissatisfaction. It took a long while for him to calm down.

His mother had put him on the floor on his back. He was drowsy but looking intently at his mother with half-closed eyes. There was again a close emotional link but there was also sadness in their relationship; it was cautious – and suddenly Ossian flung out his arms, cough-cried and wailed; he seemed still more frightened and seemed to be rejecting his mother. I became aware that Ossian was avoiding eye contact with his mother at this moment and with me as well; he closed or nearly closed his eyes. But he opened them to look out of the window or at the lamp, or he fastened his gaze on the metal tripod that formed the base of my chair. Ossian continued to whimper for the rest of the session.

Comments on the first session, Wednesday

The infant is 'interested'

Even though Ossian was a troubled and inhibited infant, he turned his attention to the analyst from the first moment, especially when the analyst was talking to him. He was interested. 'Interest' was the word that Freud proposed for 'Besetzung,' which was later translated into 'cathexis.' The infant was 'interested' and 'occupied with' the analyst and, in that moment, the infant and analyst opened up an emotional mutual link 'that x is in a state of getting to know y and y is in a state of getting to be known by x,' in abridged form 'xKy' (Bion, 1962b, p. 47). This moment of mutual interest was interrupted by Ossian; he inhibited his interest in the relationship.

The inhibition and the sudden fright

At the start of the session Ossian's mood fluctuated between interest in the relationship with the mother and the analyst, and inhibition and aversion. It was as if he was interested but didn't dare to stay in the emotional link. Ossian was overtaken by attacks of pain and terror. On both occasions it happened when there was a close emotional relationship between Ossian and his mother. The first attack was followed by his energetically sucking on his mother's blouse, indicating that his interest in his mother was still there but had taken a displaced form suggesting a defensive substitute formation. Substitution means representation and repression (Hinshelwood, 1999, p. 5). Ossian showed a need for his mother, indicating an internal libidinal object representation. During the second attack the need for the mother object was connected with fright. This time Ossian broke off eye contact, rejected the mother and didn't accept the pacifier, as if the mother was a threat. Through cutting the links with the mother he then became emotionally absent and, no longer frightened, he looked out of the window and fastened his gaze on emotionally neutral things. In this mental state there was no substitute formation, but his mental state can rather be understood as a split between the libidinal object and the frightening-bad-mother object. He cut the emotional links to the libidinal object and, thus, created no substitution, and projected the frightening-bad-mother object on his mother and then cut the link with the mother. Ossian used the lamp, the window, the base of my chair to create a lifeless environment as a 'retreat to remain relatively free from anxiety' (Steiner, 1993, p. 3). This course of events supports the idea that the two processes, splitting and repression, seemed to be 'correlated with the level of anxiety, not of development' (Hinshelwood, 1999, p. 8).

A few minutes before the first attack, Ossian's mother had shown me a few small pigmented spots on his skin, signaling the possibility that he might be seriously ill. One possibility is that the mother's unconscious/preconscious images of the ill child may have suddenly been actualized and had an impact on the child and the analyst as an intrusive projective identification. The analyst had to set to work at once on the intrusive projective identification and to transform the image of the destroyed infant into the question 'who is afraid of what?' The close emotional contact might therefore imply an emotional risk for Ossian that he would detect something threatening, and therefore his anxiety increased. The presence of the mother's fright may also have meant a momentary inhibition of the mother's emotional receptivity and reverie, which separated Ossian from a containing link with the mother. The mother's efforts to divert Ossian's attention support this interpretation.

The next day, Thursday

Ossian looked pleased when he saw me, and his mother declared that today he was content and cheerful. Ossian looked very attentively at his mother and she began to talk with him. Lying on his back, he pulled up his feet and kicked in the air. His mother laughed in a friendly way. Ossian looked at me. I said, 'I see that you are happy and lively when you are talking with your mother and that you are surprised that we are meeting here again today. We don't know each other very well.' Ossian babbled in response to me and his mother laughed quietly at our dialogue. But he didn't let his attention and interest linger in the relationship with either his mother or me. Ossian's mother and I talked for some minutes and he interjected a little sound. She began a dialogue with him and then he answered, looking at her, sometimes raising his hand and touching her face gently. It was a loving but cautious contact. Ossian played with his mother's finger, took it into his mouth, but after a while his mood changed. He began to cough and cry. His mother lifted him up and, when he came close to her face, he opened his mouth and eyes wide as if to take in all of his mother through his mouth and gaze – and then his glance moved away from her. He looked out of the window, looked at the lamp, the tapestry on the wall, and when he turned towards me he did not look at me either but at my chair. I accompanied this with my comment, 'Ossian, I see that you want to look out the window.' Ossian interjected some sounds. 'Well, what did you say? There is the lamp and you are looking at the chair I am sitting on but you don't want to look at me, and not at Mamma.' Ossian replied plaintively and I answered him. He peeped at his mother and I said, 'You see Mamma there, you are looking at her – but no, you are turning away.' Ossian averted the contact, and his mother said that she could feel that his body stiffened. Neither Ossian's mother nor I could reach him now. He was crying in a stifled, complaining way, a combination of crying and coughing.

Even though I was already aware that by his whimpering Ossian showed that he was in a state of emotional turbulence and aversion to emotional links, it was as if I was continuing anyway to search for something that was not there. Restlessness overcame me, as I couldn't find an emotional link with Ossian. I felt that it was of no use to try to use the personal pronouns 'I,' 'you' and 'we' with him. I felt like complaining. In this way, I came to reach Ossian in the state of mind where he actually was, with his coughing-crying-complaining, as I unintentionally fell into his complaining mood. We carried on a dialogue in a tone of complaint.

A: But I can somehow feel – oooh, what is Ossian crying about?
P: [Whimpers.]
A: Why is Ossian crying? Do you have anything to complain about? What is it that makes you so troubled that you have to cry?
P: [Whimpers.]
A: Mm.
P: [Whimpers.]
A: Mm. What are you whimpering about, Ossian?
P: [Whimpers.]
A: Mm.

This went on for a long while. When he recovered his balance and re-established contact with his mother and me, he was tranquil and serious, looking at her all the time, smelling her hand, sucking on her finger, feeling her face.

Towards the end of the session his mother began to talk about the illness they had heard that he might have. When Ossian was three months old a physician informed them that the seemingly trivial organic changes his parents had noticed could be signs of a serious illness. Now in the session, Ossian's mother described with remembered horror all the symptoms that are associated with this chronic, incurable disease and how she visualized Ossian as he would be, wasted by illness, and she described these intense, frightening visual images. Ossian was sitting in his mother's lap, and now and then I turned to him and formulated in my words to him what his mother was talking about. He looked at me calmly and attentively, interjecting a few sounds occasionally. His mother explained that she couldn't look at Ossian without beginning to cry, gripped by boundless grief at the thought of possibly losing him. This turned into a long, very serious and sincere emotional and verbal exchange between his mother and me. Ossian also took part through his attention, sometimes putting in small sounds; he didn't whimper, and it was remarkable that he was so calm and attentive, as if he felt safe being on firm ground. At the end of the session his mother said, 'Maybe Ossian senses how I have been feeling . . . now everything has turned out well but my feelings are, of course, there after all. I can still feel that dread.'

The session was over. This was a Thursday and the last session of the week. We agreed to continue. Now there would be a break until Monday.

Comments on the second session, Thursday

Fluctuation between libidinal object and frightening object

At the start of the session both Ossian and his mother seemed to be happy, and Ossian was attentive to me. He played with his mother in an emotionally warm manner. But Ossian began to express dissatisfaction and he showed his intensive need for his mother when she lifted him up and he met her approaching face with wide-open eyes and mouth. A moment later this libidinal object relation was replaced by rejection, aversion, splitting and projection.

The dialogue in a tone of complaint

As long as I was looking for what I expected to find in the intersubjective exchange with Ossian – something that was not there – the session got stuck, but at the same time the sense of rejection and emotional turbulence in Ossian's whimpering reached me. I was not aware of this identification until we had started our melancholy dialogue. This emotional tuning can be described as resonance (Sandler, 1993), an intercorporality where the mood in the one is also present in the other through primary recurrent identification. It can also be understood as a projective identification: Ossian couldn't stand his own dissatisfaction and I became receptive to this state and identified with it. There was a moment of acting out of my countertransference when I started the dialogue. When I said, 'But I can somehow feel – oooh, what is Ossian crying about?' I said it in a tone that conveyed a feeling of complaint about his whimpering, but his whimpering response made it immediately clear to me that we had opened a containing link, according to Bion's (1962b) formula 'xKy,' for what was actually there, an unclear, turbulent, emotional distress. One aspect of the analyst's work can be said to be to find levels of xKy communication and interaction wherever this is possible.

The opening up of the mother's anxiety

During the first two sessions the mother became aware of her anxiety and the dreadful images of a future destruction of Ossian by illness, and she became aware that 'Ossian has probably noticed it.' It had burdened her during the last three months. In the presence of the infant and the analyst as a third party creating a reverie, the mother's repressed psychic reality of 'the memories of the future' (to use a formulation alluding to Bion's *A Memoir of the Future*, 1991) emerged at the end of the second session and the transformation could take place. The mother could then open her reverie with the infant and this had an immediate impact on the infant.

Monday, after our first weekend break

Ossian conveyed a more robust, open impression. He had slept peacefully during the four nights since the last session; in fact, he had never slept so peacefully before. He also had stopped his endless whimpering and cough-crying. It was a sensation. Ossian was now talkative – with his mother and with me – but in the middle of a playful and friendly dialogue with his mother a change suddenly came over him of the same sort we had seen in the previous sessions. Ossian began to protest, crying, twisting himself away from his mother as if to escape. He was crying more and more angrily and violently, struggling against his mother with his hands and feet. In a short pause when Ossian looked at me and I could catch his attention, I said, 'Ossian, you are very angry, so angry, you are so frightened and angry that you want to push Mamma away, out with Mamma.' He was silent, sucking energetically on his pacifier. We were silent a moment.

His mother said that she was surprised that she felt so terribly unhappy when we were talking about the illness at the last session. She realized that she had been concealing those feelings, but that Ossian had probably noticed them.

Ossian and his mother talked with each other a while, calm and serious. Suddenly Ossian started a new round, the same procedure as before. In a pause, he looked at me and I talked to him.

A: Yes, Ossian, you feel Mamma's hand on your head; she is rocking you. You have been an unhappy, angry boy, Ossian, you couldn't understand what had happened, why Mamma was so different. These were such difficult feelings.

P: [Ossian is silent, sucking vehemently on his pacifier, looking at me all the time with a serious gaze, so I go on talking.]

A: You are suddenly afraid of losing your mother. Just when you and your mother are very close and you are happy you get so frightened. [Ossian replies with some sounds.] I see that you are now a serious boy. [Silence.]

Mother: Mm.

[Ossian looks at her and they come together again with warmth. His mother is talking with Ossian and he responds.
Silence.]

After a while his mother turned to me and said that he almost never sits on her lap as quietly as this. We talked about how fast his mood changed, but Ossian at once made it clear to us that he was very dissatisfied and angry. I turned to him and said that I noticed that he became disappointed and angry when his mother and I were talking to each other and not talking with him, but a new, short, intense round of rejection and rage had already begun. As I had at the end of the previous outburst, I began to talk to Ossian when he calmed down for a moment and looked at me. What then ensued was a long dialogue between Ossian and me lasting about fifteen minutes. Lying in his mother's arms, he did not take his eyes off me. Here, I can only give a short glimpse of this long conversation.

A: You were sitting so very peacefully there in your mother's arms – like this – very quietly. So serious – serious little Ossian, such a serious little fellow, a little anxious actually, ye-e-s, a little anxious, ye-e-s, a little anxious, a little troubled. Mm, and then you get so terribly angry when you feel Mamma isn't with you.

Mother: Were you so angry at me?

P: [Ossian does not turn to his mother; he is silent and continues to look at me.]

A: Mamma has been unhappy. Mamma has been very, very unhappy, because she was afraid that you were ill. Mamma may still be anxious and desperate. You have been terribly afraid when you thought that Mamma looked so sad.

Ossian did not avert his gaze from me for a moment, so I continued talking, with many long silences in between, some comments from the mother and some sounds from Ossian. Everyone was unusually serious, calm and attentive.

After more than ten minutes Ossian did something completely astonishing. He was lying in his mother's arms with his head turned towards me but he now turned his eyes – only his eyes! – as far as he could to the side to catch a glimpse of his mother's face without turning his head, as if he didn't want to reveal it to his mother. He looked at me again and I followed what he was doing with my comments. Again, he turned his eyes as he tried to catch a glimpse of his mother's face, but then he turned his head and looked into his mother's face for a long time. Ossian said something – and fell asleep. His eyes were moving rapidly back and forth; he gave a start in the dream. I said that perhaps the dream made him frightened. Ossian squinted, looked at his mother, at me, at his mother – and fell asleep again. He dreamed and I continued to talk with him; he did not wake up. He then went on sleeping until the session was over.

Comments on the third session, Monday

Ossian's symptoms disappeared from everyday life

During the break from Thursday to Monday Ossian could sleep and eat, and did not whimper day and night as he had done before. This surprising change was lasting. The question is what the three parties, the infant, the mother and the analyst, were doing to each other during this first phase of the analysis that led to the instant relief from symptoms in everyday life. According to Bion's 'container/contained' and 'K-link' model (1962b), this first phase of the work can be understood as a change in the here-and-now interaction in the analytical session, which aroused the emotional container/contained links between all of us, resulting in reverie, containment and transformations of unbearable emotional experiences and images. The analytical situation and the analyst's mind at work created a strong containing function also for the mother, who found courage to bring her part of the story back from repression and relocate it in the interaction. The rapid change of symptoms can thus be understood as an effect of two processes: 1) the mother's phantasies about the damaged infant were retrieved and contained, which changed the mental functioning so that the mother's anxiety decreased and defense by intrusive projective identification vanished; and 2) the normal, communicative projective identifications in Bion's sense (1959, 1962a, 1962b) were revitalized, allowing the container/contained link to take care of the moment-to-moment tensions. Both processes contribute to unburdening the infant's frail personality and provide room for development.

The distinction between everyday life and the sessions

But how can we understand the fact that, although the symptoms had disappeared in everyday life, the outbursts and whimpering continued in the sessions? In the Monday session the outbursts came when Ossian had a close emotional link to his mother or to me.

The recurrence of the outbursts could, of course, be said to be still dependent on the dynamics of the mother and her intrusive projective identifications, but it could rather be understood as indicating that Ossian had found an emotional safety on firm ground since the turning point in his mother's psychic reality in the Thursday session. The repression of the need for a good-mother was now lifted and his needs could be taken care of in everyday life in a way that was mutually satisfying to Ossian and his parents. This implied, for Ossian, a diminished inhibition of emotional links. The emotional heat of the triangular situation of the analytical sessions was a specific retrieval cue for the mobilization of Ossian's psychic reality of the implicit memories of the frustrating-intrusive-frightening-bad-mother internal object representation. The concept of transference seems to be relevant in the sense that 'infantile prototypes re-emerge and are experienced with a strong sensation of immediacy' (Laplanche and Pontalis, 1973, p. 455). The infantile prototypes were gathered into the analysis (Meltzer, 1967).

The fifteen-minute dialogue: Attention and dreamwork

It was a surprise that Ossian's attention was sustained for such a long time in the emotional link with me when I was talking with him at the end of the session. During the long dialogue Ossian stayed in an xKy link with me. What aspect of me was interesting to Ossian? My impression is that the analyst's mind at work, looking for and trying to find a meaning in what is going on – that is, the analyst's α-function – arouses the infant's attention and receptivity. In this situation Ossian was still suspicious of his mother. He was sitting in his mother's arms, turned towards me, as if his mother had to be only a silent background of safety (Grotstein, 2000). This indicated a split of the internal good-mother object as a defense against the internal bad-mother object and hate. He did not respond when his mother spoke, and did not turn his head towards her. When he wanted to look at her he turned only his eyes at first. When he finally turned his head and gazed at her face for a long while he fell asleep. It is possible that impressions from being face to face with his mother overwhelmed his capacity to integrate so that he fell asleep. That he began to dream just a moment after his falling asleep indicates that, in the dialogue with me, he was already in a waking, dreamy state, what Bion has called 'dreamwork-α' (1992), that went over to a dream when he fell asleep.

The analysis gathered an emotional storm: The second phase of the analysis

A lasting change had occurred in the everyday life of the family. Of course there were still problems in Ossian's life but he could sleep and eat; he was much happier and more playful, and did not whimper as he had done before. At home Ossian's father became a great discovery for him, indicating a step in his oedipal development. The analysis continued and after three weeks of analysis, four sessions a week, we had to take a break because of a holiday period lasting for one and a half weeks. Ossian and his family took a long trip abroad, and Ossian continued to be easy to live with and seemed to enjoy life. Our work in the first phase had become a turning point for Ossian's mother; she could think and talk about her old dread, and her emotional links to Ossian seemed to have recovered and evolved.

Even after the holiday break the same pattern of emotional upset as before was repeated in the sessions, but still not in everyday life. When Ossian and his mother came to the sessions they were often happy and playful together, and everything seemed to be okay, but in the middle of their lively companionship Ossian would suddenly lose his good mood. The more emotionally present his mother was, the more vigorously Ossian expressed rage and aversion towards her. He tried to push her away, and began to kick and fight with hands and feet against her. He did not whimper but rather cried and sobbed.

It was remarkable that this went on session after session without exception. In order to understand this phenomenon I am going back to the distinction between two internal objects: a need for a good-mother object; the link to that representation had been restored and was continuously revitalized in everyday life. The repression and the inhibition of emotional links with the good-mother internal object had been lifted and had been replaced by emotional links of mutual satisfaction and love. Connected with this internal object was a 'bad' object built up around expectations that unsatisfied needs implied unbearable frustration and fear of a containing link, contaminated by intrusive projective identification. These experiences were gathered into a frightening object evoking 'nameless dread' (Bion, 1962a, p. 116). The high level of anxiety and intrusive projective identification into Ossian went on between three and six months of age. Three months is a very long time for an infant and we can assume that a profound impact was left on Ossian's implicit memory. The lack of containment created in Ossian channels for unburdening his fragile personality by evacuation through splitting and non-communicative projective identification. When the dynamic changed and Ossian was no longer looked upon as a destroyed child, the emotional links of containing and love were revitalized, and Ossian found a safe ground in everyday life with his mother and father. It may seem paradoxical that, when Ossian could feel the safe ground and that the life-threatening danger was over, he was overcome by a deep despair, rejection and rage – but only in the sessions. This may indicate that the presence of the analyst in the analytical, high-frequency setting, with its focus on xKy, created a space and a heightened containment that was a specific cue for retrieval of feelings of frustration and hate and images from the past, the three months before the analysis.

After a time, something happened to the attacks of crying. Ossian was not warding off his mother and fighting her any more, and he didn't seem to be as angry with her. Sometimes he could also look at his mother and at me in the middle of his crying as if to make sure that we would not abandon him in his emotional state of total despair. Sometimes he arched his back with arms and legs straight out, leaving it completely up to his mother to hold him. He cried like a newborn, sometimes with a tremulous voice, the cry that only newborn babies have, the cry that can make a grown-up person's heart quiver. There was no longer the same hate in his voice. Subsequently, the emotional storms in the sessions became shorter. Sometimes, when Ossian had recovered from one of these storms, he looked at his mother and at me in astonishment, as if it were a surprise to him that he could land in this state of mind again and another surprise that he had suddenly recovered (Norman, 2002). In Winnicott's therapeutic consultations (1971a), he often found 'that the significant moment is that at which the child surprises himself or herself' (1971b, p. 51). Ossian was often in a playful and loving mood with his mother and the analyst, and he responded when we talked with him. His emotional links were flexible and he could divide his attention between his mother and me, and also accept the fact that his mother and I talked to each other. This indicated that the triangulation no longer meant abandonment. He was curious and could stand the frustration when things were out of his reach. He also expressed his anger and disappointment very clearly when something was wrong from his point of view. At the end of one session his mother laid him on the floor so that she herself could put on her outer clothing, and Ossian's objections were absolutely clear. He cried forcibly and angrily, but his mother said to him in a friendly way, 'Take it easy, Ossian, just a moment,' and as soon as his mother lifted him up everything was okay again. For Ossian, the working through had made available a new variety of emotional expressions, and a flexibility in his mental functioning and emotional links. And then we are back again to the 'fort-da' game.

The 'fort-da' play: A third phase of the work – the beginning of the end

Ossian's playing the 'fort-da' implied that he could create an active form for a separation from his mother as the object of his satisfaction. In Winnicott's discussion of his observations of infants' playing 'fort-da' with a spatula, his interpretation is that the infant 'externalizes an internal mother whose loss is feared, so as to demonstrate to himself that this internal mother, now represented through the toy on the floor, has not vanished from his inner world' (1941, p. 68). In the 'fort-da' play there was a circular movement: the inner world was furnished by objects from external reality, for example, the pacifier was part of the mental representation. In the 'fort-da' play the significance of the pacifier as part of the mental representations of emotional links connected with the mother and her presence and absence conjoined with the pacifier as an object in time and space in external reality. The external object/pacifier could be used by Ossian in his theatrical visual narrative on the mental representation/

pacifier. This circular movement was possible only when the inhibiting force from the repression had lost its control over the mental functioning.

It is difficult to find a relevant term for Ossian's 'fort-da' playing. The pacifier was mated with the mental representation of the containing and satisfying mother's coming and going. In a general sense it can be said to be a symbolic relationship, but 'in this sense symbolism embraces all forms of indirect representation' (Laplanche and Pontalis, 1973, p. 443), and the term is close to losing all meaning. Perhaps we should stay with the description of the development of the mental functioning that made the 'fort-da' play possible.

Discussion

The study of the process in this case indicates the good reasons to adapt the concepts of repression and unconscious to the prerequisite of the infantile personality. We can then use the concepts of 'infantile unconscious,' 'infantile repression,' 'substitute formation,' 'return of the infantile repressed' and 'infantile transference' beside the more established concepts of 'splitting,' 'projection' and 'persecutory anxiety' as some of the theoretical tools for understanding the infant's mental functioning in this clinical psychoanalytical setting. In Ossian's case, we can assume that the protective shield was partially lost because of his mother's anxiety, and that he could not get enough protection against his frustration. There was an excessive degree of excitation. When the flexibility in the emotional interaction between the infant and the environment had been inhibited, one aspect of the stability of the disturbance could be found in the environment (in the mother's anxiety) and one in the infant (in the infant's repression). When Ossian turned to his mother's shoulder it was a displacement and substitute as the mother's emotional presence/breast/face/gaze evoked threatening affects and was thus averted. This indicates an infantile repression. When the anxiety increased he even rejected the substitute and tried to ward off every link with his mother, as if the mother was frightening and dangerous. This indicates splitting and projection. He created a concrete enactment against his own projected aggressivity. When he was in a calm state he accepted the mother's emotional presence and the pacifier, looked at the mother's face and sucked the pacifier as if sucking into himself, with the gaze and the pacifier being the satisfaction of his needs.

In the presence of the analytical situation, Ossian could not resist the mobilization of his mental state, which was then gathered and transferred into the analysis, and worked through in the relationship with the analyst and the mother.

During the course of the analysis the dynamics changed in many different respects. The process can be understood as an interplay between changes in the here-and-now interaction, and changes in the intrapsychical mental functioning and psychic reality of the infant and of the mother. In the analytical setting, the analyst's mind, with its evenly suspended attention and responsiveness, receptivity and reverie directed towards the infant, captured the infant's attention and interest. This helped to lift the repression for a moment and thus aroused his aversion to emotional links, repeatedly providing opportunities to demonstrate for the analyst and the mother an emotional disturbance between the infant and his environment. A pendulum in Ossian swung between his unfulfilled needs, substitute formation and searching the mother, indicating infantile repression, and rejecting the mother when he came close to her as he could not stand the frustration. He then evacuated what he could not stand by splitting and projection that transformed the relationship with the mother and the analyst into a persecutory relationship. The analyst's mind at work in the analytical setting offered a safe ground for the infant and the mother, and the impact of the more clear-cut image of an emotional disturbance aroused the mother's self-reflection. When the mother's repressed/preconscious anxiety about her images of the damaged infant were retrieved and contained, the mother's intrusive projective identifications into Ossian vanished and did not burden Ossian any more. Ossian responded immediately by opening the mutual emotional links to his mother and the analyst, and the restored link could unburden Ossian through normal communicative projective identification.

These initial processes can be seen as an effect of the establishment of the analysis in the here-and-now interaction of the session, and the fact that the mother took the opportunity to open up for her own repressed, frightening images. This was the first phase of the analysis but, although it was very striking that the symptoms disappeared from everyday life, the main part of the analysis was still there to evolve and work through.

When the everyday containing links were restored in the first phase of the analysis, this implied that Ossian, his mother and the analyst emotionally came closer to each other, and Ossian's inhibition and repression of unsatisfied needs were lifted and transformed into the satisfaction of mutual emotional interaction and reverie. The relationship with the good-mother internal object could thrive. Every step in that direction vitalized the disturbances emanating from the hateful aspects of Ossian's repressed memories.

Through the countertransference work and the process that evolved, Ossian's endless whimpering and sudden attacks in the sessions could be understood as indicating inhibited and repressed expressions of hate and aggression. The return of the repressed unsatisfied needs created substitutes for Ossian's libidinal wishes, while the increase of anxiety connected with hate, fright and destructivity demolished substitute formation and led to splitting, projection and a further increase of Ossian's anxiety about persecution by his mother and the analyst. Since Ossian and his mother at the first phase of the analysis had recovered their mutual emotional link, the return of the repressed hate and aversion went on only in the sessions and made them into an emotional battle field, as well as a field for reparation and development. Good projective-introjective circles could internalize and build up a permeable and moveable inner world and mental functioning. Aspects of representations of mental states could be externalized and create conjunctions with external objects that could be handled within the limits of time and space. The flexibility was regained and a space for play evolved. As the frequency of sessions was so high – four sessions a week – the mother and infant were not left alone to manage the situation themselves, which may have contributed to the process that was kept alive and evolved, and the transference gathered in the sessions. This indicates that the analytical setting, with its containment of the strong emotional expressions in both mother and infant, was a prerequisite for the process to evolve and for the working through.

Fourteen months after the termination, when Ossian was twenty-one months old, his mother wrote about him, 'He is a happy little boy who seems to feel comfortable with his life.'

Acknowledgements

Special thanks to Associate Professor Karin Norman, Professor Rolf Sandell and Dr Egon Fenyö for many helpful suggestions, Sheila Smith for translation and to the Bertil Wennborg Foundation for generous economic support.

References

Bion, W.R. (1959). Attacks on linking. In: Bion, W.R. (1967). *Second Thoughts*. London: Karnac.

Bion, W.R. (1962a). A theory of thinking. In: Bion, W.R. (1967). *Second Thoughts*. London: Karnac.

Bion, W.R. (1962b). *Learning From Experience*. London: Karnac, 1984.

Bion, W.R. (1991). *A Memoir of the Future*. London: Karnac.

Bion, W.R. (1992). *Cogitations*. London: Karnac.

Bowlby, J. (1988). *A Secure Base*. London: Routledge.

Fonagy, P (2001). *Attachment Theory and Psychoanalysis*. New York: Other Press.

Fonagy, P., Gergely, G., Jurist, E.L., Target, M. (2002). *Affect Regulation, Mentalization, and the Developmental of the Self*. New York: Other Press.

Fraiberg, S. (1987). *Selected Writings of Selma Fraiberg*. Fraiberg, L. (ed.) Columbus, OH: Ohio State University Press.

Freud, S. (1915a). Repression. *SE 14*. London: Hogarth Press.

Freud, S. (1915b). The unconscious. *SE 14*. London: Hogarth Press.

Freud, S. (1920). Beyond the pleasure principle. *SE 18*. London: Hogarth Press.

Freud, S. (1926). Inhibitions, symptoms and anxiety. *SE 20*. London: Hogarth Press.

Green, A. (2000). Science and science fiction in infant research. In: Sandler, J., Sandler, A.-M., Davies, R. (eds.) (2000). *Clinical and Observational Psychoanalytic Research: Roots of a Controversy*. London: Karnac.

Grotstein, J. (2000). *Who is the Dreamer Who Dreams the Dream? A Study of Psychic Presences*. Hillsdale, NJ: The Analytic Press.

Hadley, J. (1989). The neurobiology of motivational systems. In: Lichtenberg, J. (ed.) (1989). *Psychoanalysis and Motivation*. Hillsdale, NJ: The Analytic Press, pp. 227–372.

Harrison, A.M. (2003). Affect regulation, mentalisation, and the development of the self. [Review.] *International Journal of Psychoanalysis* 84: 1382–7.

Hinshelwood, R.D. (1989). *A Dictionary of Kleinian Thought*. London: Free Association Books.

Hinshelwood, R.D. (1999). Controversy is the growing point: Repression and splitting. Unpublished manuscript. Lecture to the British Psychoanalytical Society, October 1999.

Laplanche, J. and Pontalis, J.-B. (1973). *The Language of Psychoanalysis*. London: Karnac/Institute of Psychoanalysis.

Mehler, J. and Dupoux, E. (1994). *What Infants Know: New Cognitive Science of Early Development*. Oxford: Blackwell.

Meltzer, D. (1967). *The Psycho-Analytical Process*. London: Heinemann.

Norman, J. (1997). To talk with infants: Using words in psychoanalytical practice with small children who are not yet able to speak. Paper presented at the Bion Conference, Turin, 1997. Website: http://www.sicap.it/merciai/bion/papers/norma.htm

Norman, J. (1999). Freedom to dream, play and think. *Scandinavian Psychoanalytic Review* 22: 172–88.

Norman, J. (2001). The psychoanalyst and the baby: A new look at work with infants. *International Journal of Psychoanalysis* 82: 83–100.

Norman, J. (2002). The experience of infant psychoanalysis is a surprise. In: Raphael-Leff, J. (ed.) (2002). *Between Sessions and Beyond the Couch*. Colchester: CPS Psychoanalytic Publications, pp. 94–6.

O'Shaughnessy, E. (1981). Bion's theory of thinking and new technique in child analysis. In: Bott Spillius, E. (ed.) (1988). *Melanie Klein Today. Vol. 2*. London: Routledge, pp. 177–90.

Sandler, J. (1993). On communication from patient to analyst: Not everything is projective identification. *International Journal of Psychoanalysis* 74: 1097–107.

Schore, A. (1994). *Affect Regulation and the Origin of the Self: Neurobiology of Emotional Development*. Hillsdale: LEA.

Singer, J. and Fagen, J. (1992). Negative affect, emotional expression, and forgetting in young infants. *Developmental Psychology* 28: 48–57.

Solms, M. and Turnbull, O. (2002). *The Brain and the Inner World*. New York: Other Press.

Steiner, J. (1993). *Psychic Retreats*. London: Routledge.

Stern, D. (1995). *The Motherhood Constellation: A Unified View of Parent–Infant Psychotherapy*. New York: Basic Books.

Talvitie, V. and Ihanus, J. (2002). The repressed and implicit knowledge. *International Journal of Psychoanalysis* 83: 1311–23.

Winnicott, D.W. (1941). The observation of infants in a set situation. In: Winnicott, D.W. (1987). *Through Paediatrics to Psycho-Analysis*. London: The Hogarth Press, pp. 52–69.

Winnicott, D.W. (1960). Counter-transference. In: Winnicott, D.W. (1965). *The Maturational Processes and the Facilitating Environment*. New York: International University Press.

Winnicott, D.W. (1971a). *Therapeutic Consultations in Child Psychiatry*. London: Hogarth Press.

Winnicott, D.W. (1971b). *Playing and Reality*. London: Tavistock Publications.

Chapter 12

'Talk to me baby, tell me what's the matter now'

Semiotic and developmental perspectives on communication in psychoanalytic infant treatment

Björn Salomonsson

'Talk to me baby, tell me what's the matter now.' The entreating words of Billie Holiday summarize how the mother of eight-month-old Karen[1] felt in the face of her incessant crying and demand for the breast. Like the two lovers in the blues, they seemed to be slaves to each other, desperately trying to understand what had gone wrong between them. Today, many mothers seek psychotherapy with their infants. All therapy methods relate the baby's disturbance to a derailed interaction with the mother (Baradon, 2002; Baradon *et al.*, 2005; Barrows, 2003; Berlin, 2002; Cramer and Palacio Espasa, 1993; Dolto, 1982, 1985, 1994; Fraiberg, 1987; Lieberman *et al.*, 2000; Manzano *et al.*, 1999; Stern, 1998; Watillon, 1993). One of them stands out in its focus on the baby. Here, the analyst contains the infant's anxieties by describing *to the infant* her behavior and its unconscious roots. This method, psychoanalytic work with infants (Norman, 2001, 2004), in which the analyst interprets verbally to the baby, was the one I used when treating Karen and her mother.

I argue that Karen could communicate to me many of her unresolved intrapsychic and interpersonal conflicts, such as her anger and difficulties in negotiating it with her mother. Truly, she did not respond to my interpretations by telling me 'what's the matter now.' But her ability to express herself to me and to understand my communication was so well developed that the blues title sprang to my mind as an apt metaphor for this form of psychoanalytic work. 'Talk to me baby' thus denotes the analyst's consistent way of speaking to the infant about her inner world.

There are, however, many questions as to how the infant tells the analyst 'what's the matter,' and how the analyst understands infant 'talk.' These questions can be framed as follows:

- 'In your method, the analyst speaks to the infant in interpretative work. How do you know that the infant understands what you say to her?'

- 'If she understands you, *what* does she understand?'
- 'Given the infant understands other aspects of your communication than the verbal, what are these aspects and how do you know that you two understand the same thing?'
- 'Couldn't the infant's behavior simply be unspecific and uninterpretable reactions to your presence?'
- To sum up: 'Does the infant really understand what you convey to her and do you understand what she conveys to you?'

To approach these questions, we need to tackle two tasks. First, we need to find a theoretical framework for the communication between analyst and infant. I demonstrate that the concept of symbol is used in an unclear way in psychoanalytic theory and that it serves us badly as an explanatory tool for communication in infant work. Instead, I will explicate the interchange between infant, analyst and mother in semiotic terms, and I will label the different parts of this framework.

Second, we need to account for how and when the infant develops her perceptual and cognitive communicative capacities. I describe this in terms of findings from developmental psychological research.

I use semiotics and developmental research as assistant disciplines for explicating the questions. One could argue that these disciplines are irrelevant to an analyst because in clinical practice he/she relies on countertransferential experiences. Certainly, countertransference is vital for the analyst's understanding. In infant work, our emotional reactions are, moreover, often very intense. But, since analyst and baby communicate in such different modes, the cues the baby provides for the analyst are seldom easy to understand. The analyst needs more information than what countertransference yields for understanding the clinical situation. Knowledge of investigations of the baby's communicative abilities will help us to meet the criticism that we exaggerate what can be interpreted and what the baby understands of it. In this paper, I aim to account for these investigations and link them with a theoretical framework of analyst–infant–mother communication. The two vignettes with Karen are presented to illustrate the theoretical discussion.

A comment on definitions: the term 'communication' shall denote any way of conveying meaning from one person to another. I will let 'language' denote the 'remarkably complex, flexible and powerful *system* for communication that involves the creative use of words according to the rules of a systematic grammar' (Bear *et al.*, 2001, p. 638). A linguistic utterance is paralleled by gesture, tone, rhythm, etc. and I shall specify when I refer to its verbal or non-verbal content.

Psychoanalytic work with infants and mothers

The clinical method was developed by Johan Norman (2001, 2004) and is now practiced at the Psychoanalytic Infant Reception Service in Stockholm. It proceeds from four assumptions:

1 That a relationship can be established between the infant and the analyst.
2 That the infant has a primordial subjectivity and self as a base for intersubjectivity and the search for containment.
3 That the infant has an unique flexibility in changing representations of itself and others that comes to an end as the ego develops.
4 That the infant is able to process aspects of language (Norman, 2001, p. 83).

The treatment aims at bringing 'the disturbance in the infant into the emotional exchange of the here-and-now of the session, making it available for containment in the infant–mother relationship' (ibid., p. 83). Mother *and* baby are regarded as active participants who relate to the analyst. In this respect, the method draws from Winnicott, who thought the 'fluidity of the infant's personality and the fact that feelings and unconscious processes are so close to the early stages of babyhood' (1941, p. 232) could be used therapeutically. However, Winnicott said it was essentially from the study of adult transference that we could 'gain a clear view of what takes place in infancy itself' (1960, p. 595). Norman radicalizes Winnicott's notion of infantile fantasies 'full of content and rich in emotion' (1941, p. 61) into a technique in which the analyst talks to *the infant* to contain and interpret her unconscious mental content.

The problem is that infants cannot speak and understand very dimly, if at all, the analyst's words. Not until twelve months will they understand some ten words, and they begin producing their 'first recognizable words between roughly twelve and twenty months' (Karmiloff and Karmiloff-Smith, 2001, p. 62). This developmental skew between language understanding and expression Balkányi (1964) used to explain why children faced with a trauma they cannot verbalize yet run into turmoil. To Norman, the infant's problem is not so much that she cannot verbalize the trauma but that it has not been contained. The mother might have said soothing words but at the same time emitted unconscious messages with different meanings. Since the infant 'understands the unconscious communication made to her' (Dolto, 1994, p. 177)[2] she is presented with a bewildering situation. The analyst's interpretations aim at containing this traumatic situation. The question is what the infant understands of them. I will soon return to this point.

As for infantile defense mechanisms, Norman speaks of two types; infantile repression and splitting + projective identification (2004, p. 1118).

When a mother communicates via intrusive projective identifications, her verbal and non-verbal messages will diverge, as when a depressed mother projects her sinister worldview, smiles faintly but is too absorbed or hostile to contain the distress that her projections evoke.[3] Either the baby will displace her negative affects on to a concrete thing such as mother's blouse or body (infantile repression), or she will reject the painful situation altogether and ward off every link with mother (splitting + projective identification).

Treatments are kept at a frequency of four sessions a week whenever possible. They run from a few months for babies under one year to longer analyses with children of around eighteen months, when they assume many characteristics of classical child psychoanalysis. The infants suffer mainly from disturbances of sleep, nursing, mood and contact. They cannot fall asleep or they wake up from seeming nightmares. They reject the breast or cling to it desperately. They avoid contact with mother or cannot let go of her. Some babies have additional disorders: colic, allergies, and eczema. In some, a diagnosed somatic disease has contributed to disrupting the emotional link between mother and child. It is as if neither dared attach to the other. Both parties suffer intensely, and witnessing their torment is often heartbreaking to the analyst.

To state that a baby reacts when mother's conscious and unconscious messages diverge is not controversial to an analyst. However, to state the reverse, that the baby transmits incongruent messages and that the analyst had better talk to her about these situations, is. I now lay out the theoretical justification for this technique and account for research findings on the infant's ability to understand verbal and emotional communication, respectively. I use two brief vignettes.

Case vignette 1

Karen is eight months old. She demands nursing continuously and has severe sleeping problems. It is impossible to get her to sleep unless mother yields to her demand for the breast. Any mishap makes Karen cry and her mother is exhausted and helpless. The three of us worked in a two-month psychoanalysis of four sessions a week.

In the first session, mother tells of her former worries about Karen's somatic health. She knows that, from a medical point of view, it was not serious. She is distressed, though, but her feeling contrasts with her light tone of voice. She seems unwilling to let in my suggestion that it must have been hard for her and not only for Karen. I feel she blurs their identities, substituting 'we' for either of them. If I am right that she fears her own affects about Karen's health, she cannot contain Karen's affects. I ponder whether Karen's whining for the breast is related to her mother's way of handling this affective situation. While mother speaks and I reflect on my countertransference feelings of our artificial contact, Karen whines and starts crawling. She tumbles at a little stool in my room and starts to cry. I say, 'Now you fell.' Mother says, 'Oh dear! You fell and hurt your head.'

I tell Karen, 'Well, actually you look *angry*[4] when you're looking at me. You might wonder what kind of man you have come to, with his stupid stool . . . Yes? . . . But it wasn't that dangerous.'

Karen calms down but whimpers still. Meanwhile, mother describes how Karen wakes up during the night and then only the breast will soothe her. She continues, as if telling Karen, 'When you wake up during the night, the *only* thing that helps is to get the breast *at once*, otherwise you become *So Sad*.'

I get the impression Karen is annoyed, however. I say to her, 'One could ask oneself: do you get *sad* because you don't get the breast? Or, do you get *Angry?!*' Karen roars and I comment, 'Well, *that* does sound quite *angry*, I think!' Karen stops crying.

This is a common situation in infant psychoanalytic work. The emotional climate between mother and infant gets hotter. I am drawn into the process via my countertransference and the way the two relate to me; Karen by glaring at me and the mother by conveying her need for help while covering it up. I describe what I experience and, finally, I interpret to Karen that she seems angry with me.

What entitles me to attribute such significance to Karen's communication? We are reminded of our initial questions. To frame them differently: Karen doesn't say she is angry with me. She roars. How does she convey her affect to me? Which concepts best account for her communication? Traditionally, when psychoanalysts feel the patient conveys a meaning beyond the obvious, we say she *symbolizes* this other meaning. Karen's roar would thus symbolize her anger with me. On second thoughts, however, we note that the concept of 'symbol' is used in so many ways to convey meaning. We could, for example, use 'symbol' for an infant's roar, a manifest dream content, a symptom, or a work of art. This would challenge us to clarify in each case how we use 'symbol' and 'symbolization.' This is not always done clearly in psychoanalytic theorizing. We need to go into the problems with the concepts of 'symbol' and 'symbolization.'

Problems with the concepts of 'symbol' and 'symbolization'

According to Silver, symbols are 'instruments of expressing our feelings to one another as well as being the instruments of meaning and understanding' (1981, p. 271). The psychoanalytic situation is indeed loaded with such feeling expressions and our efforts to understand them. Accordingly, 'symbol' is a concept commonly used in psychoanalytic theory. Yet, we do not always make it clear what we mean by it. This is even more regrettable in infant work, since the little patient's communication is so abstruse and hard to interpret. We need a better conceptual apparatus for how analyst and analysand convey conscious or unconscious meanings.

Colloquially, the psychoanalytical symbol implies 'constancy of the relationship between the symbol and what it symbolizes in the unconscious' (Laplanche and Pontalis, 1973, p. 442). As the jargon goes, a cigar always means a penis. The symbol is formed on an analogy with the symbolized (Gibello, 1989, p. 37), it will revolve around bodily functions and existential issues, and it will not evoke associations (Jones, 1916). This contrasts with Freud's broader original definition. Here, *any* substitutive formation is symbolic. The condition of a constant connection *Cs–Ucs* has been dropped, and the symbol is now a general semiotic entity. We could call this Freud's semiotic definition of symbolization, in which 'the deciphering of the unconscious is analogous to the one of a foreign language' (Anzieu, 1989, p. 10).

While the two definitions have been used interchangeably, a third one has slipped into clinical discussions. Statements like 'The patient has difficulties in symbolizing' imply that her words are blunt and incomprehensible, convey her affects vaguely, or that she understands interpretations concretely. This definition focuses on the formal qualities of an expression, its degree of comprehensibility, and the subject's communicative intent.

A fourth definition was introduced by Lacan, who radicalized Freud's semiotic definition of symbolization. He said that the unconscious is structured like a language since it uses linguistic mechanisms to express itself; condensation is analogous to metaphor and displacement to metonymy (1966, p. 508). His emphasis on words as the primary instrument of symbolizing unconscious meaning tended to overshadow other expressive modes. In his later writings, though, he introduced the concept of *lalangue*, infant babbling. *Lalangue* supports the language structure of the unconscious by articulating affects, which remain enigmatic to the individual. It 'articulates things which go much further than the speaking individual bears knowing that he has expressed' (Lacan, 1975, p. 175). The problem with using it as a tool for explicating phenomena in infant work is that Lacan used *lalangue* more as a metapsychological concept, and did not investigate it in infant clinical practice or research.

When Lacan defines language as part of *le symbolique*, one of three orders together with the imaginary and the real, 'the structure of the symbolic system . . . [becomes] the main consideration, while the links with what is being symbolised . . . are secondary' (Laplanche and Pontalis, 1973, p. 440). The *symbolique* system is governed by linguistic principles, which bars from it 'expressions of affects, the investment of aesthetic objects, the representation and organization of images' (Arfouilloux, 2000, p. 25). Since affective expressions are typical for the infant, *le symbolique* depends too heavily on a linguistic definition to make room for infants' crying and grimacing.

Let us now investigate if any of these four definitions of 'symbol' will help us to explicate Karen's roar. Along the first-mentioned, classical definition, the roar would constantly signify one unconscious X. This seems counterintuitive; a roar can signify many things and Karen seems conscious of her anger. According to the second, semiotic definition, the roar would symbolize Karen's defensive conflict. But, since her roar openly expresses an affect, it becomes unclear what is defensive about it. Designating Karen's roar along the third definition, that 'she has difficulties in symbolizing,' goes without saying but leaves us with the question: when is a roar complex enough to merit being called a symbol? Finally, to state that the roar belongs to the order of *le symbolique* would be incorrect, since this order obeys linguistic laws and a roar is not a linguistic expression.

If we could liberate the definition of *le symbolique* from its tie to linguistics, we might find tools for designating Karen's roar. Guy Rosolato (1978, 1985), who assumes this task, divides language into two dimensions: digital and analogical.[5] While Lacan focused on the first, which views speech as discrete units assembling in obedience to linguistic laws, Rosolato brought up the analogical dimension: non-verbal aspects of tone, intensity, and other nuances parallel to the word stream. I can grasp Karen's roar in its analogous dimension; it 'copies' her anger, and the copy corresponds to my representation of anger because it has certain characteristics, for example, a sound or a grimace. Beebe and Lachmann conclude, 'As mother and infant match each other's temporal and affective patterns, each recreates in herself a psychophysiological state similar to that of the partner, thus participating in the subjective state of the other' (2002, p. 109). This is how Karen and I participate in each other's subjective states. Our participation is bidirectional. I have noted in myself spontaneous mimic expressions that are analogous with what I feel and with what I imagine the infant feels.

Obviously, the meaning of an analogous representation is not immediately given to the receiver. How do infant and mother understand each other's emotional communication? Someone must provide a code that links the content to its expressive form. The infant must have an object to clarify the meaning. Here, Melanie Klein's work becomes indispensable since she focused on the object's role in the symbolization process. She understood children's play to symbolically express their struggle with internal and external objects, and by offering herself to be their interpreting object in the transference (Klein, 1924, 1930, 1931). Segal (1957, 1991) continued Klein's work by providing a theoretical framework for the object's role in symbolization. To her, the subject's relation with the internal object will govern her use and understanding of symbolization. In the most elaborated level, symbolic representation, typical of the depressive position, the object's separateness is recognized. It is a 'tripartite relationship: the symbol, the object it symbolizes and the person for whom the symbol is the symbol of the object' (Segal, 1991, p. 38). In a symbolic equation, however, a part of the ego identifies with the object and is confused with it. The symbol becomes cruder and harder to understand. However, since the infant's internal object relation is so difficult to ascertain, and since Segal exemplifies with more advanced symbol forms than infant expressions, it is not easy to apply her concepts to Karen's roar. It could hardly be a symbolic equation since Karen conveyed anything but a muddled border between us. Symbol would be a better candidate, but it does not differentiate the roar from a verbal account of my wrongdoings.

To bypass problems with the symbolization concept, I suggest we conceptualize infant expressions, from kicking, smiling, crying, cooing, all the way to words, with one general term. It should be unburdened by dichotomies like conscious/unconscious content, verbal/non-verbal expression, and separate/fused object. Out of this concept should branch a terminology that covers significations on different levels of consciousness, complexity, and object status. I suggest using the term *sign;* Karen's roar is a sign of her affect at whichever level it is signified. Defining that level comes at a second step. We must first define what a sign is.

'What is a sign?'

'This is a most necessary question, since all reasoning is an interpretation of signs of some kind' (Peirce, 1998, p. 4). C. S. Peirce set aside one general term for invoking meaning, irrespective of the level of signification: the sign. Out of this term branches a multitude of sign types of which 'symbol' is but one:

> A *sign* is a thing, which serves to convey knowledge of some other thing, which it is said to *stand for* or *represent*. This thing is called the *object* of the sign; the idea in the mind that the sign excites, which is a mental sign of the same object, is called an *interpretant* of the sign.
> (ibid., p. 13)

In order to perceive something as a sign, the mind sorts the experience into one of three universal categories: Firstness, Secondness and Thirdness. Firstness is an immediate experience unrelated to other experiences. 'Assert it and it has already lost its characteristic innocence' (Peirce, 1992, p. 248). Secondness is always related to other experiences. One experience stands against or is compared to another. Thirdness applies to perceptions of laws, conventions and regularities. Peirce's theory thus makes room for all human experiencing, from its crudest to its most elaborated forms.

These experiential categories can be signified in essentially three ways; as icons, indices and symbols.[6] If my impression of Karen's anger was a Firstness experience of 'Angry Face,' I experienced it as an *icon* of anger. Icons 'convey ideas of the things they represent simply by imitating them'

(Peirce, 1998, p. 5). It is fit to become an 'image of its object' (ibid., p. 273). If I compared Karen's face to faces in other situations, it would be an *index* of anger. I placed my experience in a context of dynamic interaction; her face called on me to react.

An index 'stands for its object by virtue of a real connection with it, or because it forces the mind to attend to that object' (ibid., p. 14). Finally, my words to Karen 'That does sound quite angry!' were *symbols*. They were 'associated with their meanings by usage. Such are most words, and phrases' (ibid., p. 5). 'A symbol is a sign which refers to the Object that it denotes by virtue of a law . . . which operates to cause the Symbol to be interpreted as referring to that Object' (ibid., p. 292). Signs are our building blocks for thinking; 'we think only in signs' (ibid., p. 10).

Since 'it is almost impossible to assign a period at which children do not already exhibit decided intellectual activity' (Peirce, 1992, p. 19), we are entitled to apply Peircean signs to infant thinking. This is clear also from his examples of what signs refer to: anything from color spots and images to complicated verbal relations.

Signs do not cover their referents in a fixed way; it is not always the case that X = icon or Y = index. A sign does not constantly refer to one unconscious content. Karen's cry is not automatically a sign of sadness. Any sign can be interpreted on all three levels; as icon, index and symbol. Interpreted as word symbols, 'That sounds angry!' describes a feeling state in Karen. This does not preclude Karen, however, from interpreting them on an icon level, e.g. as 'Friendly Man.'

Semiosis, the attribution of meaning, goes on endlessly. My immediate interpretant, i.e. my thinking about what Karen's roar signified, was emotional. I felt she was angry. Having made her anger clear to me, I thought of it as opposed to someone friendly, and I felt affected by her anger. Finally, I could ask myself what I mean by 'angry,' constructing a logical interpretant. This idea, in its turn, could function as an emotional interpretant in a new train of thoughts. The semiotic process can be described as an infinite series of triangles where one corner hitches on a corner in the next triangle of interpretant, object and sign. *Figure 1* is adapted from Sheriff (1994, p. 35).

The triangle places the sign in a chain of infinite meanings. Iconical, indexical and symbolical meanings mingle in a continuous associative chain, which has no fixed anchoring point. Not even icons, the most primitive sign form, can be used as a semiotic linchpin. They might seem identical to that which they represent but, actually, 'they do not own any of the characteristics of the depicted object but transcribe according to a *code* some of the conditions of the experience' (Eco, 1971, p. 208). I used my personal code when I experienced Karen's angry face. She looked like other angry people I have met. But, to Karen's mother, it was an icon of a sad baby.

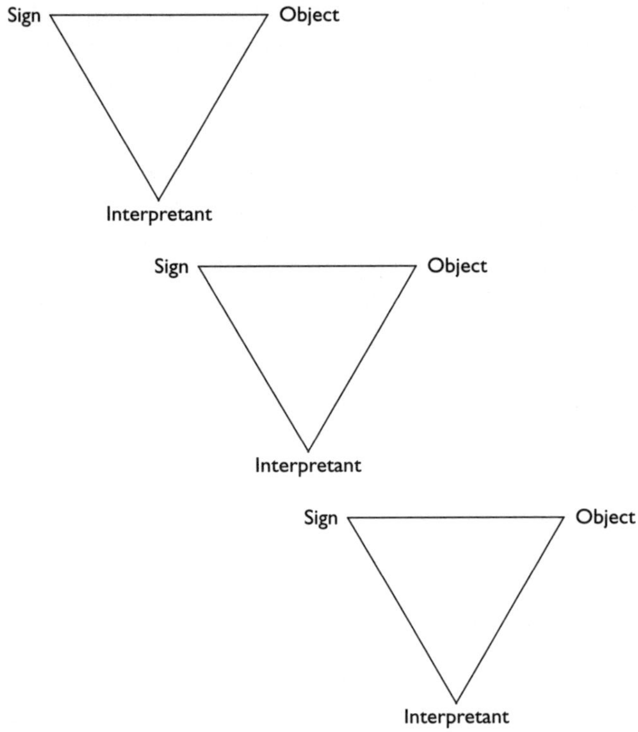

Figure 1 The semiotic process as an infinite series of triangles.

'Does the infant really understand what you convey to her and do you understand what she conveys to you?' If I need a code to interpret Karen, the answer to this question seems to be negative, since I know so little of what she understands and of her tools for perceiving my words. Infant communication would just seem impossible to understand! We will find our way out, however, by investigating the role of the object that interacts with the infant. Several models of the intersubjective process of meaning-making exist (e.g. Beebe and Lachmann, 2002; Stern, 1985; Trevarthen and Aitken, 2001; Tronick, 2005). Muller's (1996) account of how the baby develops her semiotic capacities with mother has the advantage of integrating psychoanalytic theory with research on mother–infant interaction and with Peirce's concepts of signification.

The semiotic process: mother and child, analyst and analysand

'The profound gaze of the infant is also an utterance. His happy or worried agitation when undressed is also an information. The cry, with its modalities of appeal or suffering, is a sign that speaks to the mother' (Lebovici and Stoléru, 2003, p. 254). Muller (1996) describes how infant and mother come to understand each other's utterances and cries and develop their semiotic capacities. Through mutual mirroring with the mother, the baby forms representations of icons and responds; Mom frowns and she frowns. Later, indexical signs come to the fore. Mom frowns and the baby understands that she feels something about her. She feels affected and responds. Finally, mother and child take part in a traffic of word symbols.

How does the infant make meaning out of all the expressions, including the verbal expressions, that she meets with? How do they become 'acts of meaning' (Bruner, 1990)? Bruner suggests we enter language via 'prelinguistic "readinesses for meaning" . . . certain classes of meaning to which human beings are innately tuned and for which they actively search' (1990, p. 72). They exist as 'protolinguistic representations' (ibid., p. 72), which are structured like narratives. He suggests that they 'serve as early interpretants for "logical" propositions before the child has the mental equipment to handle them by such later-developing calculi as adult humans can muster' (ibid., p. 80). Our dialogues in the session are thus little unfolding stories. 'Once there was a little girl. Then she stumbled on a stool and roared . . .'

But is it meaningful to label such infant behavior narrative? Hadn't we better reserve narration for language? Langer challenges the notion that only language can possess the 'character of symbolic expressiveness' (1942, p. 86). The idea that we can understand only what is expressed in discursive, i.e. linguistic, form is based on two misunderstandings: '1) that language is the only means of articulating thought, and 2) that everything which is not speakable thought is feeling' (ibid., p. 87). 'There are things which do not fit the grammatical scheme of expression . . . matters which require to be conceived through some symbolistic schema other than discursive language' (ibid., p. 88). Langer exemplifies this other symbolism by images, ritual, magic, dance, and music (1942, 1972). I suggest Karen's mother and I understand her expressions as forms of 'presentational symbolism,' to use Langer's term. We understand Karen similarly to how we would understand an image or a dance. Our impressions form a total, immediate experience of a 'wordless symbolism, which is non-discursive and untranslatable, does not allow of definitions within its own system, and cannot directly convey generalities' (Langer, 1942, p. 97).

In every step of this interactive understanding of meaning, an object must help the baby climb the semiotic ladder. This object is external at first but continuously internalized. A baby listens to her mother, who has discerned 'a state of mind in her infant before the infant can be conscious of it, as, for example, when the baby shows signs of needing food before it is properly aware of it' (Bion, 1962, p. 34): 'What is the trouble my dear, are you hungry?' The baby calms down when she understands mother's message as icons or indices from a containing object. Containment is thus a semiotic process in which the mother or analyst translates the infant's communications. The mother interprets an icon 'Hungry Baby' and an index 'Feed Me!' Her emotions and understanding of the baby's communications are, in their turn, conveyed as signs to the baby. Meaning is not clarified in an unequivocal and clear manner. Rather, 'meaning is made out of messiness' (Tronick, 2005, p. 311) because the 'meaning-making systems' (ibid., p. 308) of infants and adults are so different. We need infant research and clinical psychoanalysis to chart how containment comes about. It does not take place in an 'ether medium,' as Stern (1998, p. 42) wryly remarks against formulations that do not clarify through which kind of interactive behavior containment comes about.

In psychoanalysis, a derailed mother–baby semiotic development can assume new directions because the analyst adds new translations, as when I said, 'Karen, that does sound quite angry.' The semiotic model alerts the analyst to check what kind of semiotic partner he/she is to the baby and mother right now. Let me exemplify with a second vignette.

Case vignette 2

In the second session, the mother criticizes Karen's father in a pleading way.

Karen: Whines, once cooing 'Maeh-Maeh.' [Unclear icon: Sad Face + indexical request: Treat Me Like A Poor Creature + possibly an effort at forming a word symbol 'Mama.']

Analyst: Yes . . .? [Symbol-question: What Do You Mean? + encouraging index: Go On, Express Yourself, Karen! + Icon: Attentive Face.]

K: Roars. [Distinct index: I Am Angry With You! Feel It!]

A: Yes . . . Now you sound *furious*, I think. [Symbol-interpretation: You Are Angry + index: Go On, I Am Interested And I Am Not Afraid Of Your Anger.]

K: Whines again. [Resumes iconical and indexical signification to elicit analyst's response: Feel Sorry For Me! I Am Sad!]

A: Maybe there are *Two* darned people here! [Symbol-interpretation: You Two Are Angry + indexical communication: I Am Not Scared Of Your Anger.]

Mother: Mmm. [Symbol comment: I Agree + indexical comment: I Am Thinking About What's Happening Here.]

A: One mother mad with *father* . . . [Symbol-interpretation + Index: I Am Reflecting.]

K: Frowns and roars distinctly. [Icon and index now match: Angry Face And Voice + I Want To Tell You Both I Am Angry.]

A: . . . and one Karen mad with *me* and *Mom* because we talk so much. [Etc.]
K: Cries angrily.
A: Is it in a situation like this that Karen wants the breast?
Mother: Yes, now it starts getting breast-time . . .
K: Cries again.
A (to Karen): I think . . . I think you are *angry.*
K: Cries more angrily.
Mother: Yes, now she is *not* sad, now she is *angry!*
A (to Karen): Shall we try to find that out; *what are you angry with?*

Mother interprets Karen's signs differently from the first vignette. Karen creates more unequivocal signs, for example when Mom and I speak, which entitles me to interpret her anger. Let us formulate her crying and breast-craving in semiotic terms. They are distorted iconical and indexical expressions of mainly anger. This distortion arises when her affects have lost contact with explicit memories of situations when they arose. Instead, affects tie to craving the breast. One part of her psyche expresses symptoms and storms with affects. Another part is a warded-off and affectively silent part where anger is blacked out. After this cleavage, symptom and personality are fixated and an infantile repression is established. The more it is established, the more Karen becomes deadlocked in monotonous whining and her mother in stereotyped interpretations of it ('she is sad').

Some questions begin to find their answers. 'How do you know that the infant understands what you say to her?' She understands it in a developing semiotic interaction with me and mother. '*What* does she understand?' She understands me at increasingly complex sign levels, from icon through index to, with older children, symbols. 'How do you know that you two understand the same aspects of communication?' I judge it along my countertransference, which I compare to our present mode of semiotic interaction.

It now remains to account for Karen's cognitive capacities for understanding communication on different levels. How, and on what levels, would she understand when I say, 'I think you are angry'?

The infant's understanding of language: findings from developmental research

Developmental research techniques chart what the fetus and the newborn understand of language communication. During the last trimester, the fetus processes its mother's speech sounds and extracts 'invariant patterns across the complex auditory input that is filtered through the amniotic fluid' (Karmiloff and Karmiloff-Smith, 2001, p. 43). It can differentiate between language and other sounds. At birth, it recognizes its mother's voice (ibid., p. 44) and prefers it to a stranger's (DeCasper and Fifer, 1980).

Recognition of mother's voice thus begins *in utero*. Recognition, however, is not the same as understanding; 'For the newborn . . . the mother's voice is an acoustic stimulus which is familiar in some respects but is not yet associated with any other aspects of her identity in postnatal experience' (Fernald, 2004, p. 57). The infant recognizes prosodic and rhythmic patterns in mother's way of reading a story which has been presented before birth. She will prefer it to other women's readings (DeCasper and Spence, 1986). The newborn also uses prenatal impressions to differentiate her mother's language from that of another rhythmic class (Nazzi *et al.*, 1998, p. 756).

The mother and others around help the infant to develop language competence by speaking 'motherese,' in which 'stress patterns within words and sentences are exaggerated, as are intonation contours around phrases' (Karmiloff and Karmiloff-Smith, 2001, p. 47). It helps the infant 'to identify linguistic units in continuous speech' (Fernald, 2004, p. 58) and to associate it with pleasurable interaction.

'Between birth and two months infants process basic rhythmic characteristics of languages. From five months onward, they begin focusing on the specifics of their native tongue' (Karmiloff and Karmiloff-Smith, 2001, p. 46). This does not mean that a five-month-old experiences speech units as language. They are rather felt as 'groups of sounds as yet independent of meaning and grammar' (ibid., p. 49). Some months later, a child like Karen can 'extract a word that recurs in a variety of sentence-contexts' (ibid., p. 51). As I repeat 'angry,' Karen will gradually recognize its sound but she still doesn't understand its symbol import.

Not until the end of the first year do words begin to serve a 'referential function' (Fernald, 2004, p. 62). To understand this mechanism, the infant must realize that Mom's pointing finger refers to something else beyond. This is a prerequisite for understanding that a word refers to something else than what is immediately present. This ability sets in at around twelve months (Messer, 2004, p. 295).

The infant must develop yet another capacity in order to understand what words mean. Young infants link objects they see and hear only if they are presented simultaneously. Mothers intuitively 'use synchrony to teach their young infants new names for objects' (Bahrick, 2000, p. 132). Pointing at the spoon, mother says 'Spoon!' The young infant needs an object presented visually and aurally simultaneously. In Peircean terms, as long as the indexical sign and its object must be presented together, the baby cannot take the giant step of joining the object with the word symbol.

To sum up: a one-year-old child understands that words refer to things and they do not have to be uttered when she sees them to convey their reference. She understands the meaning of some ten words and maybe she has started pronouncing one or two. Thus, Karen, who is only eight months old, confronts us with a highly legitimate question: why do I use words whose symbolical (Peirce), digital (Rosolato) or lexical (Norman) meaning she cannot understand? I do it because I attribute to Karen a capacity to understand *emotional* communication. Findings from developmental psychological research support such a supposition.

The infant's understanding of emotions: findings from developmental research

The Still-Face experiment was developed by Tronick and co-workers (1978). If a mother playing with her child suddenly, at the researcher's request, keeps her face still, the effect is dramatic. The infant stops smiling and looking at her mother and becomes distressed. The Still-Face prevents mother and baby forming a 'Dyadic State of Consciousness' (Tronick, 2005). The mutual exchange and creation of meaning is interrupted. Instead, these infants 'engage in self-organized regulatory behaviours to maintain their coherence and complexity, to avoid the dissipation of their State of Consciousness' (ibid., p. 303).[7]

Muir and co-workers (2005) have refined observation methods in the Still-Face. They registered not only the infant's gaze at or away from her mother, but also her emotional reactions. By measuring gaze direction and infant smiling to mother's face shifting from a happy to a sad expression, 'D'Entremont [1995] was able to show that infants can discriminate between multiple exemplars of an adult's happy versus sad facial emotional expressions when a smiling index is used, several months earlier than visual attention measures indicate' (Muir *et al.*, 2005, p. 216). Infants of three months stop smiling, 'revealing the infant's sensitivity to a change from happy to sad emotional expressions' (ibid., p. 214). These young infants can 'read' and sort different facial emotional expressions. At eight months, Karen is already an expert reader of the emotions expressed in mine and mother's faces. Her problem is not that her mother's face is still, but that she cannot fuse what Mom conveys consciously and unconsciously or, put in another framework, what her diverging sign types mean.

Concerning auditory communication, the adult's voice 'operates primarily to maintain infant visual attention, although on its own the voice can elicit some positive affect when facial expressions become hard to decipher' (Muir *et al.*, 2005, p. 224). To create such hard-to-decipher situations, the voice of a televised adult was replaced by a synthesized voice with another emotional meaning. The results showed that infants can show signs of distress when confronted with a message in which what they see and hear do not match. In other experiments, however, infants are captured by the sight of the happy face, ignore the discrepant sad voice and remain calm. Karen seems to belong to the first group. She registers those shifts in her mother's voice that I experienced as insincere, when her wording and its affect did not match. On the other hand, this sensitivity of Karen's made her attentive when I expressed myself in an easy-to-decipher and sincere way, that is, when the wording and sound of my voice coincided with my visual appearance. I will soon return to this point. Evidence for infant sensitivity to auditory communication also comes from experiments by the musicologist Stephen Malloch. The elements of mother–infant interaction combine into a 'communicative musicality' (1999, p. 31), which Malloch investigates spectrometrically. Analyses of 'conversations' show that mother and an infant who is a few months old spontaneously find a common pulse. Mom's 'Come on!' or 'That's clever!' are taken up by the baby's cooing in an underlying shared rhythm. The mother spontaneously adjusts to infant pitch changes and her timbre changes so that messages with different meanings will sound different. When the mother is depressed, this communicative musicality is disrupted (Robb, 1999).

These experiments show that infants understand emotional visual and auditory pre-verbal communication better than they understand words. Clinically, their sensitivity implies that if my iconical and indexical expressions do not concord with my symbolic expression, the infant cannot understand me emotionally. Concordance comes about when 'the analyst's tone of voice and her gestures and the lexical meaning of the words express the same meaning' (Norman, 2001, p. 96). When I speak with Karen, the word-symbol content is irrelevant in the sense that she doesn't understand it. But it is most relevant in the sense that it concords with my emotional iconical and indexical expressions. When my expressions are fused, when I look like and sound like the words I tell her, I am sincere. This helps her to release herself from her mother's discordant communication. This is why I do not use 'motherese' with Karen. I use a plain and simple language, and I do not season it with any childish intonation.

For the analyst, there are many stumbling-blocks preventing sincere expressions. If I fear that Karen or mother can't stand any mention of anger, I will probably show this iconically even if I am silent. If I speak to mother along her logical interpretant that Karen is sad, while ignoring my emotional or energetic interpretants of her anger, I will be insincere too. If I look encouraging but feel sad about their communication, I will repeat the 'happy-face-sad-voice-experiment.' To be sincere, one must continuously examine the countertransference.

Communication and therapeutic action

The two summarizing questions were: 'Does the infant really understand what you convey to her and do you understand what she conveys to you?' I hope to have clarified my reasons and provisos when I answer both questions in the affirmative. Karen understands my communication on the iconical and indexical levels that accompany my verbal interpretations. She is affected by my attentive efforts to understand her and to express sincerely what I think goes on in her. I understand her on the basis of my countertransference and have qualified that position by sorting out my tools for understanding her. I have also accounted for infants' perceptual and cognitive tools for understanding linguistic and emotional communication.

Sometimes I am asked if this method works, not because of my interpretations but because the mother listens to my dialogue with her infant and identifies with me. Clearly, Karen's mother's pensive position and growing resistance to panic when Karen cries prove that she has identified with me. I think her identification wells forth from double sources. She is a first-hand witness when I work with Karen as the primary channel for therapeutic change. Moreover, I also interpret their interaction. Her identification with me will thus be based on her witnessing the girl's inner struggle unfolding with me, and her understanding of how she herself contributes to that emotional climate. This will give her experiences an under-the-skin quality, which promotes her identification. I will soon show this.

Another question sometimes asked is whether the infant changes because of normal development or because of interpretive work. The question is impossible to answer with certainty, but two arguments support that the infant needs interpretive work to catch up with normal development. The mothers bring their infants to us because normal development has stagnated. The infants seem helpless and immature, as if their psyche tries to delay repressions from settling. Why should development suddenly resume its normal course, as if unaffected by analytic work? Second, Karen had been crying and craving almost all her life of eight months. This changed radically during treatment. To explain this as solely due to normal development demands an account of what processes should have such powers to clear up alarming symptoms.

Does Karen really understand what I convey to her? Consider the following final snapshot. Karen arrives at the twelfth session newly awakened and a bit hungry. She is a little cross but keeps herself together. She looks at me earnestly and I wait. Unexpectedly, she crawls to a cupboard and reaches for a door knob. She knocks at it and moves her hand to her mouth, as if drinking. She gives a laugh, which mother meets. Mother says to Karen 'You're having a drink at the milk-bar, aren't you!' Karen's play shows she has integrated my interpretations of her anger with Mom's breast and her fears about it. Mother's pun 'milk-bar' shows she is not ensnared by Karen's demands. It is also a sign of her identification with me, since I sometimes use such playful language.

'Talk to me baby, tell me what's the matter now.' Or: 'Signify to me baby, and I will translate your icons and indices into more comprehensible signs and convey them to you. Your protolinguistic representations of emotions will form a narrative which we will explore together. Our dialogue becomes a dance, the presentational symbolism of which we will interpret.' The latter formulation better describes communication in infant psychoanalytic work. On the other hand, it would certainly make a lousy blues title. But that's another story.

Acknowledgements

I want to honor Johan Norman who, half a year before his death in 2005, gave me valuable points of view. I also thank Dr Alexandra Harrison and Prof. Edward Tronick for an interesting discussion. This paper forms part of a research project at the Karolinska Institute, Solna, Sweden on infant developmental problems. It compares psychoanalytic treatments of infants and mothers with more usual treatments. I want to thank the Ahrén, Ax:son Johnson, Engkvist, Groschinsky, Golden Wedding Memorial of Oscar II and Queen Sophia, Jerring, Kempe-Carlgren, Majblomman and Wennborg foundations, and the IPA Research Advisory Board, for generous grants.

Notes

1 Names and biographical data of the baby and her mother have been changed to protect anonymity.
2 There is one crucial difference between Norman and Dolto on the infant's ability to understand unconscious communication: Dolto attributed a capacity in the infant to understand words literally (see e.g. 1985, p. 211); Norman and our group do not share this position, as I argued in this paper in my discussion of the infant's understanding of language.
3 In research experiments, Tronick and Weinberg (1997) and Field *et al.* (1988) have shown similar intense infant reactions during interaction with their depressed mothers.
4 In this vignette, italic characters and capital letters indicate emphasis of words.
5 The distinction digital/analogical semiosis is also used by Eco (1971).
6 Peirce later expanded this terminology into a multitude of sign types, which I will not account for here.
7 State of Consciousness (SOC) is 'a psychobiological state with a distinct complex organization of body, brain, behaviour, and experience. It is a distinct assemblage of implicit and explicit meanings, intentions and procedures. . . . SOCs are purposive, and organize internal and external actions towards some end' (Tronick, 2005, p. 295). 'At some point in development, SOCs assemble meanings from psychodynamic processes including a psycho-dynamic unconscious' (ibid., p. 297).

References

Anzieu, D. (ed.) (1989). *Psychanalyse et Language. Du Corps à la Parole* [*Psychoanalysis and Language. From the Body to the Word*]. Paris: Dunod.

Arfouilloux, J.-C. (2000). *Guy Rosolato*. Paris: PUF.

Bahrick, L. (2000). Increasing specificity in the development of intermodal perception. In: Muir, D., Slater. A. (eds.) (2000) *Infant Development: Essential Readings*. London: Blackwell, pp. 119–36.

Balkányi, C. (1964). On verbalization. *International Journal of Psychoanalysis* 45: 64–74.

Baradon, T. (2002). Psychotherapeutic work with infants – Psychoanalytic and attachment perspectives. *Attachment and Human Development* 4: 25–38.

Baradon, T., Broughton, C., Gibbs, I.,. James, J., Joyce, A. and Woodhead, J. (2005). *The Practice of Psychoanalytic Parent-Infant Psychotherapy – Claiming the Baby*. London: Routledge.

Barrows, P. (2003). Change in parent–infant psychotherapy. *Journal of Child Psychotherapy* 29: 283–300.

Bear, M., Connors, B. and Paradiso, M. (2001). *Neuroscience: Exploring the Brain*. Baltimore, MD: Lippincott William & Wilkins.

Beebe, B. and Lachmann, F. (2002). *Infant Research and Adult Treatment: Co-constructing Interactions*. Hillsdale, NJ: Analytic Press.

Berlin, N. (2002). Parent–child therapy and maternal projections: tripartite psychotherapy – a new look. *American Journal of Orthopsychiatry* 72: 204–16.

Bion, W. (1962). *Learning From Experience*. London: Karnac.

Bruner, J. (1990). *Acts of Meaning: Four Lectures on Mind and Culture*. Cambridge, MA: Harvard UP.

Cramer, B., Palacio, Espasa F. (1993). *La Pratique des Psychothérapies Mères-Bébés. Études Cliniques et Techniques* [*The Praxis of the Mother–Infant Psychotherapies. Clinical and Technical Studies*]. Paris: PUF.

DeCasper, A.J. and Fifer, W.P. (1980). Of human bonding: Newborns prefer their mothers' voices. *Science*, 6 June; 208: 1174–6.

DeCasper, A.J. and Spence, M. (1986). Prenatal maternal speech influences newborns' perception of speech sounds. *Infant Behaviour and Development* 9: 133–50.

D'Entremont, B. (1995). One- to six-months-olds' attention and affective responding to adults' happy and sad expressions: The role of face and voice. Unpublished doctoral dissertation, Queen's University, Kingston, Ontario.

Dolto, F. (1982). *Séminaires de Psychanalyse d'Enfant* [Seminars on Child Analysis.], Vol. 1. Paris: Seuil.

Dolto, F. (1985). *Séminaires de Psychanalyse d'Enfant* [Seminars on Child Analysis.], Vol. 2. Paris: Seuil.

Dolto, F. (1994). *Les Étapes Majeures de l'Enfance* [The Major Stages of Childhood.]. Paris: Gallimard.

Eco, U. (1971). *Den Frånvarande Strukturen* [1968] [The Absent Structure]. Lund: Cavefors.

Fernald, A. (2004). Hearing, listening and understanding: Auditory development in infancy. In: Bremner, J.G. and Fogel, A. (eds.) (2004). *Blackwell Handbook of Infant Development*. London: Blackwell, pp. 35–70.

Field, T., Healy, B., Goldstein, S., Perry, S., Bendell, D., Schanberg, S., *et al.* (1988). Infants of depressed mothers show 'depressed' behavior even with non-depressed adults. *Child Development* 59: 1569–79.

Fraiberg, S. (1987). *Selected Writings of Selma Fraiberg*, Fraiberg, L. (ed.). Columbus: Ohio State University Press.

Gibello, B. (1989). Fantasme, langage, nature, trois ordres de réalité [Fantasy, language, nature, three orders of reality]. In: Anzieu, D. (ed.) (1989). *Psychanalyse et Langage* [Psychoanalysis and Language]. Paris: Dunod, pp. 25–70.

Jones, E. (1916). The theory of symbolism. In: Jones, E. (1948) *Papers on Psycho-Analysis*, 5th edition. London: Baillière, Tindall & Cox, pp. 87–144.

Karmiloff, K. and Karmiloff-Smith, A. (2001). *Pathways to Language*. Cambridge, MA: Harvard University Press.

Klein, M. (1924). The role of the school in libidinal development. *International Journal of Psychoanalysis* 5: 312–31.

Klein, M. (1930). The importance of symbol-formation in the development of the ego. *International Journal of Psychoanalysis* 11: 24–39.

Klein, M. (1931). A contribution to the theory of intellectual inhibition. *International Journal of Psychoanalysis* 12: 206-18.

Lacan, J. (1966). *Écrits*, Vol. 1. Paris: Seuil, 1999. [(2005). *Écrits*, Fink, B., translator. New York: Norton, p. 878.]

Lacan, J. (1975). *Encore: Séminaires* [On Feminine Sexuality, the Limits of Love and Knowledge: The Seminar of Jacques Lacan, Book XX, Encore], Vol. 20. Paris: Seuil.

Langer, S. (1942). *Philosophy In A New Key: A Study In The Symbolism Of Reason, Rite And Art*. Cambridge, MA: Harvard University Press.

Langer, S. (1972). *Mind: An Essay On Human Feeling*, Vol. 2. Baltimore, MD: Johns Hopkins University Press.

Laplanche, J. and Pontalis, J.B. (1973). *The Language Of Psychoanalysis* [1967], Nicholson-Smith, D., translator. London: Hogarth. [*International Psychoanalytical Library*, No 94.]

Lebovici, S. and Stoléru, S. (2003). *Le Nourisson, sa Mère et le Psychanalyste* [The Infant, the Mother and the Psychoanalyst]. Paris: Bayard.

Lieberman, A., Silverman, R. and Pawl, J. (2000). Infant–parent psychotherapy: Core concepts and current approaches. In: Zeanah, C. (ed.) (2000). *Handbook Of Infant Mental Health*, 2nd Edition. New York, NY: Guilford, pp. 472–84.

Malloch, S. (1999). Mothers and infants and communicative musicality. *Musicae Scientiae*, Special Issue, 29–58.

Manzano, J., Palacio Espasa, F. and Zilkha, N. (1999). *Les Scénarios Narcissiques de la Parentalité. Clinique de la Consultation Thérapeutique*. Paris: PUF. (*Le Fil Rouge* series.)

Messer, D. (2004). Processes of early communication. In: Bremner, J.G. and Slater, A. (eds.) (2004). *Theories Of Infant Development*. Oxford: Blackwell, pp. 284–316.

Muir, D., Lee, K., Hains, C. and Hains, S. (2005). Infant perception and production of emotions during face-to-face interactions with live and 'virtual' adults. In: Nadel, J. and Muir, D. (eds.) (2005). *Emotional Development*. Oxford: Oxford University Press, pp. 207–34.

Muller, J. (1996). *Beyond The Psychoanalytic Dyad*. London: Routledge.

Nazzi, T., Bertoncini, J. and Mehler, J. (1998). Language discrimination by newborns: Towards an understanding of the role of rhythm. *Journal of Experimental Psychology: Human Perception and Performance* 24: 756–66.

Norman, J. (2001). The psychoanalyst and the baby: A new look at work with infants. *International Journal of Psychoanalysis* 82: 83–100.

Norman, J. (2004). Transformations of early experiences. *International Journal of Psychoanalysis* 85: 1103–22.

Peirce, C.S. (1992). *The Essential Peirce, Vol. 1: 1867–1893*. Kloesel, C. and Houser, N. (eds.) Bloomington, Indiana: Indiana University Press.

Peirce, C.S. (1998). *The Essential Peirce, Vol. 2: 1893–1913*. Houser, N. (ed.) Bloomington, Indiana: Indiana University Press.

Robb, L. (1999). Emotional musicality in mother–infant vocal affect and an acoustic study of postnatal depression. *Musicae Scientiae*, Special Issue, 123–54.

Rosolato, G. (1978). Symbol formation. *International Journal of Psychoanalysis* 59: 303–13.

Rosolato, G. (1985). *Éléments de l'Interprétation* [Elements of Interpretation]. Paris: Gallimard.

Segal, H. (1957). Notes on symbol formation. *International Journal of Psychoanalysis* 38: 391–7.

Segal, H. (1991). *Dream, Phantasy and Art*. London: Routledge. [New Library of Psychoanalysis, Vol. 12.]

Sheriff, J. (1994). *Charles Peirce's Guess at the Riddle: Grounds for Human Significance*. Bloomington, Indiana: Indiana University Press.

Silver, A. (1981). A psychosemiotic model: An interdisciplinary search for a common structural basis for psychoanalysis, symbol-formation, and the semiotic of Charles S. Peirce. In: Grotstein, J.S. (ed.) (1981). *Do I Dare Disturb the Universe? A Memorial to W. R. Bion*. London: Karnac, pp. 270–315.

Stern, D. (1985). *The Interpersonal World of the Infant: A View from Psychoanalysis and Developmental Psychology*. New York: Basic Books.

Stern, D. (1998). *The Motherhood Constellation – A Unified View Of Parent–Infant Psychotherapy*. London: Karnac.

Trevarthen, C. and Aitken, K. (2001). Infant intersubjectivity: Research, theory and clinical applications. *Journal of Child Psychology and Psychiatry* 42: 3–48.

Tronick, E. (2005). Why is connection with others so critical? The formation of dyadic states of consciousness and the expansion of individuals' states of consciousness: Coherence-governed selection and the co-creation of meaning out of messy meaning making. In: Nadel, J. and Muir, D. (eds.) (2005). *Emotional Development*. Oxford: Oxford University Press, pp. 293–315.

Tronick, E., Als, H., Adamson, L., Wise, S. and Brazelton, B. (1978). The infant's response to entrapment between contradictory messages in face-to-face interaction. *Journal of the American Academy of Child and Adolescent Psychiatry* 17: 1–13.

Tronick, E. and Weinberg, K. (1997). Depressed mothers and infants: Failure to form dyadic states of consciousness. In: Murray, L. and Cooper, P. (eds.) (1997) *Postpartum Depression and Child Development*. New York: Guilford, pp. 54–82.

Watillon, A. (1993). The dynamics of psychoanalytic therapies of the early parent–child relationship. *International Journal of Psychoanalysis* 74: 1037–48.

Winnicott, D.W. (1941). The observation of infants in a set situation. *International Journal of Psychoanalysis* 22: 229–49.

Winnicott, D.W. (1960). The theory of the parent–infant relationship. *International Journal of Psychoanalysis* 41: 585–95.

Index